The Strategic Management of Intellectual Capital

The Strategic Management of Intellectual Capital

David A. Klein
Editor

Butterworth-Heinemann
Boston Oxford Johannesburg Melbourne New Delhi Singapore

Library of Congress Cataloging-in-Publication Data
The strategic management of intellectual capital / David A. Klein,
    editor.
        p.   cm. — (Resources for the knowledge-based economy)
    Includes bibliographical references and index.
    ISBN 0-7506-9850-0 (alk. peper)
        1. Creative ability in business.   2. Organizational learning.
    3. Human capital.   I. Klein, David A., 1959– . II. Series.
HD53.S77   1998
658.4—dc21   97-40130
                                                                      CIP

British Library Cataloguing-in-Publication Data
A catalogue record for this book is available from the British Library.

Contents

Introduction to Series—
Why Knowledge, Why Now?

Why is there such an upsurge of interest in knowledge? In 1996 there were at least six major conferences on the subject; three new journals focusing on knowledge (sometimes loosely called intellectual capital or organizational learning) were published; and many major firms in the United States and Europe added positions such as chief knowledge officer, organizational learning officer, and even a few vice presidents for intellectual capital!

Why the focus on a subject that, at some levels, has been around since the pre-Socratic philosophers? Is it yet another one of the multitudinous management enthusiasms that seem to come and go with the frequency of some random natural phenomena? We don't think so! Many of us doing research on this subject have seen the rise and fall of many of these varied nostrums—all of which attempted to offer firms a new road to achieving a sustainable competitive advantage. However, when much of the shouting dies down, we conclude that, excluding monopolistic policies and other market irregularities, there is no sustainable advantage other than what a firm knows, how it can utilize what it knows, and how fast it can learn something new!

However, this still does not answer the questions why knowledge, why now? Let us list some very broad trends that seem to be playing a significant role in the current development of knowledge:

A) The globalization of the economy, which is putting terrific pressure on firms for increased adaptability, innovation, and process speed.

B) The awareness of the value of specialized knowledge, as embedded in organizational processes and routines, in coping with the pressures of globalization.

C) The awareness of knowledge as a distinct factor of production and its role in the growing book value to market value ratios within knowledge-based industries.

D) Cheap networked computing, which is at last giving us a tool for working with and learning from each other.

While many can argue for and against the significance of these trends, we feel that the preponderance of evidence points to the increasing substitution of brain for brawn within our organizations and our social lives. Yet we have developed few conceptional tools to better work with "wetware."

It is with these forces in mind that we offer the following volume to you. While there are, as yet, few agreed-upon standards and analytic frames and definitions, there are enough serious articles and books to help managers get some real traction in dealing with the crucial yet elusive subject of knowledge.

After all, we have had about 500 years of thought concerning the other major factors of production, for example, land, labor, and capital. Let these volumes start the process of codifying knowledge about knowledge in order for us to better manage in the twenty-first century.

Laurence Prusak,
Series Editor

1

The Strategic Management of Intellectual Capital: An Introduction

David A. Klein

Organizations increasingly compete on the basis of their intellectual assets. We hear it echoed in the buzzwords of the day: Companies compete in a "knowledge economy," skilled functions are performed by "knowledge workers," and firms that improve with experience are "learning organizations." We see it in some of the innovative management agendas of recent times: Reengineering involved doing more with less by working smarter; continuous quality improvement derived from learning how to do things better and better over time; and the development of new core competencies entailed building fresh organizational know-how. In an environment where innovations are replicated by competitors expeditiously and where smaller firms often gain market share from larger ones by introducing superior products and services, it is firms' *intellectual capital*—their knowledge, experience, expertise, and associated soft assets, rather than their hard physical and financial capital—that increasingly determines their competitive positions.

And with this shift in competitive emphasis has come an explicit recognition by a growing number of organizations that their intellectual capital is an essential source of competitive advantage that should be managed more systematically. In particular, organizations are devising enterprise strategies and portfolios of initiatives to capture and disseminate what they learn over time, to facilitate the sharing of new ideas and experiences across functional and organizational boundaries, to leverage their best practices, and to manage their intellectual capital by other deliberate means rather than continuing to rely on haphazard approaches. And they are finding, for example, that insights captured on the factory floor, when properly cataloged, interpreted, and disseminated, can lead to changes in processes that yield cost advantages; that a re-examination of what every player in the industry knows versus what their particular organizations know uniquely can lead to new knowledge-sharing partnerships with competitors; and that performance-measurement systems designed to reward the creation and exchange of ideas can enhance the firm's decision making and increase innovation. In short, firms adopting a strategic approach to managing their intellectual capital see an opportunity to enhance their market positions relative to organizations that continue to manage such capital opportunistically: If indeed "knowledge is power," then harnessing it and channeling it make better business sense than simply letting the sparks fly.

ELEMENTS AND CHALLENGES OF MANAGING INTELLECTUAL CAPITAL

To manage its intellectual capital more systematically, the firm must devise an agenda for transforming from an organization simply comprising knowledge-able *individuals* to a knowledge-focused *organization* that stewards the creation and sharing of knowledge within and across internal business functions and that orchestrates the flow of know-how to and from external firms. The fabric of such an agenda comprises many threads—people, incentives, technology, processes, and other elements—that need to be woven together carefully in a fashion commensurate with the organization's particular strategy, culture, capabilities, and resources. Although each firm's program will be likewise unique, a common set of themes, issues, and challenges underlies the objectives and implementation of such programs.

Understanding the Strategic and Operational Roles of Intellectual Capital in the Organization, and the Links Between Them

What kinds of know-how could improve the organization's products and services today? What intellectual capital is required to support its key processes and functions more effectively? What knowledge will be needed in the future? Does the firm currently possess this intellectual capital, and if not, how should the firm develop or acquire it? How can the firm share selected intellectual capital with customers, suppliers, and competitors to create cost and performance advantages? Meeting the firm's strategic intellectual-capital requirements has broad competitive implications, but historically such requirements have not occupied center stage in boardrooms. Firms that expressly consider the strategic role of intellectual capital in their businesses by addressing such questions increase the likelihood of taking the actions needed to meet their intellectual-capital requirements.

Ultimately, the firm's strategy for managing intellectual capital is embodied in a portfolio of management and technology initiatives at the operating level. In part, management's challenge is to orchestrate the transformation of raw intellectual material generated by individuals into intellectual capital—knowledge packaged in forms that can be invested directly in the same spirit as the firm's hard assets. For example, the sales force that employs an explicit intranet-based repository for capturing and disseminating the competitive rumors of the day as soon as they become known is harnessing and channeling knowledge that might otherwise be shared by only a small collection of colleagues, rendering it available for direct investment in lead generation, product positioning, and executive decision making; the engineering firm that establishes regular forums for sharing design insights enables their reinvestment in product-development cycles beyond their discovery. Organizations possess immense unstructured storehouses of informal know-how, which in the absence of intellectual-capital programs is physically distributed in a haphazard fashion across the minds of individuals and a plethora of recording media, such as memos, books, voice-mail messages, paper files, and databases. And even less-tangible intellectual assets are embedded implicitly in the workings of the organization itself—in its culture and in its informal routines and processes. By more deliberately forming intellectual capital from this sea of unstructured intellectual material, management can more readily invest such capital in opportunities targeted to meet strategic knowledge requirements.

But how does a firm decide what set of operating-level initiatives would best meet its strategic goals? In the context of knowledge-based competition, management faces the new challenge of linking strategy with execution at the knowledge level by supporting scanning for strategic opportunities to form investable intellectual capital from raw intellectual material, by monitoring and measuring its intellectual capital to evolve its intellectual-capital programs, and by designing other such processes and initiatives to connect the strategic and operational elements of intellectual capital.

Creating an Infrastructure for Cultivating and Sharing Intellectual Capital

The strategic management of intellectual capital necessitates a fundamental shift in thinking about the dissemination of the firm's intellectual assets. In particular, firms are accustomed to delineating such assets largely in the context of rigid legal definitions of intellectual property, which focus on restricting the use, sale, and transfer of intellectual capital in forms such as patents and copyrights. In contrast, leveraging intellectual capital generally requires that managers cautiously promote rather than restrict its use, reflecting an expansionist approach rather than a reductionist one that includes deliberately seeking out opportunities to form and leverage such capital throughout and across organizations. At the implementation level, capturing large volumes of knowledge and facilitating such orchestrated broadcasting are enabled by an explicit management and technology infrastructure for capturing and leveraging intellectual capital.

Although the designs of particular infrastructures naturally will vary with the firm's particular goals and initiatives, there are at least three general characteristics that such infrastructures should embody. First, a firm's intellectual-capital infrastructure should connect the unconnected, providing a foundation for creating and linking communities of knowledge workers with similar interests and tasks. Second, an intellectual-capital infrastructure should be designed to facilitate the capture of know-how in context. In particular, firms cannot pragmatically pursue approaches that require professionals to address general questions about their knowledge as a process outside normal workflows. Rather, firms need to build a community-based model of organizational knowledge acquisition that integrates seamlessly into knowledge work and that embodies the richness of the particular business contexts at hand. Finally, the flip side of capturing intellectual capital in context is delivering it directly to the point of execution. Well-formed, investable intellectual capital is of relatively little value unless it is delivered to where it is needed at the time it is needed.

More broadly, the prospect of creating an explicit infrastructure for managing intellectual capital raises new implementation issues at the intersection of management thinking and technology innovation. In particular, a shift to an intellectual-capital focus provides an opportunity to rethink the roles of people and machines in designing knowledge work to incorporate organizational memory, explicit knowledge sharing, and other elements of managing intellectual capital. Beyond straightforward design decisions to employ foundational technology, such as email, groupware, and discussion groups, the synthesis of a competitive infrastructure design evokes new questions about what knowledge is flowing through a firm, how it can be collected and formalized, and how most appropriately to allocate intellectual work to people and machines as processors of knowledge at various stages of knowledge work.

Framing the capabilities and benefits of machines as knowledge media and as the foundational glue of a knowledge-based enterprise boils down largely to questions concerning the representation of knowledge. In effect, the technology infrastructure must provide a mirror view of how knowledge is used in the organization, but formalizing that view remains an art rather than a science. In an analytical sense, issues of organizational knowledge representation evoke some of the fundamental enduring questions: What, exactly, is knowledge? What are the uses of knowledge? How can knowledge be formalized and organized? In that the use of knowledge recommends its representation in technology infrastructures, the design of competitive knowledge technology is driven largely by the capability of the firm to match tools with tasks in the context of a knowledge-centric view of how the firm actually uses knowledge in performing knowledge work, and by the firm's ability to devise new representations to meet new knowledge requirements.

Also germane is the extent to which the firm's infrastructure balances the benefits of systematizing intellectual capital with the flexibility to meet unanticipated requirements. As firms depart from opportunistic approaches to managing their intellectual capital, they likewise need to exercise caution not to venture too far toward rigid infrastructures under which knowledge work is constrained rather than enlightened. In designing an intellectual-capital infrastructure, management must seek balances between the directed and the undirected, between the specified and the unspecified.

To create a management and technology infrastructure for forming and investing intellectual capital, designers and managers need to address these and related questions concerning the interplay between knowledge work and supporting foundational tools and management structures.

Creating a Culture That Encourages Intellectual-Capital Formation and Investment

Although the firm's strategy and supporting infrastructure for managing intellectual capital may be newly conceived, its existing web of attitudes, reward systems, and behaviors often are inconsistent with the firm's goals for managing intellectual capital, reflecting yesterday's competitive environment. Asking consultants, lawyers, and other professionals who compete essentially by selling intellectual capital to share it in up-or-out environments for the good of the firm has its obvious obstacles; so does expecting engineers and researchers to reuse each other's work after they've been socialized in graduate school to exalt innovation and shun rote application; and asking any sort of knowledge worker to play an active role in the conversion of his or her personal intellectual assets to corporate assets begs questions of incentive. The achievement of the firm's knowledge strategy and the success of its operating-level intellectual-capital initiatives must be enabled by fostering a culture that values and rewards the creation and sharing of intellectual capital.

The nature of the firm's current culture in large part suggests its transformation path. For example, in organizations where personal intellectual achievement is at center stage, managers may focus on creating an environment where professionals also attain special recognition for influencing the work of others. In firms where autonomous decision making is particularly emphasized, managers may afford special attention to the process of nurturing change in the processes by which intellectual capital is created and shared, rather than imposing change. A firm's culture also has implications for the preferred means by which its intellectual-capital programs are marketed internally: In some firms, visible support from top management for intellectual-capital programs is among the most critical success factors, whereas other firms have deliberately pursued their intellectual-capital efforts as grass-roots initiatives to facilitate knowledge-worker buy in from the bottom up.

Beyond firm-specific concerns in effecting transformation to a knowledge culture, participation in any firm's intellectual-capital programs necessitates that knowledge workers see value in them, and the need to close the gap between new knowledge objectives and old knowledge behaviors gives rise to new questions: What sorts of programs can facilitate the creation of environments that embody the cultivation and sharing of intellectual capital as core values? How can management communicate the importance of intellectual-capital formation and investment toward supporting the behaviors of the knowledge workers who ultimately need to integrate learning, sharing, and innovating into the fabric of the firm's operations? Organizations that address such issues explicitly take essential steps toward making viable their agendas for managing intellectual capital.

Monitoring, Valuing, and Reporting Intellectual Capital

In tandem with the cultivation of an appropriate knowledge culture and infrastructure, management can give knowledge workers incentive to contribute to the firm's base of intellectual capital by supporting such contributions with explicit transactions. From an economic standpoint, the challenge is to create an internal market for intellectual capital, where buyers and sellers can exchange it at fair market prices. The firm that pays a royalty or otherwise recognizes the author of a frequently referenced model work product, for example, provides greater incentive for the author to make that work product widely available.

Beyond rewarding knowledge workers for their intellectual-capital contributions, management needs to monitor the formation and investment of intellectual capital toward evolving the firm's intellectual-capital programs and work processes over time. By more systematically accounting for organizational know-how, firms also provide a basis for reporting intellectual assets to external stakeholders and for valuing selected repositories of intellectual capital for sale or transfer to other organizations.

But how should intellectual capital be measured? How can management determine its value? Our established disciplines have surprisingly little to say about these issues. Intellectual-property law makes a contribution only in its treatment of the most well-delineated intellectual assets, such as patents and trademarks. At the firm level, the disparity between the market and book values of firms in intellectually intensive industries underscores the associated limitations of modern accounting, which focuses on measuring physical and financial capital. What is needed is a more expressive system that defines the component elements of intellectual capital and provides a calculus for valuing and aggregating them.

But what are these building blocks of intellectual capital? In our traditionally unsystematic treatment of intellectual capital, we have employed gross proxies for delineating and valuing such intangibles: We retain professionals as storehouses of intellectual capital and measure their intellectual capital by rough indicators, such as education and years on the job. We count proposals produced, papers published, and take other uncompelling inventories of work products to measure intellectual output. We mostly ignore the problem of depreciating such intellectual assets in a systematic fashion, missing unseen signals to *un*learn processes, techniques, and general know-how that have expired. To support the monitoring, valuation, and reporting of intellectual capital, management ultimately will need systems and processes that support knowledge accounting with a rigor comparable to our traditional systems for managing hard assets.

PURPOSE AND ORGANIZATION OF THIS READER

The strategic management of intellectual capital involves rethinking how the organization creates value from a knowledge-centric perspective and redesigning and orchestrating the role of intellectual assets in the firm's strategy and operations. Firms of different character naturally will pursue correspondingly different approaches, but a growing community of managers and researchers has articulated general ways of thinking about the nature of the enterprise, its essential challenges, and emerging methods toward design and implementation that can be matched with the requirements of particular firms. The papers included in this volume explicate some of that thinking, which I have organized in terms of the classes of challenges in managing intellectual capital that I described earlier in this introduction.

In Part One of this volume, which focuses on understanding the strategic and operational roles of intellectual capital in the organization, Ann B. Graham and Vincent G. Pizzo describe case studies in managing intellectual capital and address issues underlying the design and execution of knowledge-driven business strategies. Henry W. Chesbrough and David J. Teece present a framework to assist managers in determining appropriate strategies and organizational structures associated with different types of competitive innovation.

Part Two includes papers that address issues pertinent to creating a management and technology infrastructure for cultivating and sharing intellectual capital. Daniel H. Kim explores how learning at the individual level is transferred to an organization and proposes a model that can guide the search for new tools to support organizational learning. Arthur Armstrong and John Hagel III offer a view of the internet as a community-building vehicle, presenting a taxonomy of internet-based communities and addressing their roles in the generation of returns. Randall Whitaker explores the management of context in enterprise knowledge processes. James Brian Quinn et al. propose a multilevel model of the organization's professional intellect and address issues in its development and leverage.

Part Three comprises works that address the challenges of creating a culture that encourages intellectual-capital formation and investment. Thomas H. Davenport et al. propose a view of organizational information and knowledge as currency and delineate models of information politics that firms can implement to govern its exchange. Edwin C. Nevis et al. describe a model of organizations as learning systems and prescribe directions for enhancing learning. A broader view of corporate transformation processes provided by Sumantra Ghoshal and Christopher A. Bartlett offers a perspective on the creation of new behavioral environments toward corporate renewal.

The chapters in Part Four focus on issues underlying the monitoring, valuing, and reporting of intellectual capital. Sydney G. Winter explicates a view of knowledge and competence as strategic assets, supported by a perspective on the basic definition and nature of organizational assets. Linda Argote et al. address the persistence of learning in organizations and elucidate foundational concepts for depreciating intellectual capital. Looking beyond the perspectives of firms and markets, Paul M. Romer discusses the roles of intellectual capital and ideas in the economic growth of nations.

Collectively, these pieces provide perspectives, case studies, frameworks, models, and tools toward laying a foundation for organizations developing agendas for managing intellectual capital. It is my intention that executives leverage the knowledge provided in this book toward gaining a richer understanding of the emerging field of intellectual capital and developing competitive programs for the strategic management of intellectual capital in their own organizations.

Part One

Understanding the Strategic and Operational Roles of Intellectual Capital in the Organization and the Links between Them

2

A Question of Balance: Case Studies in Strategic Knowledge Management

Ann B. Graham and Vincent G. Pizzo

INTRODUCTION

In a recent essay, Peter Drucker (1994) wrote: "management as a practice is very old. The most successful executive in all history was surely that Egyptian who, 4,500 years or more ago, first conceived the pyramid, without precedent, designed it, and built it, and did so in an astonishingly short time." Here the Egyptian demonstrated the essence of effective knowledge management—the ability to balance creative activities that cultivate the raw materials of the mind with the disciplined execution needed to transform good ideas into valuable goods.

This balancing act was a central theme in interviews with 38 companies for *The Learning Organisation: Managing Knowledge for Business Success* (Graham, 1996). In this research, we examined knowledge management in two organisational domains (see Figure 2-1). In the fluid domain, knowledge originates and grows from individual intuition, personal networks that form outside formal organisation charts, chance encounters between people, and improvisation that ignores standard procedures to discover better ways of doing things. In the institutional domain, work is structured, controlled, and measured. Knowledge is clearly defined in procedures, reports, memos, and databases. It is usually shared selectively through official chains-of-command.

If the environment is too fluid, creative work lacks a solid connection to business goals and accountability is unclear. As a result, many great ideas never make it to market. At the other extreme, too much formality stifles the initiative and open communication necessary to conceive unique products and services and seize new opportunities quickly. The alternative is to manage with just-enough-

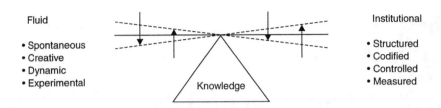

FIGURE 2-1   Challenge of Balancing Knowledge Management

discipline (JED) to maintain the right balance between the fluid and institutional domains. In this way, a company is constantly adjusting the mix of freedom and control to achieve innovation and flexibility and the operating efficiencies to succeed in today's complex marketplace.

STUDY BACKGROUND

The primary research for the EIU-IBM study consisted of a mail survey and detailed personal interviews with executives at companies based in North America, Europe, and Asia.[1] The survey focused primarily on executive familiarity with organisational learning (OL) theory and techniques and practical barriers to knowledge sharing. Field interviews explored how OL theory and other post-industrial age management ideas play out in the real world. We started by looking for examples of learning organisation features that are cited frequently in the management literature, such as learning from mistakes, open information flows, connecting knowledge creation and use with organisational agility and so on (Senge, 1990; Peters and Waterman, 1982; Garvin, 1993). Communities-of-Practice (CoP) is another key learning concept we examined (Hedberg, 1991; Seely Brown and Duguid, 1991; Wenger, 1991; Seely Brown and Solomon Gray, 1995). CoPs, which operate alongside but independently of formal structures, emerge wherever people share knowledge and rely on one another to perform work. Some are formal, such as project teams and task forces. Most are informal and constantly evolving relationships and networks. Theorists argue that companies need to better understand the social dynamics of CoPs and how the learning and work that occurs in these communities supports business goals.

The Nonaka-Takeuchi concept of the knowledge-creation spiral also helped us understand the balance issue. The spiral refers to different "modes of knowledge conversion" that occur through interactions between an individual's tacit knowledge ("personal, context-specific, and difficult to articulate") and explicit knowledge ("transmittable in formal systemic language") which is shared at the group, organisational, and inter-organisational levels (Nonaka and Takeuchi, 1995).

LEADERS IN LEARNING

The companies in our research that manage the fluid-institutional balance most effectively are those that make knowledge management central to their business strategy. Less than a third of the 38 firms fall into this category. Among those on the learning edge, nine identify learning or knowledge management goals as explicit elements of corporate strategy. Most established these goals within the past five years due to changing competitive dynamics in their markets. Several appointed an individual at the vice-president level to fill the role of "chief knowledge officer."[2] These firms have also pursued cultural change and business process reengineering programs to achieve greater organisational fluidity.

A second, rare group of companies are highly evolved learning organisations but do not consciously refer to their learning skills. They learn and share knowledge intuitively because their business purposes and values have historically and consistently guided them in this direction. As such, their ability to create a cultural milieu and management systems that promote learning is a genetic advantage that distinguishes them from those companies trying to become more learning-oriented. Three companies in the study fall into this category.

For the purposes of exploring the balance theme in this article, we chose four case examples. Buckman International, a specialty chemical manufacturer based in Memphis, Tennessee, falls into the category of companies undergoing cultural change. The other three have a genetic advantage. They include Minnesota Mining and Manufacturing (3M) and Kao Corporation, Japan's leading manufacturer of household packaged goods and chemical products. The fourth, AES Corporation (AES), is a US-based multinational independent power producer.

FLUID INTO INSTITUTIONAL

Despite major differences in size and industry, AES, 3M, Buckman, and Kao share common cultural and learning bonds. Each strives for consistency between their chosen core values, business strategy, and actual work environment. They do this by making knowledge of values a shared guide to appropriate behaviour in the company. Equally significant, they share values that stress personal freedom, cooperation, and community. Written statements are only a starting point for managing culture. The values are imbedded in structures, daily management routines, unique corporate rituals and language, and behavioural and business performance measures. In all cases, top leaders say they are the principal stewards of the values and strive to practice what they preach.

In turn, clear articulation and centralised management of values and business purposes allows the fluid environment to flourish. In each company, bureaucracy is minimal, CoPs thrive, and sharing of knowledge and information is broad and efficient. The emphasis on value-based leadership clearly liberates individuals from excessive command-and-control management. At the same time, measures of performance, closely correlated with core values and business goals, impose operational and financial accountability. This combination sustains employee focus on *all* the knowledge that is most critical to the company's success.

AES: DOING WELL BY DOING GOOD

AES has pushed the limits of conventional business wisdom to be sure that each of its employees uphold the values—of integrity, fairness, fun, and social responsibility—even when the decision involves a trade-off favouring values over profit. The values embody the founders' twin missions. Never aiming to make a fortune, their dream was to create a business to satisfy the world's need for environmentally sound, safe, and low-cost electricity, and the individual's desire for productive, fulfilling work. In fact, and to many people's surprise, AES has far surpassed its original financial goals. In 1991 and 1993, AES was the second fastest-growing company among the 4,700 NASDAQ-listed firms. In 1994, net income rose for the 11th consecutive year to $100 million. The company has 680 employees and operates plants in the US, Europe, Latin America, and Asia.

AES values are central to the evaluation of prospective employees and the content of training programs for new employees. Corporate and individual performance measures that track adherence to values are as important as financial measures. Each year employees fill out a survey rating the company's support of its values. For example, AES defines "fun" in its formal value statement as follows: "AES wants people employed by the company and those with whom the company interacts to have fun in their work. AES's goal has been to create and maintain an environment in which each person can flourish." In the survey, the criterion for having fun includes how well the company creates "an environment where people can grow and develop by using their gifts and skills to the maximum extent possible" *or* "decentralizes authority and responsibility for getting a job done to the level of the person actually doing the job."

Employee attitude surveys are a common evaluation tool but AES has taken its values survey further than most companies. Survey data are reviewed closely by top management (and upon request by other employees); the value survey is the first item on the agenda at the annual strategy meeting and values are discussed frequently in ongoing dialogues at all levels. Values also come first in the annual report's letter to shareholders. Dennis Bakke, co-founder and current CEO, says, "our values are the only thing that is centrally managed in the company."

One result is that decentralisation is taken to an extreme, unheard of, in most businesses. While many firms are trying to delegate centralised staff functions (e.g., human resources, finance) to the line, AES never centralised these functions in the first place. Instead, multi-disciplinary project teams in the plants run the operations and handle all the support tasks. For instance, there is a small finance staff at headquarters but line employees structure all project finance deals. When the company had to raise £200 million to acquire a stake in two privatised plants in Northern Ireland, two control-room operators handled the project with AES's chief financial officer (CFO) coaching from the sidelines. Over the past eight years, the CFO has raised only $300 million of the $4 billion dollars of funding for AES's plants.

All facilities are organised in "families" (e.g., the turbine family or the coal pile family) consisting of 10–20 people who manage and lead themselves. The concept of organizing around multiple family units, known as the "honeycomb," was the inspiration of a manager at AES's first plant. Families take charge of personnel management, capital budgeting, purchasing, and safety inspections. The honeycomb is also used at headquarters, where only 75 of the firm's 680 employees work (Mavrinac, 1994).

Task forces are everywhere; they include cross-company, intra-plant, and inter-plant teams. Some are temporary and address specific issues. For example, one group recently conducted an historical study of the company's 10 biggest mistakes. Others are permanent, such as those for the audit functions and strategic planning. (Permanent task force membership rotates every few years.) Corporate has a strategy task force, but operating units have almost total flexibility to draw up budgets and set strategy as long as what they do is consistent with AES's purposes and principles. Plant employees also provide direct input in the annual strategic planning process. "Our strategy is whatever the people decide," says Mr. Bakke. In lieu of a headquarters operating committee, plant and project teams convene each quarter on a companywide basis for a two-day "project review." The meeting allows people from different plants to share what they are doing and get advice on problems.

Overall, pervasive team-based management and emphasis on front-line responsibility has eliminated most of AES's formal hierarchy. There are only three layers between entry-level employees and the CEO. Most plants have only two levels. Thus, with the passing of authority to the operating level, management effectiveness—not hierarchy—guides decisions according to shared values and a sense of responsibility towards colleagues. Compensation is also tied to values and behavioural performance. Individual compensation is based on a roughly even split between technical performance and adherence to values, with a strong emphasis on qualitative self-evaluation and peer feedback.

At the same time, precise operational measurement systems and widely-shared, detailed business performance data are the critical complement to AES's fluid work environment. One of the primary jobs of the headquarters staff is to provide real-time information to the plants on all critical business issues (e.g., policies or regulatory changes related to environmental or personnel management). Detailed data is provided on key operating variables (e.g., environmental, health and safety, daily levels of power availability and costs). Such measures are not only used in managing individual plants, but are also routinely discussed via staff communication between plants.

3M: "THOU SHALT NOT KILL IDEAS"

The Economist has called 3M's balancing approach "conservatism with creativity." CEO Livio DeSimone characterises it as "innovation and stability."

(Stewart, 1996) While learning values keep 3M's inventors on the creative edge, management is vigilant about linking continuous learning and innovation to revenues. A well-known corporate target demands that 30 per cent of 3M's annual sales come from products less than four years old. Compensation for senior and division managers is also tied to the percentage of sales from new products. Other aggressive annual financial goals including 10 per cent growth in earnings per share, 27 per cent return on capital employed and an 8 per cent rise in sales per employee. Beyond the discipline of financial measures, 3M's creativity and productivity is sustained by the firm's institutional management of two key knowledge areas: (1) core technology competencies that keep the new product pipeline full and diverse; (2) corporate values that honour the needs of the innovators.

At the heart of the innovation process is the notion that 3M's 60,000 products belong to business sectors, groups, and divisions. Technology, however, belongs to the company. Approximately 33 technologies (e.g., adhesives and microreplication) are organised in "platforms" that generate "multiple products for multiple markets." Platforms are represented in product portfolios across the company. For instance, the surface texturing technique, microreplication, was first applied three decades ago to create a lens for overhead projectors. Currently, it generates over $1 billion in a multimarket family of products ranging from an abrasive that polishes golf clubs to reflective materials used on road signs.

With centralised "ownership" of the core technologies, 3M promotes knowledge transfer and entrepreneurial management unmatched among most firms its size. More than 8,000 scientists and researchers in over 100 laboratories work together without the secrecy typical of the not-invented-here syndrome. Scientists have always encouraged colleagues to try out their discoveries.

Today, a vast computerized database allows scientists to share their expertise more systematically and enables other employees to easily connect with the technology experts. Cross-fertilisation of ideas and technology is also facilitated through two institutional groups that support personal networking among scientists.

On the cultural side, values captured in corporate maxims and stories express unusual support for individual creativity. The phrase "grow and divide" describes how 3M has been able to retain the entrepreneurialism that is often lost in large organisations by encouraging employees to develop their product ideas in small, dynamic teams. Indeed, many of 3M's most lucrative profit centres began as project teams consisting of an individual with an idea and a few supporters. If the divisions grow large enough, they may break apart again to restore the dynamism.

The sanctity of time is embodied in the infamous "15 per cent rule," which allows all employees to set aside 15 per cent of their work time to pursue personal research interests. Another familiar 3M homily, "Thou shall not kill new ideas for products," is known as the 11th commandment. It is the source of countless stories, including the one that tells how Mr. DeSimone tried five times (and failed) to kill the project that yielded the 3M blockbuster, Thinsulate.™

3M's corporate language and story telling traditions are part of training programmes that teach newcomers and remind old timers about unwritten rules and informal ways work actually gets done. For instance, the 11th commandment reinforces the acceptance of challenging superiors or the patience required to shepherd projects for years before they yield results.

Leaders in the company see themselves as the keepers of the values. Mr. DeSimone says "the primary role of senior management is to create an internal environment in which people understand and value our way of operating." More specifically, he says "Our job is one of creation and destruction—supporting individual initiative while breaking down bureaucracy and cynicism. It all depends on developing a personal trust relationship between those at the top and the lower levels" (Bartlett and Ghoshal, 1995).

In addition to its corporate financial measures, 3M's conservatism emerges in rigorous checks and balances in the project development and funding systems. For example, once a product development team receives its first round of funding, it must meet clear objectives and be able to market its ideas to coaches and supporters in management to qualify for the next round. And while project champions do not need top brass approval to get started, when the costs or market potential are high, the project must pass the toughest scrutiny of 3M's top executives. Another mechanism, "pacing programs," selects high potential projects for accelerated funding. For instance, Apex, an abrasive material made from a microreplication application, was evolving slowly on a researcher's 15 per cent time, until it was recognised as a potential half billion dollar business. A "pacing program" accelerated the Apex launch from 1998 to 1995 (Stewart, 1996).

At a time when many companies have underestimated the downside of downsizing for morale, 3M has stood by its belief that knowledge is best cultivated through personal loyalty and trust built through long-term associations. Until recently, the company resisted layoffs due to business fluctuations; employee turnover has historically been limited to about 3 per cent a year. However, in the face of today's competitive pressures, even 3M is questioning whether it can sustain their record. That it may no longer be able to so was implied in the 1995 reorganisation announcement that will require a work force reduction of 5,000 jobs, at least 1,000 of which may be layoffs.

KAO—ADDING VALUE IN A KNOWLEDGE NETWORK

Almost 90 per cent of Kao's sales come from such consumer products as soaps and toiletries. In this highly competitive market, even a small improvement in quality or one new feature can translate into multi-billion yen gains in sales and profits. Thus, for Kao the key to organisational learning is understanding the needs and desires of the customer.

Kao is similar to 3M in its focus on cultural messages and core technology. For example, Kao chairman, Yoshio Maruta, cites his Buddhist faith, not managerial theory, as the inspiration for three principles of knowledge that guide his stewardship of Kao (Nonaka and Takeuchi, 1995). The first principle, "contribution to the consumer," says Kao's purpose is to provide consumers with products they want, not to compete on market share. The third principle, "the search for truth and unity," says the collective intelligence of the organisation comes from sharing and building on the knowledge of all its members. But it is the responsibility of leaders to create the right environment so that such knowledge exchange can occur.

Kao also achieves product diversity and innovation through its proprietary expertise and the cross-application of technologies in these areas: fat and oil science; surface science; polymer science; biological science; and applied physics. For instance, the study of surface tension has led to innovations in products ranging from shampoos to floppy disks.

Guided by its unifying philosophy and scientific knowledge, Kao organises its roughly 7,000 employees into a structure of top management committees, business divisions, and functions. Interaction occurs, not through the hierarchy, but through a constantly changing mix of horizontal, vertical, and multi-functional activities. Kao likens its organizational structures to a self-perpetuating and controlling biological system referred to as the "bio-function" organisation model. Mr. Maruta compares the desired work environment at Kao to the way in which parts of the human body respond to other parts' signals. The flatness, flexibility, and interconnectedness of the bio-function system is designed to maximise responsiveness to the complexity inside and outside the organisation (Nonaka and Takeuchi, 1995).

Much of the company's business—from high-level strategic decisions on new product development to business-process improvement, problem-solving, and even traditional staff work (e.g., human resources)—is done by cross-functional project teams and committees. Senior managers also strive for continuous interaction with employees at lower levels. Every meeting at Kao is open to any employee who wants to attend. Top management meetings are no exception. For example, at the quarterly R&D conference, Kao's most senior executives learn about projects directly from researchers. The conference is also open to and well-attended by non-R&D people.

The human networks are supported by a company-wide computer information system, known as the value-added network (VAN). The key characteristics of the computer network are its comprehensive store of company information and knowledge and its accessibility to all employees. VAN makes all business information on the system immediately available to everyone.

Computer terminals are located throughout the company, including large open meeting areas called "decision spaces." Offices are configured around these spaces, which have tables and chairs that invite people to join in discussions. On a typical day, executives rarely stay in their offices. Instead, they assemble in decision spaces for impromptu brainstorming sessions as well as scheduled meetings.

Employees work with several VAN databases that are integrated through a company-wide local area network. These include databases in sales, marketing, production, distribution, and a network covering all the offices in Japan. The integration of and open access to the knowledge databases allows rapid co-ordination between production, marketing, distribution, and product design specialists. For example, marketers make detailed advertising plans, budgets, and schedules available to everyone through the marketing database.

The VAN's customer knowledge is augmented by a nation-wide customer service system, known as the "Echo of Consumers' Helpful Opinions" (ECHO). Operators handle an average of 250 calls daily from consumers, which are archived on ECHO the same day. Relevant information from ECHO is also digested in reports sent to managers in R&D, production, marketing, and sales.

Kao's innovative use of multi-tier team management and computer-based networks is best illustrated by a highly successful foray into the cosmetics market. In the 1980s, a group working in the surface and biological sciences developed a skin care line called Sofina. Its success helped Kao expand in just seven years to become the number-two cosmetics maker in Japan. For this project, the computer network not only provided the engineers with information from the company's extensive databases on fats, oils, surfactants, and polymers but also gave marketing personnel detailed consumer data. Some team members assembled sales data from the retail outlets, while others tried to match customer needs with ideas and technologies developed in Kao's R&D labs. At the same time, the network compared findings from market research with unsolicited consumer comments from the ECHO hot-line.

BUCKMAN'S VIRTUAL KNOWLEDGE TRANSFER

Buckman Laboratories' business is to sell specialty chemicals and support services used in treatment of water and industrial processes. The privately-held company sells its services in 90 countries. It has a workforce of 1,200 people, approximately half of whom are field salespeople ("associates") and technical service experts engaged in front-line sales and technical support of customers.

Today, Buckman employees worldwide communicate through a global electronic communications network called K'Netix™—the Buckman Knowledge Network. While traditional management information systems (MIS) tend to support the formal structures in a company, K'Netix™ is a leading edge model for social computing (Seely Brown and Solomon Gray, 1995) or MIS applied to facilitate knowledge that grows and flows in CoPs. As use of K'Netix™ has increased, and proven its contribution to business results, it has legitimized work done in the non-bureaucratic, fast-paced world of CoPs in cyberspace.

The beauty of K'Netix™ is its close alignment with the company's core business strategy. Chairman and CEO Bob Buckman believes company sales are directly proportional to the number and quality of the sales professionals serving customers. The corporate goal by the year 2000 is to have 80 per cent of employees "effectively engaged" in work that supports front-line interaction with the customer. Thus K'Netix™ is designed to focus everyone's attention on the needs of the front-line sales and technical professionals and work that maximizes the competitive benefits of Buckman's knowledge strategy in the marketplace.

To meet these objectives, Buckman Labs has steadily increased the number and academic qualifications of associates around the world. K'Netix™ complements their investment in people with the computer network that enables employees operating in 90 countries to jointly build Buckman's knowledge database and rapidly coordinate daily business activities. Everyone in the company can access and enter information in most parts of the system. People, with all levels of computer literacy, use it with ease. It operates across time and space—that is, the knowledge base is available, globally, 24 hours a day, seven days a week so that the company never closes.

The network consists of e-mail, seven "Forums," which are the repositories of most institutional knowledge and considerable fluid knowledge. Some Forums are open to everyone while others are limited. Each Forum includes a message bulletin board, a library, and virtual conference rooms. Since the majority of salespeople spend less than 14 per cent of their time in the office, the system is connected through a modem link to the CompuServe network. Combining knowledge databases, virtual work areas, and e-mail in one system creates an automatic incentive for people to use K'Netix™. Most employees log on the Forums at least once a day.

The success of the network can be illustrated in countless stories. In one instance, field personnel in Asia used K'Netix™ to transmit questions about a problem at a steel mill in Malaysia to Buckman experts worldwide. Within 48 hours, discussions were held with experts in South Africa, Europe, Brazil, and the US and the source of the problem was identified. During the course of developing a treatment program, Buckman installed the K'Netix™ software on the customer's laptop so that he could join in the cyberspace discussions among the account manager and company experts.

Buckman has also trademarked the K'Netix™ name so it can be used as a brand to convey not only the powers of the computer network but also the broader benefits of the knowledge transfer management philosophy. Branding of services is common in marketing specialty chemicals, but K'Netix™ is unique because it is associated with the intangible knowledge investments in Buckman's management processes and corporate culture.

Qualitative observations about the network confirm the influence K'Netix™ has had on the company's culture. Indeed, managers say that before the network existed, communications might have passed through several levels before the front-line could move ahead. With the network, it doesn't matter if you are a sales associate, a regional or district manager or a corporate VP—everybody talks to everybody. As the technology expands nonhierarchical decision-making, it has also exposed people whose status is inconsistent with their contribution. Mr. Buckman observes: "When we opened up the communications system, the old smoke blowers got shut off because people wouldn't listen to them. Now, those who really have something intelligent to say are getting more attention and their influence is growing."

K'Netix™ has unleashed powerful decentralising and democratic forces in Buckman's world of work. Still, the elements most crucial to Buckman's strategy—the computer network and the culture—are managed centrally. Thus, the vice-president of knowledge transfer, Victor Baillargeon, is one of the most senior executives in the formal hierarchy, reporting to the CEO. Since his appointment in 1991, Mr. Baillargeon has overseen the development of the network and managed crucial cultural issues, including a shift in the traditional mindset of IT staff from technology design to knowledge generation.

When it comes to matters of culture, Mr Buckman says, "the climate leaders create has a major impact on our ability to share knowledge across time and space." That ideal climate is embodied in a Buckman code of ethics which he calls the "waterline" for freedom of expression on the network. Excerpts from the code shown below emphasise the respect for the individual, community commitment, and customer focus that are crucial to the success of K'Netix.™

> *Because we are separated—by many miles, by diversity of cultures and languages—we at Buckman need a clear understanding of the basic principles by which we will operate our company. These are:*
>
> - *That the company is made up of individuals—each of whom has different capabilities and potentials—all of which are necessary to the success of the company.*
> - *That we acknowledge that individuality by treating each other with dignity and respect—striving to maintain continuous and positive communications among all of us.*
> - *That we will make decisions in the light of what is right for the good of the whole company rather than what is expedient in a given situation.*
> - *That our customers are the only reason for the existence of our company. To serve them properly, we must supply products and services which provide economic benefit over and above their cost.*

The bigger challenge has been to create a culture where people accept the authenticity of electronic communications in the same way they do telephone or face-to-face dialogue. That is where Mr. Buckman believes his leadership, with or without a code of conduct, makes the difference. "Everyone in the organisation is watching the CEO," he says. "If the CEO does not use it [the K'Netix™ system] then others will not think it is important."

CONFIGURING FOR KNOWLEDGE

Based on our research and other industry experience, we have developed a framework to help companies position and manage knowledge for competitive advantage. We call the framework "Configuring for Knowledge" (see Figure 2-2). The tool can be used by people throughout an organisation. However, senior

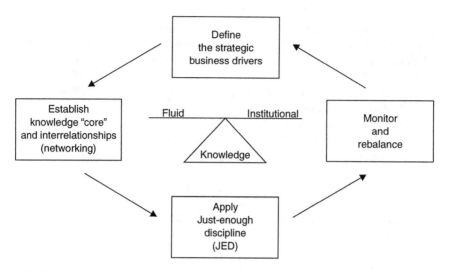

FIGURE 2-2 "Configuring for Knowledge" Framework

management must first set the stage by defining the overarching strategic context for the business and the role of knowledge management. By establishing knowledge management as a strategic business process, the tool will have greater credibility at other levels in the company.

The process of applying the framework has four elements. We purposely depict these elements not as sequential steps but as four interdependent and dynamic elements in a closed loop system. Depending on the strategic direction and variables, the framework can be applied in different sequences. For example, a strategy to change marketplace dynamics might emphasise a different sequence of elements than one where the focus is to add value over current competitors.

We also present this model as an integrating framework that can help executives explore different applications and combinations of business improvement tools from TQM, reengineering, and organisational learning. Thus "Configuring for Knowledge" may combine different management tools and techniques but is always focused on the balance between fluid and institutional domains that will yield operating efficiencies and strategic flexibility. Below are brief explanations of each element.

IDENTIFY THE STRATEGIC BUSINESS DRIVERS

Understanding the business battleground, be it the product or service dimensions (e.g., cost, precision, value, quality) or environmental factors (e.g., competitive forces, regulations, socio-economic trends) is a logical starting point for deciding how to organise and manage knowledge assets.

3M's recent decision to spin off its data storage and imaging division, and shut down the magnetic storage unit (audio and video tape and diskettes) is a good example. Although manufacturing of computer diskettes, audiotape, and videotape generated about $650 million in sales, there was long-term evidence that the once high-value-added products had become commodities. As competition shifted from innovation to price, 3M stuck with the magnetic market because it was supported by core technologies needed by other businesses. Eventually, however, 3M saw that it could not win the cost battle, especially as raw materials for tape soared.

Another critical factor in the decision to pull out of tape and diskettes was based on changes in its core technology knowledge. Specifically, the magnetic storage unit had been supporting chemistry-based color capabilities in videotape that were also used in film and x-rays. When 3M realised that they had developed knowledge of digital colour technology to the point where they no longer needed to invest in chemistry-skills, they were ready to go ahead with the reorganisation plan (Stewart, 1996).

ESTABLISH THE KNOWLEDGE "CORE" AND INTERRELATIONSHIPS

With the strategic context well-understood, attention can shift to the core knowledge assets needed to maximise value for customers, shareholders, employees, and other stakeholders. That knowledge core includes both tangible and intangible assets in values and culture, people, technology, and business capabilities.

A second step in this analysis is to determine what and where business critical knowledge exists (in the fluid or institutional domain), how it is used (by specific segments or across the enterprise) and how spontaneously or routinely it is applied (i.e, predetermined or unknown/dynamic). Mapping knowledge flows in the organisation provides important insights regarding the fluid-institutional balance a company requires.

Once the characteristics and locations of knowledge assets have been identified, a company can begin to construct a knowledge value chain that traces the patterns of knowledge use and movement through the informal and formal sides of the organisation. For example, 3M's technology communities, AES's plant families, and Kao's key cross-functional committees may be starting points to track sources and movements of knowledge important to specific areas or the entire organisation.

Other key information from the analysis of core knowledge includes the gaps in competencies needed to meet business goals. Decisions on how to fill gaps tie back to an understanding of the market drivers. A simple example is a market situation where speed is paramount. If a company does not have the time to create the knowledge on their own, they might choose a strategic alliance and acquisition to fill the gap. On the other hand, if the situation involves an innovation need that requires scale and a high degree of internal integration and coordination, the company will be better off developing their own knowledge.

APPLY JUST-ENOUGH-DISCIPLINE (JED)

As the examples in this article have shown, we believe JED begins with a highly centralised focus on culture. The financial success of the business contrarians at AES offers especially compelling proof that values and purpose can liberate companies from the constraints of industrial age management without sacrificing business discipline. Other dimensions of JED require consideration of variables such as the speed or precision with which knowledge is disseminated. For example, is the particular type of knowledge standard and repetitive or does it change often? Is its propensity for reuse frequent or occasional? These are all questions that influence how JED is applied. In turn, answers to such questions will influence how business process improvements involving reengineering and other disciplines are planned and executed.

As suggested in the Kao and Buckman cases, opportunities to apply new information technologies (e.g., client/server, groupware, audio, video, and the Internet) to support strategic knowledge transfer and social computing are exciting, vast, and unfamiliar territory. Here the balance question is critical. One of the most fundamental challenges for IT strategists and systems designers is containing the fluid on-line environment so that people are not overwhelmed by too much information. As one executive in the study noted, "technology tends to be useful for information sharing. The question is how good is it at supporting idea generation. That's a different level of interaction."

MONITOR AND REBALANCE

Although rates of change and market risks vary widely by company and industry, all businesses are equally vulnerable to errors. And once the mistakes are made, recovery is difficult. Thus, in this world of hyperchange, the monitor and rebalance mechanism is an ongoing process that helps companies stay on top of changing marketplace signals and business performance trends. Such just-in-time market information might be the trigger that leads to a rapid reconfiguration or expansion of a company's knowledge assets that, in turn, leads to a groundbreaking product. For example, companies like Kao, recognised for their skill in knowledge conversion (the time it takes to convert R&D knowledge into a product), sustain this advantage by staying close to customers and the market and continuously relaying frontline information to and from key players in R&D, manufacturing, marketing, and sales. Their approach utilises continuous monitoring and rebalancing of strategies and flexible management systems, which is a vastly different approach from the usual strategic planning and budgeting processes that most firms employ. Indeed, traditional strategic plans and budgets often pose constraints just at the moment when flexibility is most critical. By monitoring the relationship between knowledge competence, operating performance, and strategic resiliency, a company is less likely to falter.

CONCLUSION

Concepts like the learning organisation and strategic knowledge management are considered part of a new wave of ideas in business. In many ways, however, they represent a home for best practices that have stood the test of time. As Peter Drucker's Egyptian suggests, the question of balance has always represented a critical management challenge.

Presenting the question of balance in a different way, Drucker also suggests that the contemporary struggle for companies in the knowledge age is to revive the social art of management that was neglected in the industrial age. "The essence of management is not techniques and procedures. The essence of management is to make knowledge productive. Management, in other words, is a social function. And its practice is truly a liberal art." (Drucker, 1994).

As companies look to technologies to achieve new heights of agility in the marketplace, they must also build and apply knowledge of the human-centered management practices that enable people to be all that they can be. We began our research with the premise that the most critical business challenge in the new economy is creating the social contexts that maximise human creativity and productivity. We found that the firms with the most sustainable records share that belief. These organisations are flexible, innovative and effective because their people are.

NOTES

1. A survey was sent to approximately 3,000 executives in 26 countries. Final calculations were based on 345 responses. Companies chosen for field interviews consisted primarily of large multinationals. However, several smaller firms (with fewer than 2,000 employees) and one government agency were also included. Twenty of these companies are featured in case studies.

2. Five firms had senior level executives responsible for knowledge. However, each of these individuals are from different functions and are engaged in different activities. For example, the top knowledge executive at Buckman Laboratories is an IT specialist whose primary responsibility is to oversee the company's computer-based knowledge network. At the Swedish insurance company, Skandia, the director of intellectual capital has a finance background and is currently leading the development of a knowledge-driven performance measurement tool.

REFERENCES

Bartlett, C.A. and Ghoshal, S. (1995), Changing the Role of Top Management: Beyond Structure to Process, *Harvard Business Review,* January/February, 86–96.

Bartlett, C.A. and Ghoshal, S. (1995), Changing the Role of Top Management: Beyond Systems to People, *Harvard Business Review,* May/June, 132–142.

Drucker, P.F. (1994), The Age of Social Transformation, *The Atlantic Monthly,* November.

Garvin, D.A. (1993), Building a Learning Organization, *Harvard Business Review,* July/August.

Graham, A.B. and Pizzo, V. (1996), *The Learning Organisation: Managing Knowledge for Business Success,* New York: The Economist Intelligence Unit.

Hedberg, B. (1991), How Organizations Learn and Unlearn, in P.C. Nystrom and W. H. Starbuck, *Handbook of Organizational Design, Vol. 1: Adapting Organizations to Environments,* New York: Oxford University Press.

Mavrinac, S.C. (1994), AES Honeycomb, Harvard Business School case study N9-395-132, December 9.

Nonaka, I. and Takeuchi, H. (1995), *The Knowledge-Creating Company: How Japanese Companies Create the Dynamics of Innovation,* New York: Oxford University Press.

Peters, T.J. and Waterman, R.H., Jr. (1982), *In Search of Excellence: Lessons from America's Best Run Companies,* New York: Harper & Row.

Seely Brown, J. and Duguid, P. (1991), Organisational Learning and Communities-of-Practice: Toward a Unified View of Working, Learning, and Innovation, *Organizational Science,* 2(1), 40–56.

Seely Brown, J. and Solomon Gray, E. (1995), The People Are the Company, *Fast Company,* 1(1), 78–82.

Senge, P.M. (1990), *The Fifth Discipline: The Art and Practice of the Learning Organization,* New York: Doubleday.

Stewart, T.A., (1996), 3M Fights Back, *Fortune,* February 5, 94–99.

Wenger, E. (1991), Communities-of-Practice: Where Learning Happens, *Benchmark,* Fall 1991, 7–9.

3

When Is Virtual Virtuous?
Organizing for Innovation

Henry W. Chesbrough and David J. Teece

Champions of virtual corporations are urging managers to subcontract anything and everything. All over the world, companies are jumping on the bandwagon, decentralizing, downsizing, and forging alliances to pursue innovation. Why is the idea of the virtual organization so tantalizing? Because we have come to believe that bureaucracy is bad and flexibility is good. And so it follows that a company that invests in as little as possible will be more responsive to a changing marketplace and more likely to attain global competitive advantage.

There is no question that many large and cumbersome organizations have been outperformed by smaller "networked" competitors. Consider the eclipse of IBM in PCs and of DEC in workstations by Packard Bell and Sun Microsystems. But while there are many successful virtual companies, there are even more failures that don't make the headlines. After many years of studying the relationship between organization and innovation, we believe that the virtues of being virtual have been oversold. The new conventional wisdom ignores the distinctive role that large integrated companies can play in the innovation process. Those rushing to form alliances instead of nurturing and guarding their own capabilities may be risking their future.

WHAT'S SPECIAL ABOUT VIRTUAL?

What gives the virtual company its advantage? In essence, incentives and responsiveness. Virtual companies coordinate much of their business through the marketplace, where free agents come together to buy and sell one another's goods and services; thus virtual companies can harness the power of market forces to develop, manufacture, market, distribute, and support their offerings in ways that fully integrated companies can't duplicate. As William Joy, vice president of research and development at Sun Microsystems, puts it, "Not all the smart people [in the workstation industry] work for Sun." Because an outside developer of workstation software can obtain greater rewards by selling software to Sun customers than by developing the same software as a Sun employee, he or she will move faster, work harder, and take more risks. Using high-powered, market-based incentives such as stock options and attractive bonuses, a virtual company can quickly access the technical resources it needs, if those resources are available. In situations where technology is changing rapidly, large companies that attempt to do everything inside will flounder when competing against small companies with highly trained and motivated employees.

But the incentives that make a virtual company powerful also leave it vulnerable. As incentives become greater and risk taking increases, coordination among parties through the marketplace becomes more and more difficult, precisely because so much personal reward is at stake. Each party to joint development activity necessarily acts in its own self-interest. Over time, innovation can generate unforeseen surprises that work to the advantage of some parties and to the disadvantage of others. The result: Once-friendly partners may be unwilling or unable to align strategically, and coordinated development activity falters. In contrast, integrated, centralized companies do not generally reward people for taking risks, but they do have established processes for settling conflicts and coordinating all the activities necessary for innovation.

This trade-off between incentives and control lies at the heart of the decision that managers must make about how to organize for innovation. If virtual organizations and integrated companies are at opposite ends of the spectrum, alliances occupy a kind of organizational middle ground. An alliance can achieve some of the coordination of an integrated company, but, like players in a virtual network, the members of an alliance will be driven to enhance their own positions, and over time their interests may diverge. The challenge for managers is to choose the organizational form that best matches the type of innovation they are pursuing.

TYPES OF INNOVATION

When should companies organize for innovation by using decentralized (or virtual) approaches, and when should they rely on internal organization? The answer depends on the innovation in question.

Some innovations are *autonomous*—that is, they can be pursued independently from other innovations. A new turbocharger to increase horsepower in an automobile engine, for example, can be developed without a complete redesign of the engine or the rest of the car. In contrast, some innovations are fundamentally *systemic*—that is, their benefits can be realized only in conjunction with related, complementary innovations. To profit from instant photography, Polaroid needed to develop both new film technology and new camera technology. Similarly, lean manufacturing is a systemic innovation because it requires interrelated changes in product design, supplier management, information technology, and so on.

The distinction between autonomous and systemic innovation is fundamental to the choice of organizational design. When innovation is autonomous, the decentralized virtual organization can manage the development and commercialization tasks quite well. When innovation is systemic, members of a virtual organization are dependent on the other members, over whom they have no control. In either case, the wrong organizational choice can be costly.

Consider what happened to General Motors when the automobile industry shifted from drum brakes to disc brakes, an autonomous innovation. General Motors was slow to adopt disc brakes because it had integrated vertically in the production of the old technology. GM's more decentralized competitors relied instead on market relationships with their suppliers—and the high-powered incentives inherent in those relationships. As a result, they were able to beat GM to market with the new disc brakes, which car buyers wanted. When companies inappropriately use centralized approaches to manage autonomous innovations, as GM did in this case, small companies and more decentralized large companies will usually outperform them.

To understand why the two types of innovation call for different organizational strategies, consider the information flow essential to innovation. Information about new products and technologies often develops over time as managers absorb new research findings, the results of early product experiments, and initial customer feedback. To commercialize an innovation profitably, a tremendous amount of knowledge from industry players, from customers, and sometimes from scientists must be gathered and understood. This task is easier if the information is codified.

Codified information—for example, specifications that are captured in industry standards and design rules—can often be transferred almost as effectively from one company to another as it can within a single company. Because such information is easily duplicated, it has little natural protection. Sometimes bits and pieces can be protected by intellectual property rights, but those pieces, especially trade secrets and patents, are small islands in a broad ocean of knowledge.

Other information does not travel as easily between companies. Tacit knowledge is knowledge that is implicitly grasped or used but has not been fully articulated, such as the know-how of a master craftsman or the ingrained perspectives of a specific company or work unit. Because such knowledge is deeply embedded in individuals or companies, it tends to diffuse slowly and only with effort and the transfer of people. Established companies can protect the tacit knowledge they hold, sharing only codified information. They can be quite strategic about what they disclose and when they disclose it.

The information needed to integrate an autonomous innovation with existing technologies is usually well understood and may even be codified in industry standards. Systemic innovations, on the other hand, pose a unique set of management challenges regarding information exchange. By their very nature, systemic innovations require information sharing and coordinated adjustment *throughout an entire product system.* Here is where a market-based, virtual approach to innovation poses serious strategic hazards. Unaffiliated companies linked through arm's-length contracts often cannot achieve sufficient coordination. Each company wants the other to do more, while each is also looking for ways to realize the most gain from the innovation. Information sharing can be reduced or biased, as each seeks to get the most at the other's expense. In most cases, the open exchange of information that fuels systemic innovation will be easier and safer within a company than across company boundaries. The inevitable conflicts and choices that arise as a systemic innovation develops can best be resolved by an integrated company's internal management processes.

THE CASE FOR INDUSTRY STANDARDS

Coordinating a systemic innovation is particularly difficult when industry standards do not exist and must be pioneered. In such instances, virtual organizations are likely to run into strategic problems. Consider how technical standards emerge. Market participants weigh many competing technologies and eventually rally around one of them. There are winners and losers among the contestants, and potential losers can try to undermine the front-runner or to fragment the standard by promoting a rival. Until a clear winner emerges, customers may choose to sit on the sidelines rather than risk making the wrong choice.

By virtue of its size and scope, an integrated company may be able to advance a new standard simply by choosing to adopt a particular technology. If a large company commits itself to one of a host of competing technologies, consumers as well as companies promoting rival technologies will probably be persuaded to follow suit. Virtual companies, however, which may be struggling to resolve conflicts within their networks, won't be able to break a deadlock in a complicated standards battle. Players in a network won't be able to coordinate themselves to act like a large company.

Once a new standard has been established, virtual organizations can manage further innovation quite well. But when an industry begins to advance technology to a new level, the cycle can begin anew. Again, technically feasible choices present new strategic trade-offs. Suppliers, competitors, and customers may fail to agree on a common path. Unless a big player emerges to break the logjam among rival technologies, the existing standard will prevail long past its usefulness.

Today computer floppy disks are frozen in an old standard because no single company has been able to establish a new one. IBM pioneered the 3.5-inch hard case diskette in 1987 when it introduced its new line of PS/2 personal computers. Within two years, the memory capacity of 3.5-inch diskettes doubled from 720 kilobytes to 1.44 megabytes, where it has remained ever since.

Why? The technical capability to expand diskette capacity is available, but no company has the reputation and strength to set a new standard. Through the 1980s, IBM was large enough to coordinate standards among the key participants in the industry: personal computer manufacturers, diskette makers, and software publishers. If IBM told the industry it would use a particular capacity on its next generation of machines, others did the same. But in the 1990s, IBM's leadership of the PC market came to an end, perhaps permanently. Today IBM is not strong enough to move the industry by itself, and it won't move ahead of the other industry players and risk being stranded if they don't follow.

A simple rule of thumb applies: When innovation depends on a series of interdependent innovations—that is, when innovation is systemic—independent companies will not usually be able to coordinate themselves to knit those innovations together. Scale, integration, and market leadership may be required to establish and then to advance standards in an industry.

THE IBM PC: VIRTUAL SUCCESS OR FAILURE?

IBM's development of the personal computer is a fascinating example of both the advantages and disadvantages of using virtual approaches to pursue innovation. When IBM launched its first PC in 1981, the company elected to outsource all the major components from the marketplace. By tapping the capabilities of other companies, IBM was able to get its first product to market in only 15 months. The microprocessor (the 8088) was purchased from Intel, and the operating system (which became PC-DOS) was licensed from a then fledgling software company, Microsoft. In effect, the IBM PC had an "open" architecture: It was based on standards and components that were widely available. The high-powered incentives of the marketplace could coordinate the roles of component manufacturers and software vendors. IBM successfully promoted its open architecture to hundreds of third-party developers of software applications and hardware accessory products, knowing that those products would add to the appeal of the PC.

IBM also relied on the market to distribute the product. Although IBM launched its own IBM Product Centers as retail storefronts and had its own direct sales force for large corporate customers, the majority of the company's systems were distributed through independent retailers, initially ComputerLand and Sears. Eventually, there were more than 2,000 retail outlets.

By using outside parties for hardware, software, and distribution, IBM greatly reduced its investment in bringing the PC to market. More important, those relationships allowed IBM to launch an attack against Apple, which had pioneered the market and was growing quickly. The IBM PC was an early success, and it spawned what became the dominant architecture of the entire microcomputer industry. By 1984, three years after the introduction of the PC, IBM replaced Apple as the number one supplier of microcomputers, with 26% of the PC business. By 1985, IBM's share had grown to 41%. Many observers attributed the PC's success to IBM's creative use of outside relationships. More than a few business analysts hailed the IBM PC development as a model for doing business in the future.

Indeed, IBM's approach in its PC business is exactly the kind of decentralized strategy that commentators are urging large, slow-moving companies to adopt. The early years of the IBM PC show many of the benefits of using markets and outside companies to coordinate innovation: fast development of technology and tremendous technological improvements from a wide variety of sources.

With the passage of time, though, the downside of IBM's decentralized approach has become apparent. IBM failed to anticipate that its virtual and open approach would prevent the company from directing the PC architecture it had created. The open architecture and the autonomy of its vendors invited design mutinies and the entry of IBM-compatible PC manufacturers. At first, competitors struggled to achieve compatibility with IBM's architecture, but after several years compatibility was widespread in the industry. And once that happened, manufacturers could purchase the same CPU from Intel and the same operating system from Microsoft, run the same application software (from Lotus, Microsoft, WordPerfect, and others), and sell through the same distribution channels (such as ComputerLand, BusinessLand and Micro-Age). IBM had little left on which to establish a competitive advantage.

To maintain technological leadership, IBM decided to advance the PC architecture. To do that, IBM needed to coordinate the many interrelated pieces of the architecture—a systemic technology coordination task. However, the third-party hardware and software suppliers that had helped establish the original architecture did not follow IBM's lead. When IBM introduced its OS/2 operating system, the company could not stop Microsoft from introducing Windows, an application that works with the old DOS operating system, thereby greatly reducing the advantages of switching to OS/2. And third-party hardware and software companies made investments that extended the usefulness of the original PC architecture. Similarly, Intel helped Compaq steal a march on IBM in 1986, when Compaq introduced the first PC based on Intel's 80386 microprocessor, an enhancement over the earlier generations of microprocessors used in IBM and compatible machines. Even though IBM owned 12% of Intel at the time, it couldn't prevent Intel from working with Compaq to beat IBM to market. This was the beginning of the end of IBM's ability to direct the evolution of PC architecture.

By the third quarter of 1995, IBM's share of the PC market had fallen to just 7.3%, trailing Compaq's 10.5% share. Today its PC business is rumored to be modestly profitable at best. Most of the profits from the PC architecture have migrated upstream to the supplier of the microprocessor (Intel) and the operating system (Microsoft), and to outside makers of application software. The combined market value of those suppliers and third parties today greatly exceeds IBM's.

IBM's experience in the PC market illustrates the strategic importance of organization in the pursuit of innovation. Virtual approaches encounter serious problems when companies seek to exploit systemic innovation. Key development activities that depend on one another must be conducted in-house to capture the rewards from long-term R&D investments. Without directed coordination, the necessary complementary innovations required to leverage a new technology may not be forthcoming.

THE VIRTUOUS VIRTUALS

How have the most successful virtual companies accomplished the difficult task of coordination? The virtual companies that have demonstrated staying power are all at the center of a network that they use to leverage their own capabilities. Few virtual companies that have survived and prospered have outsourced everything. Rather, the virtuous virtuals have carefully nurtured and guarded the internal capabilities that provide the essential underpinnings of competitive advantage. And they invest considerable resources to maintain and extend their core competencies internally. Indeed, without these companies' unique competencies and capabilities, their strategic position in the network would be short-lived.

Consider the well-known battle between MIPS Technologies and Sun Microsystems for control of workstation processors. (See Benjamin Gomes-Casseres, "Group Versus Group: How Alliance Networks Compete," HBR July-August 1994.) MIPS was trying to promote its Advanced Computing Environment (ACE) against Sun's Scalable Processor Architecture (SPARC). Sun had strong internal capabilities, whereas MIPS tried to compete as a more virtual player, leveraging off of the competencies of partners such as Compaq, DEC, and Silicon Graphics. MIPS had a good technical design, but that was literally all it had, and this hollowness left the company at the mercy of its partners. As soon as DEC and Compaq reduced their commitment to the ACE initiative, the network fell apart and pulled MIPS down with it. The very reliance of virtual companies on partners, suppliers, and other outside companies exposes them to strategic hazards. Put another way, there are plenty of small, dynamic companies that have not been able to outperform larger competitors. In particular, a hollow company like MIPS is ill equipped to coordinate a network of companies. Although Sun also worked with alliance partners, it had strong internal capabilities in systems design, manufacturing, marketing, sales, service, and support. As a result, Sun can direct and advance the SPARC architecture, a dominant technology in the industry.

Many companies with superior capabilities have prospered as the dominant player in a network. Japanese keiretsu are structured that way. Consider Toyota, whose successful introduction of the lean production system—a truly systemic innovation—required tremendous coordination with its network of suppliers. Because Toyota was much larger than its suppliers, and because, until recently, it was the largest customer of virtually all of them, it could compel those suppliers to make radical changes in their business practices. In a more egalitarian network, suppliers can demand a large share of the economic benefits of innovations, using what economists call hold-up strategies. Strong central players like Toyota are rarely vulnerable to such tactics and are thus in a better position to drive and coordinate systemic innovation.

The most successful virtual companies sit at the center of networks that are far from egalitarian. Nike may rely on Asian partners for manufacturing, but its capabilities in design and marketing allow it to call all the shots. In the computer industry, Intel has effective control of the 80X86 microprocessor standard, Microsoft dominates PC operating systems, and Sun is driving the SPARC architecture. Those companies control and coordinate the advance of technologies in their areas, and in this regard they function more like integrated companies than like market-based virtuals.

CHOOSING THE RIGHT ORGANIZATIONAL DESIGN

Today few companies can afford to develop internally all the technologies that might provide an advantage in the future. In every company we studied, we found a mix of approaches: Some technologies were "purchased" from other companies; others were acquired through licenses, partnerships, and alliances; and still other critical technologies were developed internally. Getting the right balance is crucial, as IBM's disastrous experience in PCs illustrates. But what constitutes the right balance?

Consider how a successful innovator such as Motorola evaluates the trade-offs. Motorola, a leader in wireless communications technology, has declared its long-term goal to be the delivery of "untethered communication"—namely, communication anytime, anywhere, without the need for wires, power cords, or other constraints. In order to achieve that goal, Motorola must make important decisions about where and how to advance the required technologies. Those decisions turn on a handful of questions: Is the technology systemic or likely to become systemic in the future? What capabilities exist in-house and in the current supplier base? When will needed technologies become available?

For Motorola, battery technology is critical because it determines the functionality that can be built into a handheld communications device and the length of time that the device can be used before recharging. Batteries have been a pacing technology in this area for many years.

As Motorola scans the horizon for improved battery technology, it encounters a familiar trade-off between the degree of technological advancement and the number of reliable volume suppliers. Conventional battery technologies such as nickel cadmium (Ni-Cd) have become commodities, and there are many suppliers. But few if any suppliers can offer the more advanced technologies Motorola needs. And the most exotic technologies, such as fuel cells and solid-state energy sources, are not yet commercially viable from any supplier. How should Motorola organize to obtain each of the technologies it might need? Under what circumstances should the company buy the technology from a supplier and when should it form alliances or joint ventures? When should Motorola commit to internal development of the technology?

For Ni-Cd technology, the clear choice for Motorola is to buy the technology, or to use the market to coordinate access to this technology, because Motorola can rely on competition among many qualified suppliers to deliver what it wants, when needed, for a competitive price. Motorola faces a more complex decision for fuel cells and solid-state battery technologies. Should Motorola wait until those technologies are more widely available, or should the company opt for a joint venture or internal development?

Before deciding to wait for cutting-edge battery technologies to be developed, Motorola must consider three issues. One is that Motorola could lose the ability to influence the direction of the technology; the early commercial forms may be designed for applications that do not benefit Motorola, such as electric automobiles. The second problem is that Motorola might lose the ability to pace the technology, to bring it to market at a competitively desirable time. The third issue is that if such technologies are—or become—systemic and Motorola has no control over them, the company may not be able to advance related technologies and design features to achieve its goal of untethered communication.

Those issues suggest that Motorola cannot simply wait for the technologies to be provided by the market. Rather, Motorola needs to build strong ties to suppliers with the best capabilities, thus increasing its ability to direct the path of future systemic innovation. Where Motorola itself has strong capabilities, the company should pursue the technologies on its own.

To retain its leadership over the long term, Motorola must continue to develop the critical parts of its value chain internally and acquire less critical technologies from the market or from alliances. Although networks with their high-powered incentives may be effective over the short term for an unchanging technology, they will not adapt well over the long term as technology develops and companies must depend on certain internal capabilities to keep up. The popularity of networked companies and decentralization arises, in part, from observations over a time horizon that is far too short. Remember the enthusiasm that greeted IBM's early success in PCs.

SCALE AND SCOPE

Business history presents us with a lesson of striking relevance to the organizational decisions managers face today. In the classic *Scale and Scope,* Alfred Chandler details how the modern corporation evolved in the United States, Germany, and Great Britain at the end of the nineteenth century. Managers who invested the capital to build large-scale enterprises blazed the trail for the leading industries of the second industrial revolution. Markets in railroads, steel, chemicals, and petroleum were developed and shaped by major companies, not the other way around. The most successful of those companies were the first in their industries to make the massive investments in manufacturing, management, and distribution that were needed to realize the gains from innovation.

Companies that failed to make such coordinated, internal commitments during this period were soon thrust aside. The experience of British companies provides a cautionary tale for the champions of the virtual company. Many enjoyed early technological leads in their industries, but the reluctance of those family-run companies to relinquish control to outside investors prevented them from investing to build the capabilities they needed to commercialize their technologies. When German or U.S. competitors made the requisite investments, British companies lost their leadership position. In chemicals, for example, the British lead in the

1870s was completely lost by 1890. History even provided British chemical companies with a second chance when Germany's defeat in World War I temporarily cost German chemical manufacturers their plants and distribution networks. But by 1930, German chemical companies regained the lead because the British again failed to invest adequately. The lesson is that companies that develop their own capabilities can outperform those that rely too heavily on coordination through markets and alliances to build their businesses.

The leading industries of the late nineteenth and early twentieth centuries—chemicals, steel, and railroads—all experienced rapid systemic innovation. The winners were the companies that made major internal investments to shape the markets, rather than those that relied on others to lead the way. While business conditions have certainly changed, many of the principles that worked a century ago still pertain.

Today leading companies like Intel and Microsoft make extensive investments to enhance their current capabilities and spur the creation of new ones. Because so many important innovations are systemic, decentralization without strategic leverage and coordination is exactly the wrong organizational strategy. In most cases, only a large company will have the scale and scope to coordinate complementary innovations. For both the chemicals industry 100 years ago and the microcomputer industry today, long-term success requires considerable and sustained internal investment within a company. The lessons of the second industrial revolution apply to the third: Adept, well-managed companies that commit the right internal resources to innovation will shape the markets and build the new industries of the twenty-first century.

Ameritech's Strategy for Emerging Technologies

Ameritech, a Regional Bell Operating Company with wire and fiber assets in the Midwest, has the potential to be a major player in the development of on-demand video and interactive information services for home use. In emerging technologies such as multimedia, no one has all the information to determine what capabilities a company must develop internally or access through the market. The only certainty is that the promise of this market will depend on the co-development of many technologies, including data formats, throughput rates, wiring topologies, billing systems, and user interfaces.

Because the eventual configuration of the multimedia industry is unknown (and arguably unknowable ex ante), organizations such as Ameritech must become insiders to the discussions among a range of potential industry players. In emerging markets that are dependent on evolving technologies, considerable information sharing among a wide variety of companies will ultimately result in a road map for the industry. Virtual organizations can serve as catalysts to the development of industry directions and standards in ways that fully integrated organizations cannot.

Consider the role of alliances in Ameritech's multimedia strategy. By allying its own capabilities with those of companies with relevant and complementary skills, Ameritech can participate directly in defining and developing an architecture that will ultimately manage the emerging technologies. One such alliance is with Random House, a leading print publisher of books and magazines, with properties such as the *New Yorker,* Condé Nast, Fodor's, and Arthur Frommer Travel Guides. Random House is capable of supplying significant "content" over Ameritech's wires into the home. This alliance allows both companies to begin to explore the business and technical requirements of providing content into the home.

Ameritech and Random House have formed a joint venture to acquire a start-up virtual company called Worldview Systems, which publishes an electronic monthly current events database of travel information about more than 170 destinations around the world. While Worldview Systems products are now sold primarily through travel agents and an 800 telephone number, Ameritech and Random House believe that this type of product may turn out to be ideal for delivery to the home. As Thomas Touton, Ameritech Development's vice president for venture capital, notes, such exploratory investments "require support from senior management willing to move fast in investing but be patient in waiting for returns, and an investment focus that is strongly synergistic with the company's operations."

When and if the promise of the multimedia market becomes real, Ameritech will doubtless be competing against other powerful players. But Ameritech may already have an inside track in the race to deliver information and video on demand into the home. Through alliances such as the one with Random House and exploratory investments in virtual companies such as Worldview Systems, Ameritech has been able to share information and know-how with other potential industry participants and become an insider with the potential to influence the direction of this nascent industry. Until a technological direction becomes clear, companies must invest in capabilities and become active participants in the information dissemination process. Virtual organizations can be an extremely valuable tool at this early stage of market evolution.

Part Two

Creating an Infrastructure
for Cultivating and Sharing
Intellectual Capital

4

The Link between Individual and Organizational Learning

Daniel H. Kim

All organizations learn, whether they consciously choose to or not—it is a fundamental requirement for their sustained existence. Some firms deliberately advance organizational learning, developing capabilities that are consistent with their objectives; others make no focused effort and, therefore, acquire habits that are counterproductive. Nonetheless, all organizations learn.

But what does it mean that an organization learns? We can think of organizational learning as a metaphor derived from our understanding of individual learning. In fact, organizations ultimately learn via their individual members. Hence, theories of individual learning are crucial for understanding organizational learning. Psychologists have studied individual learning for decades, but they are still far from fully understanding the workings of the human mind. Likewise, the theory of organizational learning is still in its embryonic stage.[1]

The purpose of this paper is to build a theory about the process through which individual learning advances organizational learning. To do this, we must address the role of individual learning and memory, differentiate between levels of learning, take into account different organizational types, and specify the transfer mechanism between individual and organizational learning. This transfer is at the heart of organizational learning: the process through which individual learning becomes embedded in an organization's memory and structure. Until now, it has received little attention and is not well understood, although a promising interaction between organization theory and psychology has begun.[2] To contribute to our understanding of the nature of the learning organization, I present a framework that focuses on the crucial link between individual learning and organizational learning. Once we have a clear understanding of this transfer process, we can actively manage the learning process to make it consistent with an organization's goals, vision, and values.

Reprinted from "The Link between Individual and Organizational Learning" by Daniel H. Kim. *Sloan Management Review,* Fall 1993, pp. 37–50 by permission of publisher.

INDIVIDUAL LEARNING

The importance of individual learning for organizational learning is at once obvious and subtle—obvious because all organizations are composed of individuals; subtle because organizations can learn independent of any specific individual but not independent of all individuals. Psychologists, linguists, educators, and others have heavily researched the topic of learning at the individual level. They have made discoveries about cognitive limitations as well as the seemingly infinite capacity of the human mind to learn new things.[3] Piaget's focus on the cognitive-development processes of children and Lewin's work on action research and laboratory training have provided much insight into how we learn as individuals and in groups.[4] Some of these theories are based on stimulus-response behaviorism. Some focus on cognitive capabilities, and others on psychodynamic theory. Numerous other theories have been proposed, debated, and tested, such as Pavlov's classical conditioning, Skinner's operant conditioning, Tolman's sign learning, Gestalt theory, and Freud's psychodynamics.[5]

Despite all the research done to date, we still know relatively little about the human mind and the learning process. It seems that the more knowledge we gain, the more we realize how little we know. But let's start at the beginning—we need a common definition of the word "learning" on which to build.

A Working Definition of Learning

Jaques has noted that most words in the field of organizational development—even "manager," "plan," and "work"—are ill defined. Such words have "so many meanings that they have value only as vague slogans."[6] Such is the case with the word "learning," a term whose meaning varies widely by context.

Levels of Learning: Operational and Conceptual. The dictionary definition states that learning is "the acquiring of knowledge or skill." Thus learning encompasses two meanings: (1) the acquisition of skill or *know-how,* which implies the physical ability to produce some action, and (2) the acquisition of *know-why,* which implies the ability to articulate a conceptual understanding of an experience. A number of theorists make this connection between thought and action.[7] Argyris and Schon argue that learning takes place only when new knowledge is translated into different behavior that is replicable.[8] For Piaget, the key to learning lies in the mutual interaction of accommodation (adapting our mental concepts based on our experience in the world) and assimilation (integrating our experience into existing mental concepts).[9] As Kolb states: "Learning is the process whereby knowledge is created through the transformation of experience."[10] Thus both parts of the definition are important: what people learn (know-how) and how they understand and apply that learning (know-why).

For example, a carpenter who has mastered the skills of woodworking without understanding the concept of building coherent structures like tables and houses can't utilize those skills effectively. Similarly, a carpenter who possesses vast knowledge about architecture and design but who has no complementary skills to produce designs can't put that know-why to effective use. Learning can thus be defined as *increasing one's capacity to take effective action.*

Another way to think about the two facets is as operational and conceptual learning. This distinction is an important part of the model developed here.

Experiential Learning Model.   Experiential learning theory is the school of thought that best accommodates these two aspects of learning.[11] One of the theorists associated with this school is Lewin, whose learning cycle is represented in Figure 4-1.[12]

As Lewin describes it, a person continually cycles through a process of having a concrete experience, making observations and reflections on that experience, forming abstract concepts and generalizations based on those reflections, and testing those ideas in a new situation, which leads to another concrete experience. This basic cycle has appeared in a variety of settings. In the total quality management (TQM) literature, it shows up as the Deming cycle of plan-do-check-act.[13] Deming himself refers to it as the Shewhart cycle of plan-do-study-act.[14] In organizational development, Schein calls his version the observation-emotional reaction-judgment-intervention cycle.[15] Argyris and Schon refer to a discovery-invention-production-generalization cycle of learning.[16]

At the risk of added confusion, I have based my model of individual learning on Kofman's version of the learning cycle, as shown in Figure 4-2.[17] The observe-assess-design-implement (OADI) cycle preserves the salient features of the versions mentioned above, but the terms have clearer connections to activities

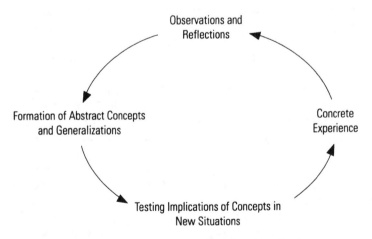

Source: D.A. Kolb, *Experiential Learning: Experience as the Source of Learning and Development* (Englewood Cliffs, New Jersey: Prentice-Hall, 1984), p. 21.

FIGURE 4-1   The Lewinian Experiential Learning Model

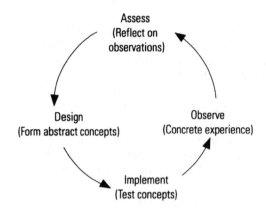

FIGURE 4-2
The Observe-Assess-Design-Imple-
ment (OADI) Cycle of Individual
Learning

Source: Adapted from F. Kofman, lecture slides
(Cambridge, Massachusetts: MIT Sloan School of Management, 1992).

conducted in an organizational context. In the OADI cycle, people experience concrete events and actively observe what is happening. They assess (consciously or subconsciously) their experience by reflecting on their observations and then design or construct an abstract concept that seems to be an appropriate response to the assessment. They test the design by implementing it in the concrete world, which leads to a new concrete experience, commencing another cycle.

The Role of Memory

Although the OADI cycle helps us understand learning, for our purposes it is incomplete. It does not explicitly address the role of memory, which plays a critical role in linking individual to organizational learning. Integrating the role of memory will require us to make a more explicit distinction between conceptual and operational learning.

Psychological research makes a distinction between learning and memory.[18] Learning has more to do with acquisition, whereas memory has more to do with retention of whatever is acquired. In reality, however, separating the two processes is difficult because they are tightly interconnected—what we already have in our memory affects what we learn and what we learn affects our memory. The concept of memory is commonly understood to be analogous to a storage device where everything we perceive and experience is filed away. However, we need to differentiate between stored memory like baseball trivia and active structures that affect our thinking process and the actions we take. That is, we need to understand the role of memory in the learning process itself A good way to understand these active structures is the concept of mental models.

Individual Mental Models.   In Figure 4-3, mental models are added to the OADI learning cycle. Senge describes mental models as deeply held internal im-

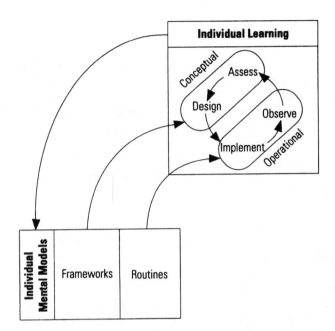

FIGURE 4-3
Simple Model of
Individual Learning:
OADI-Individual Mental
Models (MM) Cycle

ages of how the world works, which have a powerful influence on what we do because they also affect what we see.[19] Troubles can arise when we take actions on the basis of our mental models as if they were reality. The concept of mental models differs from the traditional notion of memory as static storage because mental models play an active role in what an individual sees and does.

Mental models represent a person's view of the world, including explicit and implicit understandings. Mental models provide the context in which to view and interpret new material, and they determine how stored information is relevant to a given situation. They represent more than a collection of ideas, memories, and experiences—they are like the source code of a computer's operating system, the manager and arbiter of acquiring, retaining, using, and deleting new information. But they are much more than that because they are also like the programmer of that source code with the know-how to design a different source code as well as the know-why to choose one over the other.

Mental models not only help us make sense of the world we see, they can also restrict our understanding to that which makes sense within the mental model. Senge gives this example:

> *Have you ever heard a statement such as, "Laura doesn't care about people," and wondered about its validity? Imagine that Laura is a superior or colleague who has some particular habits that others have noted. She rarely offers generous praise. She often stares off into space when people talk to her and then asks, "What did you say?" She sometimes cuts people off when they speak. She never comes to office parties. . . . From these particular behaviors, Laura's colleagues have concluded that she doesn't care much about*

people. It's been common knowledge—except, of course, for Laura, who feels that she cares very much about people. . . . Once Laura's colleagues accept as fact that she doesn't care about people, no one questions her behavior when she does things that are "non-caring," and no one notices when she does something that doesn't fit the [mental model]. The general view that she doesn't care leads people to treat her with greater indifference, which takes away any opportunity she might have had to exhibit more caring.[20]

People's untested assumptions about Laura play an active role in creating the set of interactions that make their mental model of her a self-fulfilling prophecy. Whenever we take actions on the basis of stereotypes, we risk committing the same error as Laura's colleagues.

Frameworks and Routines.   The two levels of learning—operational and conceptual—can be related to two parts of mental models. Operational learning represents learning at the procedural level, where one learns the steps in order to complete a particular task. This know-how is captured as routines, such as filling out entry forms, operating a piece of machinery, handling a switchboard, and retooling a machine. Not only does operational learning accumulate and change routines, but routines affect the operational learning process as well. The arrows going in both directions in the diagram represent this mutual influence.

Conceptual learning has do with the thinking about why things are done in the first place, sometimes challenging the very nature or existence of prevailing conditions, procedures, or conceptions and leading to new frameworks in the mental model. The new frameworks, in turn, can open up opportunities for discontinuous steps of improvement by reframing a problem in radically different ways.

To make the dynamics of the link between learning and mental models clearer, let's consider a simple example of driving a car home from work. Most of us probably know several ways to get home. The route we use most often has been chosen based on our beliefs about what makes a "good" route home from work. These belief systems are our frameworks that guide our choice between a route with the fewest stoplights and the one with the most scenic views. Once we have settled on a route, it becomes a routine that we execute whenever we want to go home. Now we can drive home on automatic pilot. If we encounter road construction that blocks our normal route or if our route becomes consistently congested, however, we rethink our criteria of what the best route home means and select a new route. This is our model, then, of individual learning—a cycle of conceptual and operational learning that informs and is informed by mental models.

ORGANIZATIONAL LEARNING

Organizational learning is more complex and dynamic than a mere magnification of individual learning. The level of complexity increases tremendously when we go from a single individual to a large collection of diverse individuals. Issues of motivation and reward, for instance, which are an integral part of human learning, become doubly complicated within organizations. Although the meaning of the term "learning" remains essentially the same as in the individual case, the learning *process* is fundamentally different at the organizational level. A model of organizational learning has to resolve the dilemma of imparting intelligence and learning capabilities to a nonhuman entity without anthropomorphizing it.

The Individual-Organization Learning Dilemma

What do we mean by organizational learning? In the early stages of an organization's existence, organizational learning is often synonymous with individual learning because the organization consists of a small group of people and has minimal structure. As an organization grows, however, a distinction between individual and organizational learning emerges, and a system for capturing the learning of its individual members evolves. Argyris and Schon posed one of the main dilemmas shared by all who tackle this issue:

> *There is something paradoxical here. Organizations are not merely collections of individuals, yet there are no organizations without such collections. Similarly, organizational learning is not merely individual learning, yet organizations learn only through the experience and actions of individuals. What, then, are we to make of organizational learning? What is an organization that it may learn?*[21]

Clearly, an organization learns through its individual members and, therefore, is affected either directly or indirectly by individual learning. Argyris and Schon present a theory whereby organizational learning takes place through individual actors whose actions are based on a set of shared models.[22] They argue that most organizations have shared assumptions that protect the status quo, preclude people from challenging others' troublesome or difficult qualities and characteristics, and provide silent assent to those attributions; hence, very little learning is possible. For example, when confronted with a leader's tendency to steamroll over any opposition, people tend to accept it with resignation as "the way X is," rather than to point out the occasions when the steamrolling occurs. Furthermore, we assume that the person is aware and doing it on purpose, or we assume that the person doesn't want to talk about it. We don't make our own mental models explicit. We don't test our assumptions with that person. Whenever we interact with such people, we "know" they will steamroll, so we act in ways that make it easy for them to do it.

There is little agreement on what constitutes "appropriate" learning, those actions or lessons that should be incorporated into an organization's memory. Organizational routines, such as standard operating procedures (SOPs), are generally viewed as an important part of an organization's memory and a repository of its past learning. However, some argue that SOPs are dangerous because they become so institutionalized that they delay the search for new procedures when the environment changes radically.[23] These theorists advocate minimal levels of consensus, contentment, affluence, faith, consistency, and rationality. Levitt and March, on the other hand, caution that such a situation can lead people to make mistakes faster by, for example, specializing prematurely in inferior technologies.[24]

In reality, both views are correct to a degree; the crux of the matter is knowing when organizational routines such as SOPs are appropriate and when they are not. As Winter argues:

> *Routinized competence clearly does not dictate inattention to considerations that fall outside of the scope of the routines; in fact, it should make possible higher levels of attention to such considerations. But the wider the range of situations subsumed by the routines and the better the routinized performance, the fewer reminders there are that something besides routinized competence might on occasion be useful or even essential to survival.*[25]

But how does an organization decide when once-appropriate routines are no longer the correct actions to take? Can an organization anticipate obsolescence of their SOPs, or must it always learn by first making inappropriate decisions in the face of changing conditions? Are organizational SOPs different from individual routines? These are the types of issues that a model of organizational learning must address.

Organizations as Behavioral Systems

Simon proposed the following hypothesis:

> *A man, viewed as a behaving system, is quite simple. The apparent complexity of his behavior over time is largely a reflection of the complexity of the environment in which he finds himself.*[26]

This behavioral perspective can be extended to organizations. For example, Cyert and March see the organization as an adaptively rational system that basically learns from experience.[27] A firm changes its behavior in response to short-term feedback from the environment according to some fairly well-defined rules and adapts to longer-term feedback on the basis of more general rules. At some level in this hierarchy, they suggest, lie "learning rules."

March and Olsen make a distinction between individual and organizational action in their model of organizational learning (see Figure 4-4).[28] In this model, individual actions are based on certain individual beliefs. These actions, in turn, lead to organizational action, which produces some environmental response. The

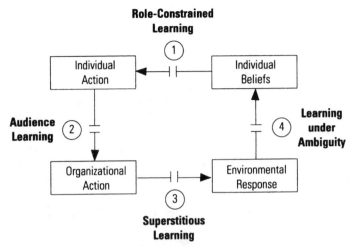

Source: Modified from J.G. March and J.P. Olsen, "The Uncertainty of the Past: Organizational Learning under Ambiguity," *European Journal of Political Research* 3 (1975): 147-171.

FIGURE 4-4 Model of Organizational Learning

cycle is completed when the environmental response affects individual beliefs. Tracing this loop, we see that if the environmental response is static and unchanging, individual beliefs, actions, and therefore organizational actions will also remain unchanged. If there are changes in the environment, however, individual beliefs about the nature of the environment could change, thus precipitating a different set of individual and organizational actions. This will, in turn, set off a new cycle of learning.

March and Olsen's model also addresses the issue of incomplete learning cycles, where learning in the face of changing environmental conditions is impaired because one or more of the links is either weak or broken. They identify four cases where the learning cycle is incomplete and leads to dysfunctional learning. *Role-constrained learning* can occur when individual learning has no effect on individual action because the circle is broken by the constraints of the individual's role. *Audience learning* occurs when the individual affects organizational action in an ambiguous way. In *superstitious learning,* the link between organizational action and environmental response is severed. Thus, actions are taken, responses are observed, inferences are drawn, and learning takes place, but there is no real basis for the connections made between organizational action and environmental response. With *learning under ambiguity,* the individual affects organizational action, which affects the environment, but the causal connections among the events are not clear. That is, operational learning occurs but conceptual learning does not. Effective organizational learning requires a balance of conceptual and operational learning.

Organizations as Interpretation Systems

The behavioral view above is consistent with the view of organizations as interpretation systems. Daft and Weick propose a model that represents the overall learning process of an organization: scanning, interpretation, and learning (see Figure 4-5).[29] *Scanning* involves monitoring and obtaining data about the environment. *Interpretation* is the process of translating events and developing concepts consistent with prior understanding of the environment. *Learning* is knowledge about the interrelationships between the organization's actions and the environment as well as the actions that are taken on the basis of such knowledge.

Although Daft and Weick likened interpretation to an individual learning a new skill, I would again separate know-how from know-why and say that interpretation occurs more at the conceptual than the operational level. Their typology of four different interpretation types—undirected viewing, conditioned viewing, discovering, and enacting—is shown in Figure 4-6. The horizontal axis, organizational intrusiveness, is a measure of an organization's willingness to look outside its own boundaries. For example, a technology-focused company's efforts may be inwardly directed (intensive research in core technologies) whereas a marketing-focused company's efforts are outwardly focused (customer focus groups and market surveys). The two axes represent an organization's assumptions about the world and its role in it, the combination of which captures an organization's worldview or *weltanschauung*. An organization's *weltanschauung* determines how it interprets environmental responses, whether it will act on them, and what specific means it will employ if it chooses to act.

The Missing Link: From Individual to Organizational Learning

Various theories of organizational learning have been based on theories of individual learning.[30] However, if a distinction between organization and individual is not made explicit, a model of organizational learning will either obscure the actual learning process by ignoring the role of the individual (and anthropomorphizing organizations) or become a simplistic extension of individual learning by glossing over organizational complexities.

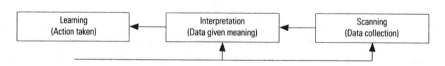

Source: R.L. Daft and K.E. Weick, "Toward a Model of Organizations as Interpretation Systems," *Academy of Management Review* 9 (1984): 286.

FIGURE 4-5 Relationships among Organizational Scanning, Interpretation, and Learning

	Passive ← **Organizational Intrusiveness** → Active	
Unanalyzable **Assumptions about Environment** **Analyzable**	**Undirected Viewing** Constrained interpretations. Nonroutine, informal data. Hunch, rumor, chance opportunities.	**Enacting** Experimentation, testing, coercion, invent environment. Learn by doing.
	Conditioned Viewing Interprets within traditional boundaries. Passive detection. Routines, formal data.	**Discovering** Formal search. Questioning, surveys, data gathering. Active detection..

Source: R.L. Daft and K.E. Weick, "Toward a Model of Organizations as Interpretation Systems," *Academy of Management Review* 9 (1984): 289.

FIGURE 4-6   Types of Organizational Interpretation Systems

Daft and Weick's model of organizations as interpretation systems does not explicitly deal with individual actors at all. March and Olsen's model also largely ignores the interactions between individual learning and learning at the organizational level. In their model, individual learning is driven primarily by environmental responses, and organizational learning occurs when the whole cycle is completed. It implies that all organizational learning must be driven in some measure by what is happening in the environment and does not explain what learning occurs within a firm, independent of the outside environment. Other theorists equate organizational learning with the actions of a group of individuals, such as a top management group.[31] They do not identify an explicit transfer process through which individual learning is retained by the organization. Hence, if individuals should leave, the organization is likely to suffer a tremendous loss in its learning capacity. In the next section, I will attempt to build an integrated model that will address some of these shortcomings.

AN INTEGRATED MODEL OF ORGANIZATIONAL LEARNING

An integrated model of organizational learning organizes all of the elements discussed thus far into a cohesive framework (see Figure 4-7). I call it the OADI-SMM model: observe, assess, design, implement—shared mental models.[32] It addresses the issue of the transfer of learning through the exchange of individual and shared mental models. Analogous to individual learning, organizational learning is defined as *increasing an organization's capacity to take effective action.*

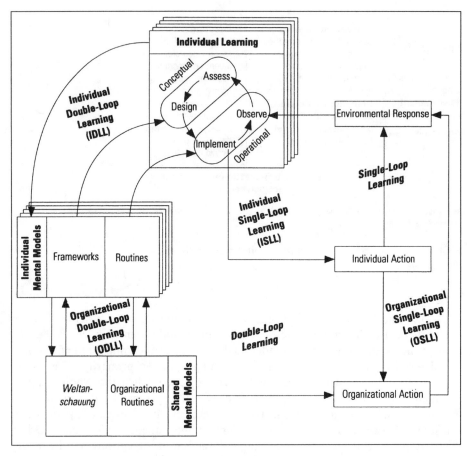

FIGURE 4-7 An Integrated Model of Organizational Learning: OADI-Shared Mental Models (SMM) Cycle

The Role of Individuals in Organizational Learning

In the OADI-SMM model, I have substituted "individual beliefs" in March and Olsen's model with the OADI-IMM model of individual learning. The individual learning cycle is the process through which those beliefs change and those changes are then codified in the individual mental models. The cycles of individual learning affect learning at the organizational level through their influence on the organization's shared mental models. An organization can learn only through its members, but it is not dependent on any specific member, as denoted in Figure 4-7 by the multiple boxes representing individual learning. Individuals, however, can learn without the organization.

Individuals are constantly taking actions and observing their experience, but not all individual learning has organizational consequences. A person may enroll in a dance class and learn a new dance step, but we would not expect such actions to be relevant to organizational learning.

Although such influences as the development and enforcement of group norms, group polarization, and other factors have an effect on individuals, group effects are not explicitly included in the model.[33] However, if we view a group as a mini-organization whose members contribute to the group's shared mental models, then the model can represent group learning as well as organizational learning. A group can then be viewed as a collective individual, with its own set of mental models, that contributes to the organization's shared mental models and learning. This is consistent with the notion that groups themselves are influenced by organizational structure and type of management style and, therefore, can be treated as if they were "extended individuals."[34]

The Transfer Mechanism: Shared Mental Models

Organizational memory, broadly defined, includes everything that is contained in an organization that is somehow retrievable. Thus storage files of old invoices are part of that memory. So are copies of letters, spreadsheet data stored in computers, and the latest strategic plan, as well as what is in the minds of all organizational members. However, as with individual learning, such a static definition of memory is not very useful in the context of organizational learning.

The parts of an organization's memory that are relevant for organizational learning are those that constitute active memory—those that define what an organization pays attention to, how it chooses to act, and what it chooses to remember from its experience—that is, individual and shared mental models. They may be explicit or implicit, tacit or widely recognized, but they have the capacity to affect the way an individual or organization views the world and takes action. Organizational learning is dependent on individuals improving their mental models; making those mental models explicit is crucial to developing new shared mental models. This process allows organizational learning to be independent of any specific individual.

Why put so much emphasis on mental models? Because *the mental models in individuals' heads are where a vast majority of an organization's knowledge (both know-how and know-why) lies.* Imagine an organization in which all the physical records disintegrate overnight. Suddenly, there are no reports, no computer files, no employee record sheets, no operating manuals, no calendars—all that remain are the people, buildings, capital equipment, raw materials, and inventory. Now imagine an organization where all the people simply quit showing up for work. New people, who are similar in many ways to the former workers but who have no familiarity with that particular organization, come to work instead. Which of these two organizations will be easier to rebuild to its former status?

Most likely, retaining all the people will make it easier to rebuild than retaining only the systems and records. In the first scenario, the organizational static memory is eliminated, but not the shared mental models of the people. In the second scenario, individual mental models and their linkages to the shared mental models are obliterated. Thus when new individuals come in, they have their own mental models that have no connection to the remaining organizational memory.

Even in the most bureaucratic of organizations, despite the preponderance of written SOPs and established protocols, there is much more about the firm that is unsaid and unwritten; its essence is embodied more in the people than in the systems. Comparatively little is put down on paper or stored in computer memories.[35] The intangible and often invisible assets of an organization reside in individual mental models that collectively contribute to the shared mental models. The shared mental models are what make the rest of the organizational memory usable. Without these mental models, which include all the subtle interconnections that have been developed among the various members, an organization will be incapacitated in both learning and action.

This assertion is not as radical as it may sound. There is some empirical support for it in the form of turnover data. As everyone knows, high turnover is costly in terms of time and money because new recruits have to "learn the ropes" while being paid and consuming an experienced person's time. In fact, the second scenario described above is precisely the case of high turnover taken to an extreme. Companies with a 40 percent to 50 percent annual turnover rate have a hard time accumulating learning because their experience base is continually being eroded. Radical changes brought about by a new CEO or by a hostile takeover are examples of the first scenario. In many such cases, the organization is completely gutted of its previous management style, procedures, and structures and replaced with a different one altogether. Although transitions are times of great upheaval, the organization as a whole usually remains intact.

Weltanschauung and SOPs. As stated earlier, mental models are not merely a repository of sensory data; they are active in that they build theories about sensory experience. Each mental model is a clustering or an aggregation of data that prescribes a viewpoint or a course of action. Conceptual learning creates changes in frameworks, which lead to new ways of looking at the world. Operational learning produces new or revised routines that are executed in lieu of old ones. The revised mental models contain not only the new frameworks and routines but also knowledge about how the routines fit within the new frameworks.

Individual frameworks become embedded in the organization's *weltanschauung*. The organization's view of the world slowly evolves to encompass the current thinking of the individuals within. In similar fashion, individual routines that are proved to be sound over time become standard operating procedures. Like an individual driving a car, the routines become the organization's autopilot reflexes. The strength of the link between individual mental models and shared mental models is a function of the amount of influence exerted by a particular individual or group of individuals. CEOs and upper management groups are influential because of the power inherent in their positions. A united group of hourly workers can have a high degree of influence due to its size.

For example, Procter & Gamble's *weltanschauung* can be characterized as one in which the company has a sense of community responsibility and believes in the importance of corporate and product brand image. Its *weltanschauung* is also a reflection of its culture, deep-rooted assumptions, artifacts, and overt behavior rules. All of these things moderate its decision making as it encounters unpredictable, nonroutine events. Its SOPs, on the other hand, may include things like a marketing plan to launch a new product, procedures for paying suppliers, employee performance reviews, and hiring criteria. These SOPs allow the organization to respond to routine needs in predictable ways.

Double-Loop Learning

The OADI-SMM model also incorporates Argyris and Schon's concept of single-loop and double-loop learning on both the individual and organizational levels. Double-loop learning involves surfacing and challenging deep-rooted assumptions and norms of an organization that have previously been inaccessible, either because they were unknown or known but undiscussable. Individual double-loop learning (IDLL) is traced out in Figure 4-7 as the process through which individual learning affects individual mental models, which in turn affect future learning.

Organizational double-loop learning (ODLL) occurs when individual mental models become incorporated into the organization through shared mental models, which can then affect organizational action. In both cases, double-loop learning provides opportunities for discontinuous steps of improvement where reframing a problem can bring about radically different potential solutions. The distinctions between conceptual and operational learning and between *weltanschauung* and organizational routines are also integrated throughout the different stages. There is a box around the diagram to emphasize that the whole model is required to represent organizational learning.

Incomplete Learning Cycles

March and Olsen identified four possible disconnects whereby organizational learning would be incomplete. I have identified three additional types of incomplete learning cycles that affect organizational learning: situational, fragmented, and opportunistic (see Figure 4-8).

Situational Learning. An individual encounters a problem, improvises on the spot, solves the problem, and moves on to the next task. Situational learning occurs when the individual forgets or does not codify the learning for later use; the link between individual learning and individual mental models is severed. Regardless of whether the learning occurs at the conceptual or operational level, it does not change the person's mental models and therefore has no long-term impact—

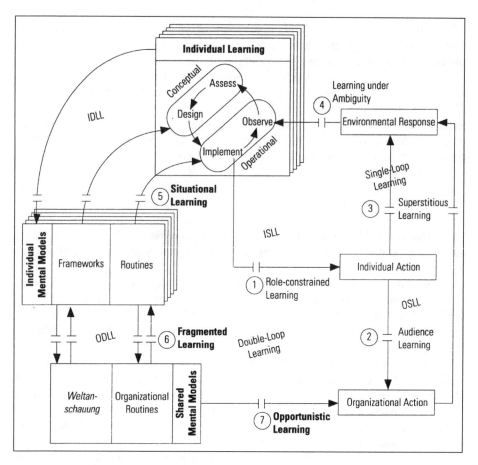

FIGURE 4-8 Incomplete Learning Cycles

the learning is situation specific. Because the individual's mental model is not changed, the organization does not have a way of absorbing the learning either.

Crisis management is an example of situational learning. Each problem is solved, but no learning is carried over to the next case. Quality improvement is a counterexample; it focuses on minimizing situational learning through systematic data gathering, analysis, and standardization.

Fragmented Learning. There are many instances in which individuals learn, but the organization as a whole does not. When the link between individual mental models and shared mental models is broken, fragmented learning occurs. In such a case, loss of individuals means loss of the learning as well. Universities are a classic example of fragmented learning. Professors within each department may be the world's leading experts on management, finance, operations, and marketing, but the university as an institution cannot apply that expertise to the running of its own affairs. Very decentralized organizations that do not have the networking capabilities to keep the parts connected are also susceptible to fragmented learning.

Opportunistic Learning. There are times when organizations purposely try to bypass the standard procedures because their established ways of doing business are seen as an impediment to a particular task. They want to sever the link between shared mental models and organizational action in order to seize an opportunity that cannot wait for the whole organization to change (or it may not be desirable for the whole organization to change). Opportunistic learning occurs when organizational actions are taken based on an individual's (or small group of individuals') actions and not on the organization's widely shared mental models (values, culture, myths, or SOPs).

The use of skunk works to develop the IBM personal computer is a good example. The company bypassed its normal bureaucratic structure and created an entirely separate, dedicated team to develop the PC, which it was able to do in record time. General Motors' Saturn is an example on a grander scale, as are joint ventures when appropriately structured.

IMPLICATIONS FOR RESEARCH

In the OADI-SMM model, individual mental models play a pivotal role, yet that is precisely an area where we know little and there is little to observe. One challenge is to find ways to make these mental models explicit; another is to manage the way these mental models are transferred into the organizational memory. Clearly, this involves creating new devices and tools for capturing a wide range of knowledge.

Making Mental Models Explicit

If what matters is not reality but perceptions of reality, then fundamental to learning is a shared mental model. However, mental models are a mixture of what is learned explicitly and *absorbed implicitly*. That's why it's so difficult to articulate them and share them with others. Making mental models explicit requires a language or tool with which to capture and communicate them.

Some progress is being made in this area.[36] However, most efforts at mapping mental models result in static representations of what are usually highly dynamic and nonlinear phenomena. New tools, such as causal loop diagrams and system dynamics computer models, are proving more effective. They allow us to address the problem of incomplete learning cycles.

Beyond Situational Learning. To close the loop on situational learning, individuals must learn to transfer specific insights into more general maps that can guide them in future situations. This requires having the appropriate tools for the type of knowledge that is being mapped. Although the English language is useful for communicating on many different levels, imprecise words can lead to ambiguous meanings or inadequate descriptions of complex, dynamic phenomena. Thus English may be perfectly adequate for making one's mental model of a Shakespearean play explicit but be grossly ineffective in explicating a mental model of how the wage-price spiral affects capital investment decisions.

The analysis of dynamic systems, in particular, requires a new set of tools. Senge makes an important distinction between *dynamic* complexity and *detail* complexity.[37] A system can have hundreds, perhaps thousands, of parts that have to be managed, but the dynamics of the whole system may be relatively simple. On the other hand, a system with only a dozen or so pieces can be extremely complex and difficult to manage.[38] The complexity lies in the nature of the interrelationships among the parts whose cause-effect relationships are highly nonlinear and distant in space and time.

Some of the new tools for mapping such phenomena are systems archetypes, a collection of systemic structures that recur repeatedly in diverse settings.[39] Archetypes can help to elicit and capture the intuitive understanding of experienced managers about complex dynamic issues. They are particularly powerful for advancing conceptual learning because they help explicate know-why and offer guidelines for operationalizing those insights into know-how.

To illustrate, let's look at an archetype called "tragedy of the commons" and how it was used in a car product development team at Ford.[40] In a tragedy-of-the-commons structure, each individual pursues actions that are individually beneficial but that, over time, deplete a common resource and result in a worse situation for everyone. At Ford, component design teams were competing for a limited amount of alternator power output. It made sense for each component team to draw as much power as it required to maximize the functionality of its part. The collective result was an impasse in the design process, as no team could concede what it saw as in the best interest of its own component.

What typically happens in situations like this is that the teams will continue to struggle among themselves until the program timing is jeopardized and someone has to make a decision. This usually means that the program manager has to step in and dictate what each team can have. This makes the teams unhappy because they don't make the decision themselves and some of them don't get what they want. The manager is not happy about having to intervene. The teams think the problem is a heavy-handed manager; the manager thinks the problem is poorly aligned teams. There is no general framework for them to learn from.

The tragedy-of-the-commons structure provides a framework for solving the issue and for transferring learning to the next problem. When the teams saw their situation in this structure, they realized that the problem could not be solved at the individual level; only a collective governing body or an individual with the authority to impose constraints on all the teams could resolve the situation. The course of action was obvious. The program manager would consider all the component designs and decide how much power to allocate to each of them. Those who had to give up some functionality did not like it, *but they understood why.* Subsequent teams looked at other common resources, such as available torque, and realized that they too fell into the tragedy-of-the-commons structure. A systemic understanding is emerging among the teams that a heavy-weight program manager with wide authority over the entire car program makes sense (most Japanese car programs are structured that way).

Mapping the teams' interrelationships allowed them to make explicit the underlying dynamic structure. Once there was a shared understanding of that structure, they could prescribe a course of action. The archetype provides a way of mapping the individual instance to a general framework to guide future learning.

From Fragmented to Organizational Learning.   Capturing individual mental models alone is not sufficient to achieve organizational learning. There needs to be a way to get beyond the fragmented learning of individuals and spread the learning throughout the organization. One way is through the design and implementation of microworlds or learning laboratories.[41] Senge describes them as the equivalent of fields where teams of managers can practice and learn together.[42]

The spirit of the learning lab is one of active experimentation and inquiry where everyone participates in surfacing and testing each other's mental models. Through this process, a shared understanding of the organization's key assumptions and interrelationships emerges. The use of an interactive computer "flight simulator" offers the participants an opportunity to test their assumptions and to viscerally experience the consequences of their actions. Management flight simulators represent mental models that have been translated into a more formalized and explicit computer model.

The Ford product development team described above has been running a learning lab codeveloped with MIT's Center for Organizational Learning. The learning lab is now spreading the Ford/MIT core learning team's insights among the rest of the car program members. The learning lab participants worked in pairs with a computer simulator to manage a product development project to meet cost, timing, and quality objectives. Encouraged to make the reasoning behind their decisions explicit, they surfaced the mental models that drove their decision making. They discovered, for example, how their assumptions about the right pace of staffing and the coordination between product and process engineering led to missing all three targets.

At Hanover Insurance, a property and casualty insurance company, groups of claims managers went through a three-day learning lab on claims management. Through the use of the simulator, managers surfaced tacit assumptions about what constituted "right" performance numbers and learned how those mental models directly affected the strategies and decisions they made. In short, they began to see how their actions created their own reality.

Wide use and successive iterations of a learning lab are expected to affect the organization's shared mental models through changes in its *weltanschauung* and SOPs. People leave a learning lab with tools they can use in their work settings; these advance operational learning. The principles embodied in such tools help advance conceptual learning as individuals use them. In terms of the OADI-SMM model, systems archetypes and computer simulators make mental models explicit, thus improving the transfer mechanism and reducing situational and fragmented learning.

Building Shared Meaning

I believe that the process of surfacing individual mental models and making them explicit can accelerate individual learning. As mental models are made explicit and actively shared, the base of shared meaning in an organization expands, and the organization's capacity for effective coordinated action increases. Johnson & Johnson's handling of the Tylenol poisoning incident is a vivid example of how a deeply shared belief (or *weltanschauung*) on the value of a human life can have a powerful effect on an organization's ability to mount a coordinated response quickly.

On a less grand scale, systems archetypes provide a glimpse of the possibility of developing a similar capability for enhancing coordinated action. As more people understand the meaning behind the tragedy-of-the-commons archetype, for example, the use of the term itself will conjure up the whole story line behind it as well as its implications for action.

At this point, my discussion is more a set of assertions based on anecdotal evidence and preliminary research than a set of facts that has been supported by extensive longitudinal studies and rigorous research. Little empirical work has been done on the construct of organizational memory and shared mental models. Further work is needed for a better understanding of the role of mental models in individual and organizational learning, the types of mental models that are appropriate for representing dynamic complexity, the methods with which to capture the understanding of such complexity, and the means through which new learning can be transferred to the whole organization. I propose the model developed in this article as a guide for pursuing these goals.

NOTES

1. H.P. Sims et al., *The Thinking Organization* (San Francisco: Jossey-Bass, 1986); and G.P. Huber, "Organizational Learning: The Contributing Processes and the Literature," *Organization Science* 2 (1991): 88–115.

2. See B. Hedberg, "How Organizations Learn and Unlearn," in *Handbook of Organizational Design*, ed. P.C. Nystrom and W.H. Starbuck (London: Oxford University Press, 1981), pp. 3–27; and M.D. Cohen, "Individual Learning and Organizational Routine: Emerging Connections," *Organization Science* 2 (1991): 135–139.

3. On limitations, see: H.A. Simon, *Models of Man* (New York: John Wiley, 1957). On capacity to learn, see: R.M. Restak, *The Mind* (New York: Bantam, 1988).

4. D.A. Kolb, *Experiential Learning: Experience as the Source of Learning and Development* (Englewood Cliffs, New Jersey: Prentice-Hall, 1984).

5. E.R. Hilgard and G.H. Bower, *Theories of Learning* (New York: Appleton-Century-Crofts, 1966). See also: G.A. Miller. "The Magic Number Seven, Plus or Minus Two: Some Limits on Our Capacity for Processing Information," *The Psychology Review* 63 (1956): 81–97; Simon (1957); and A. Tversky and D. Kahneman, "Rational Choice and the Framing of Decisions," in *Rational Choice: The Contrast between Economics and Psychology,* ed. R.M. Hogarth and M.W. Reder (Chicago: University of Chicago Press, 1987).

6. E. Jaques, *Requisite Organization* (Arlington, Virginia: Cason-Hall Associates, 1989).

7. E.H. Schein adds a third dimension—emotional conditioning and learned anxiety—that can have a powerful effect on the first two types of learning. See: E.H. Schein, "How Can Organizations Learn Faster? The Challenge of Entering the Green Room," *Sloan Management Review,* Winter 1993, pp. 85–92.

8. C. Argyris and D. Schon, *Organizational Learning: A Theory of Action Perspective* (Reading, Massachusetts: Addison-Wesley, 1978).

9. J. Piaget, *Structuralism* (New York: Basic Books, 1970).

10. Kolb (1984), p. 38.

11. Other schools include hehavioral and rationalist learning theory. See: Kolb (1984), p. 38.

12. Ibid., p. 21.

13. K. Ishikawa, *What Is Total Quality Control?* (Englewood Cliffs, New Jersey: Prentice-Hall, 1985), p. 59.

14. W.E. Deming, *Quality, Productivity, and Competitive Position: Dr. W Edwards Deming's Seminar Notes* (Ford Quality Education and Training Center, 1992).

15. E.H. Schein, *Process Consultation, Volume II: Lessons for Managers and Consultants* (Reading, Massachusetts: Addison-Wesley, 1987), p. 64.

16. Argyris and Schon (1978), p. 141.

17. F. Kofman, lecture slides (Cambridge, Massachusetts: MIT Sloan School of Management, 1992).

18. L Postman, "Methodology of Human Learning," in *Handbook of Learning and Cognitive Processes,* Vol. 3., ed. W.K. Estes (New York: John Wiley, 1976),pp. 11–69.

19. P.M. Senge., *The Fifth Discipline* (New York: Doubleday, 1990a). See also: J.W. Forrester, *World Dynamics* (Cambridge, Massachusetts: Productivity Press, 1971).

20. Senge (1990a), pp. 192–193.

21. Argyris and Schon (1978), p. 9.

22. Ibid., p. 17.

23. Ibid.; S.C. Winter, "The Case for 'Mechanistic' Decision Making," in *Organizational Strategy and Change,* ed. H. Pennings (San Francisco: Jossey-Bass, 1985), pp. 99–113; C. Perrow, *Complex Organizations* (New York: Random House, 1986); and B.L.T. Hedberg, P.C. Nystrom, and W.H. Starbuck, "Camping on Seesaws: Prescriptions for a Self-Designing Organization," *Administrative Science Quarterly* 21 (1976): 41–65.

24. B. Levitt and J.G. March, "Organizational Learning," *Annual Review of Sociology* 14 (1988), pp. 319–340.

25. Winter (1985), p. 111.

26. H.A. Simon, *Sciences of the Artificial* (Cambridge, Massachusetts: MIT Press, 1981), p. 65.

27. E.M. Cyert and J.G. March, *A Behavioral Theory of the Firm* (Englewood Cliffs, New Jersey: Prentice-Hall, 1963).

28. J.G. March and J.P. Olsen, "The Uncertainty of the Past: Organizational Learning under Ambiguity," *European Journal of Political Research 3* (1975): 147–171.

29. R.L. Daft and K.E. Weick, "Toward a Model of Organizations as Interpretation Systems," *Academy of Management Review 9* (1984): 284–295.

30. For example, adaptation theories can be viewed as analogs of individual stimulus-response theories and strategic choice models having similarities with psychodynamic theories.

31. R.E. Miles et al., "Organizational Strategy, Structure, and Process," *Academy of Management Review 3* (1978): 546–563.

32. For a fuller treatment of this model, see: D. Kim, "A Framework and Methodology for Linking Individual and Organizational Learning: Application in TQM and Product Development" (Cambridge, Massachusetts: MIT Sloan School of Management, Ph.D. Diss., 1993).

33. See D.C. Feldman, "The Development and Enforcement of Group Norms," *Academy of Management Review 9* (1984): 47–53; D.J. Isenberg, "Group Polarization: A Critical Review and Meta-analysis," *Journal of Personality and Social Psychology 50* (1986): 1141–1151; and J.R. Hackman, "Group Influences on Individuals in Organizations," in *Handbook of Industrial and Organizational Psychology,* e.d. M.D. Dunnette (Chicago: Rand-McNally, 1976).

34. R.E. Walton and J.R. Hackman, "Groups under Contrasting Management Strategies," in *Designing Effective Work Groups,* ed. P.S. Goodman (San Francisco: Jossey-Bass, 1986).

35. H.A. Simon, "Bounded Rationality and Organizational Learning," *Organization Science 2* (1991): 125–134; and J.W. Forrester, "System Dynamics and the Lessons of Thirty-Five Years," in *Systems-Based Approach to Policy Making,* ed. K.B. DeGreene (Norwell, Massachusetts: Kluwer Academic Publishers, 1993).

36. See, for example: A. Bostrom, B. Fischhoff, and G.M. Granger, "Characterizing Mental Models of Hazardous Processes: A Methodology and an Application to Radon," *Journal of Social Issues 48* (1992): 85–100.

37. Senge (1990a).

38. J.D. Sterman, "Modeling Managerial Behavior: Misperceptions of Feedback in a Dynamic Decision-Making Experiment," *Management Science 35* (1989): 321–339.

39. Senge (1990a); and D.H. Kim, *Toolbox Reprint Series: Systems Archetypes* (Cambridge, Massachusetts: Pegasus Communications, 1992).

40. N. Zeniuk, "Learning to Learn: A New Look at Product Development," *The Systems Thinker 4* (1993): 1.

41. P.M. Senge, "The Leader's New Work: Building Learning Organizations." *Sloan Management Review,* Fall 1990b. pp: 7–23: and D.H. Kim, *Toward Learning Organizations: Integrating Total Quality Control and Systems Thinking* (Cambridge, Massachusetts: Pegasus Communications, 1990).

42. Senge (1990b).

5

The Real Value of On-Line Communities

Arthur Armstrong and John Hagel III

The notion of community has been at the heart of the Internet since its inception. For many years, scientists have used the Internet to share data, collaborate on research, and exchange messages. In essence, scientists formed interactive research communities that existed not on a physical campus but on the Internet. Within the last few years, millions of computer users worldwide have begun to explore the Internet and commercial on-line services such as Prodigy and America Online. Many have joined one or more of the communities that have sprung up to serve consumer needs for communication, information, and entertainment. One of the oldest virtual communities is the Well, launched in 1985 by a group of high-tech enthusiasts located primarily near San Francisco. Over the past decade, thousands of computer users have communicated with one another through the Well and, over time, developed strong personal relationships off-line.

Commercial enterprises—relative newcomers to the on-line world—have been slow to understand and make use of the unique community-building capabilities of the medium. Usually, businesses on the Internet today do little more than advertise their wares on the World Wide Web in the hope that somebody will buy something. For instance, flower distributors, booksellers, liquor companies, durable-goods manufacturers, and other businesses have sites on the World Wide Web where visitors can obtain information about the company and its products and send electronic messages to the company. Some of the more sophisticated sites allow visitors to play games and order products electronically. But rarely do these sites encourage communication among visitors to the site. (Meanwhile, most existing communities, such as the Well, are not business oriented; in fact, most strongly oppose the very idea of commercial activity on the Internet.)

By adapting to the culture of the Internet, however, and providing consumers with the ability to interact with one another in addition to the company, businesses can build new and deeper relationships with customers. We believe that commercial success in the on-line arena will belong to those businesses that organize electronic communities to meet multiple social and commercial needs. By creating strong on-line communities, businesses will be able to build customer loyalty to a degree that today's marketers can only dream of and, in turn, generate strong economic returns.

CONSUMERS' NEEDS FOR COMMUNITY

Electronic communities meet four types of consumer needs.

Communities of transaction primarily facilitate the buying and selling of products and services and deliver information related to those transactions. They are not communities in the traditional social sense. Participants are encouraged to interact with one another in order to engage in a specific transaction that can be informed by the input of other members of the community. Visitors to communities of transaction may want to buy a used car or a vintage wine, and they may want to consult with other community members before doing so.

Virtual Vineyards, a Web-based service that sells wines, is a community of transaction. The Virtual Vineyards site offers visitors information on wines and lists special deals on attractively priced offerings. Most of the wines that are listed are from small vineyards and are usually difficult to obtain. Visitors can purchase the wines directly from Virtual Vineyards, using an on-line form, or they can call the on-line service. Although visitors can post E-mail to the organizer of the site (and wine neophytes can post questions to the Cork Dork), they cannot yet trade information with one another. Adding that capability might add value for the site's visitors, making it a true community.

The organizer of a community of transaction does not need to be a vendor. Community organizers may simply bring together a critical mass of buyers and sellers to facilitate certain types of transactions. For example, a community organizer might offer electronic classified ads or provide a "marketspace" where everything from used construction machinery to financial investment products and services could be bought and sold.

Communities of interest bring together participants who interact extensively with one another on specific topics. These communities involve a higher degree of interpersonal communication than do communities of transaction. One community of interest is Garden Web, where visitors can share ideas with other gardeners through Garden Web forums, post requests for seeds and other items on the Garden Exchange, and post queries on electronic bulletin boards. Garden Web also provides direct electronic links to other Internet gardening resources, including directories of sites relating to gardening. Participants communicate and carry out transactions with one another, but their interactions are limited to gardening. They do not discuss topics such as car care or parenting—topics which bring together people in other communities of interest. Nor do they share intensely personal information.

One of the most successful communities of interest is the Motley Fool, an electronic forum that two charismatic brothers, David and Tom Gardner, host on America Online. The Gardners began the Motley Fool for people interested in personal financial investment. They developed a portfolio of stock investments and invited people to comment on the choices made. The Motley Fool has become an engaging blend of information and entertainment. For example, in an area known as Today's Pitch, the organizers recently offered a short tutorial on why insider trading by managers of a company may be an important indicator of potential changes in stock value. They then provided a selection of companies in which insider trading had been particularly active and invited community participants to bet on which company would have the largest change in stock value over the next several weeks. The winner received several hours of free on-line time on America Online.

The Motley Fool has also aggressively leveraged user-generated content. Because the number of users and the extent of their participation have grown, the Motley Fool now offers extensive message boards organized by company, industry, and investment strategy. The forum also provides opportunities for participants to chat. The Motley Fool is one of the most rapidly growing communities within America Online, and it has spun off new communities that focus on entertainment (Follywood), sports (Fooldome), and popular culture and politics (Rogue).

Many people on-line today participate in *communities of fantasy*, where they create new environments, personalities, or stories. On America Online, a participant can pretend to be a medieval baron at the Red Dragon Inn. In this fantasy area, visitors exercise their imagination and participate (through typed, electronic chat) in the creation of an ongoing story of life at the inn. On ESPNet, an Internet-based sports community, participants can indulge their need for fantasy by creating their own sports teams (using the names of real players), which then compete against teams created by other participants. Winners are determined based on the performance of the real players during the season. Participants' real identities are not important in many of these communities, but interaction with others is at the heart of the appeal.

Finally, groups of people may feel a need to come together in *communities of relationship* around certain life experiences that often are very intense and can lead to the formation of deep personal connections. In communities of relationship, people often are aware of one another's actual identities—exceptions being communities formed around addictions (there is even a community of Internet addicts!), whose participants may prefer anonymity. The Cancer Forum on CompuServe, for instance, provides support for cancer patients and their families. Participants talk about how they deal with the disease and exchange information on medical research, pain medication, test results, and protocols. The forum's library features literature on cancer, which participants can download. However, the primary value of this sort of community is that it gives people the chance to come together and share personal experiences. Other communities of relationship on the Internet include groups focused on divorce, widowhood, and infertility.

Clearly, the four sorts of community are not mutually exclusive. When consumers shop for goods and services, they often seek advice from others before they buy, essentially blending the needs met by communities of transaction with those met by communities of interest. But currently, most communities target only one of the four needs. In so doing, they are missing an opportunity to exploit the on-line mediums fully. Imagine an on-line toy store that allows visitors only to enter, buy a toy, and then exit without giving them the opportunity to connect with one another—an experience that might encourage them to return. Now consider Parents Place, an Internet based community for parents. Parents can turn to the community for advice on such matters as whether an infant should be put on a schedule for meals and sleep. Parents Place also has a shopping mall equipped with catalogs, stores, and services such as on-line diaper ordering. Price and selection being equal, it is more likely that parents will shop at Parents Place than at a competing site that allows only for transactions.

Organizers offer participants the greatest range of services when they address all four needs within the same community. In practice, this may not be possible, but community organizers should strive to meet as many of the four needs as they can. By doing so, they will be able to develop new and stronger relations with participants. A travel community, for instance, could allow visitors to search for information about museums and special events in, say, London, and even to purchase airline tickets and make hotel reservations (community of transaction). The site could offer bulletin boards filled with tips from people who have traveled to London recently; it also could offer the opportunity to chat with travel experts, residents of London, and others (community of interest). Travelers might be invited to join a game hosted by an airline running a special deal (community of fantasy). The site even could make it possible for single travelers, such as elderly widows and widowers, to chat and perhaps find compatible travel companions for a trip to London (community of relationship).

By fostering relationships and networks of interest, organizers can make their communities highly competitive. First movers can build a critical mass of participants that has the potential to make it difficult for new entrants to lure customers away. When Apple Computer introduced its on-line service, eWorld, to compete with America Online, CompuServe, and Prodigy, media and industry reviews generally agreed that it was an appealing environment and easy to use. But eWorld was not popular with consumers, who were frustrated to discover that when they entered chat areas, they could find no one to chat with, and when they accessed bulletin boards, they found few postings. A community full of half-empty rooms offers visitors a very unsatisfactory experience. The value of participating in a community lies in users' ability to access a broad range of people and resources quickly and easily.

CREATING VALUE IN COMMUNITIES

What will be the likely sources of economic value in electronic communities? Most companies investing in an Internet presence today are doing so cautiously because they are uncertain about the payoff. Pundits point out that the only businesses currently making money on the Internet are those selling products and services to enable companies to develop their own sites. Certainly, even under the best of circumstances, electronic communities may take a decade to grow to sufficient scale to be significant contributors to the overall profitability of a large company.

In the short run, however, businesses that create communities that satisfy both relational and transactional needs will reap the benefits of greater customer loyalty and may gain important insights into the nature and needs of their customer base. In the long run, electronic communities are likely to create value in four different ways.

First, communities can charge *usage fees*. This is how on-line services such as America Online and Internet access providers such as Netcom make most of their revenues. (Typically, customers pay a fixed price to access the service for a certain number of hours per month; when customers use the service for additional hours, they are charged additional fees.) Time-based fees may make sense in the short run, given the relative absence of other sources of revenue. They make less sense in the long run. Communities will need to maximize the number of members and encourage them to spend increasingly more time on-line—posting messages on bulletin boards and chatting, for example—in order to make the community attractive to others. Usage fees do not encourage members to venture on-line and discourage them from lingering there. For this reason, we believe that most electronic communities will eventually turn away from usage fees.

Second, communities can charge users *content fees* for downloading an article or a picture from the service's library or for obtaining access to material. *Encyclopaedia Britannica* offers on-line access to its content and varies its fees depending on how much information the user wants. Bill Gates has been assembling the electronic rights to a vast library of photographic and artistic images over the last several years, and one way for him to derive value from those assets is through content fees.

Third, communities can draw revenues from *transactions and advertising*. Advertising is already a significant source of revenue for many popular Internet sites. In 1995, on-line revenue from placement of advertising amounted to roughly $50 million to $60 million, according to best estimates. (The actual amount spent is not yet systematically tracked.) Still, this amount pales in comparison with the $140 billion spent annually in the United States on advertising overall to reach consumers in the home. It is even more difficult to assess—or define—the volume of transactions conducted in on-line environments. For instance, should estimates include business-to-business transactions conducted over private electronic-data-interchange networks? Jupiter Communications, a research company, has suggested that the value of all shopping transactions that took place over the Internet or through on-line services in 1994 amounted to roughly $500 million.

For most communities, revenue from transactions probably will be slimmer than those from advertising. Community organizers could take a substantial share of advertising revenues (although if they choose to offer their communities through an on-line service such as America Online, with its existing audience of 5 million subscribers, they may have to share the revenues with the service), but they will have to share a much greater portion of transaction revenues with the manufacturers and distributors of goods and services to the community. Currently, on-line services such as CompuServe usually receive commissions of 3% to 5% on transactions—not much more than commissions taken by credit card companies. These limited commissions reflect the fact that once the retailer's margins are factored in, additional margins are slim. Community organizers may be able to increase their cut of transaction revenues if they bypass retailers entirely and strike deals directly with product and service vendors. By doing so, a community organizer can become, in effect, the merchandiser and distribution channel for products and services and can command a retailer's share of the revenues (as much as 50%).

Finally, some electronic communities may be in a position to take advantage of *synergies* with other parts of their business. For a software company such as Microsoft Corporation, that could mean saving the cost of physically distributing new software or software upgrades. For some companies, it may mean reducing customer service costs. Federal Express Corporation allows customers to track a package on-line. This is convenient for the customer and saves money for Federal Express because it reduces the number of expensive calls to customer service representatives. Companies can benefit by following this model and moving activities from the physical world to the electronic world. (See "Exploiting the Virtual Value Chain," by Jeffrey F. Rayport and John J. Sviokla, HBR November–December 1995.)

How communities adopt these four models of value creation will vary, depending on the blend of needs the community addresses. Consider again the travel community that meets multiple needs. This community will probably derive most of its value from transactions and advertising, but it also may charge an access fee. A community for substance abusers, on the other hand, will probably have to derive its value primarily or even entirely from fees, given that its members are interested in a mutual support network rather than in buying goods or services.

Yet even though communities will rely primarily on just one of the four models of value creation, innovative community organizers will blend models. A canny organizer of the community of substance abusers, for instance, might find other sources of value to subsidize the cost of managing the community. Perhaps synergies for providers of health care services could be identified, for example.

MANAGEMENT CHALLENGES

Before they can capture new sources of value, aspiring community organizers face a daunting array of issues, whether they are assessing strategies for competition or designing and managing the communities. Everyone needs to learn the new rules for managing in on-line communities.

Assessing Strategies for Competition. There are two strategic questions that a would-be community organizer must face up front: How large is the economic potential of the community and how intense is the competition likely to be?

The elements that make a community economically attractive include the potential for a large number of participants, the likelihood of frequent use and intense interaction among participants, the attractiveness the participants hold for advertisers and the expectation that participants will want to engage in frequent or valuable transactions. When assessing those elements, managers might look to specialty-magazine advertising or product-category retail sales for indications of the overall economic potential of a target community. Additionally, they might explore whether the community they are considering could draw provocative gurus or personalities who would attract a broader range of participants and spur discussion on bulletin boards or chat lines.

When assessing potential competition, organizers must recognize that some communities may have "natural owners." For example, magazine publishers are likely to have a head start in some areas because of their strong understanding of particular groups of people (young women, for instance) or of a specific subject (such as boating). A boat manufacturer intent on launching a community could end up competing with a magazine in which its advertisements regularly appear. The magazine, for its part, could view the development of a community not simply as an opportunity but also as a mechanism for defending an existing business—because through an electronic community it would be able to collect, package, and offer to advertisers more detailed information about participants than it could before. If, however, the magazine fails to allow communication among members of its audience, or if it blocks participation by competing publishers, it will create opportunities for competitors. More fundamentally, natural owners of a community are those businesses that have a substantial economic incentive to exploit synergies between an on-line community and a preexisting business. For example, can the Walt Disney Company afford not to organize one of the leading on-line communities that target children?

Designing the Community. In order to decide how to structure their community, organizers must look at how they might segment the community over time. The finer the segmentation, the easier it will be to appeal to people's narrow (and probably more passionate) interests, but the smaller the community's size. For example, organizers of a travel community could divide the community by continent (Europe) or by type of travel (cruises). They could divide each continent into subcommunities for each country of interest (Italy) and sub-subcommunities for cities (Venice).

Another design dilemma the organizer faces is whether to locate the community directly on the Internet or within a proprietary service. On the one hand, a proprietary service provides, among other benefits not yet available on the Internet, a ready audience, a technology infrastructure, security for transactions, and billing processes. On the other hand, it also is a powerful business entity standing between the community organizer and subscribers. A proprietary service that builds a critical mass of subscribers and erects barriers to prevent those sub-scribers from switching may be able to renegotiate what share of revenues it takes from participating communities. At an extreme, the proprietary service could "backward integrate" by establishing communities of its own to compete with the communities it serves. Or it might try to disintermediate certain communities. For example, it might bypass a successful personal financial-investment community and offer subscribers direct access to checking accounts, credit cards, or mutual funds at an attractive discount.

Operating the Community.   Electronic communities will involve a number of new roles. The "producer" (general manager) of any community or sub-com-munity will play or oversee at least six roles, of which the first three are the most important.

The *executive moderator* will manage a large number of system operators ("sysops"), who in turn will moderate discussions on bulletin boards and chat lines. Sysops—such as the Gardner brothers—resemble radio or television talk-show hosts in that they are, at their best, conversation managers. They help to keep the discussion focused on the topic at hand, inject new topics or provocative points of view when discussion lags, and seed the discussion with appropriate facts or content. Sysops must be able to transform the random, low-quality inter-actions that one often finds on cyberspace chat lines and bulletin boards into en-gaging and informative forums that will keep people coming back for more.

Community merchandisers will identify goods and services that are likely to be attractive to community members, negotiate with the providers of those goods and services, and then market them creatively and unobtrusively to community members. The *executive editor* will develop a programming strategy for the community (including content, special events, and the overall look and feel of the community) and manage the external providers of content, information, and serv-ices.

That leaves the *archivist,* who will maintain and organize the content gener-ated by participants over time; the *usage analyst,* who will study data on partici-pants' behavior within the community and develop programming or editorial recommendations for the producer; and the *new-product developer,* who will keep the community fresh and distinct from its rivals.

Partnering to Compete.   Organizers must decide whether to build commu-nities by themselves or to form alliances. Given the broad range of distinctive skills needed to manage a community successfully, it may make sense for many businesses to work with partners. For example, a magazine publishing company intent on forming a community will know its subscribers' interests and possess a large body of content, but will it know how to foster interaction among members of the potential community? The magazine may look to a large society, such as the American Association of Retired Persons, or to a smaller society focused on a spe-cific hobby (depending on the nature of the community) for help. It also may look to those manufacturers or service providers that understand the key transactional needs of the members.

The value of successful electronic communities will be in the intense loyalty they generate in their participants, which is what favors first movers into this area. The organization of successful electronic communities will depend on skills and the right iconoclastic mind-set, not capital. As a consequence, this arena may favor bold entrepreneurs with constrained resources over established corporate titans.

Those titans who are tempted to wait and buy later should be warned that this market will not wait for slow learners. The skills required to participate successfully will be hard to learn quickly and the premiums required to buy successful businesses will be very high. We therefore believe that any business marketing to consumers should make the small investment required to "buy an option" on electronic communities so that it can better understand both the potential value of communities and the radical changes they may cause.

6

Managing Context in Enterprise Knowledge Processes

Randall Whitaker

In the current passage from physical production to "knowledge work," enterprises are increasingly dependent upon data, information, and the means to communicate and manipulate these resources—especially *information technology* (IT). Because competitive advantage accrues to those enterprises that effectively generate, maintain, and exploit "knowledge" of their task domains and themselves, there is a need for a viable organizational epistemology (von Krogh and Roos, 1995). Such an epistemology entails a stance on the nature of enterprise knowledge, the individual and social processes realizing it, and boundary conditions on these processes. The "epistemological challenge" I shall discuss is the slippery but critical notion of "context." The following sections will address four key propositions. First, as "that which imparts meaning," context is inherently important to epistemological enquiry generally and enterprise knowledge processes specifically. Second, context's significance for enterprise (re-) engineering and "organizational learning" corresponds to trends in three relevant fields applied to such efforts: (a) systemic theories for addressing enterprises; (b) representational tools for modeling enterprise features; and (c) linguistic interactions as vehicles for enterprise change. Third, dealing with contextual issues from a systemic perspective requires redefining it as a process (*contexture*) embedded in the intrinsic "situatedness" of a system's mode of operation. Finally, this shift from "context" to "contexture" can be facilitated in practice by reconfiguring the procedures by which enterprise knowledge activities are conducted.

Reprinted with permission from *European Management Journal,* Volume 14, Number 4, August 1996. Copyright © 1996 Elsevier Science Ltd., Oxford, England.

CONTEXT'S EPISTEMOLOGICAL AND OPERATIONAL IMPORTANCE

What is meant by context, and what is its relevance to enterprise knowledge building? For the sake of brevity, let me proceed from a conventional information-processing perspective addressing an observing system (e.g., an enterprise) within its milieu. We typically treat context as a thing " . . . which environs the object of our interest and helps by its relevance to explain it" (Scharfstein, 1989, p. 1). In this view, "context" denotes background or "meta-level" information which constrains or determines the interpretation of other data. To serve a contextualizing function, such information must be present to or known by the observer/interpreter. The construct of "context" is an explanatory device by which we acknowledge that anything the observer/interpreter " . . . learns, or can learn, from a signal (event, condition, or state of affairs), and hence the information carried by that signal, depends in part on what one already knows about the alternative possibilities" (Dretske, 1981, p. 43).

Operationally, contextual information is taken to accomplish two functions. First, it supports observation of individual data by facilitating discrimination of discrete object elements and relationships among them. In this sense, "context" refers to the means by which an observing system acknowledges specifics of novelty or details in its milieu. Second, contextual information supports orientation to incoming data by providing a basis for evaluating coherence and consistency (of both the perceived milieu and the system's attitude toward it). In this sense, "context" refers to the means by which an observing system acknowledges viable stability in reciprocal interactions with the milieu. When an observing system exhibits an increased effectiveness in discriminating aspects of—and reaching a viable stability within—its environment, we attribute "learning" to its operations. When the observing system is an enterprise, effectiveness in handling "context" is therefore a critical element in the process of "organizational learning."

The operational relevance of context is illustrated by Figure 6-1, which models the progress through a problem-solving cycle from the occurrence of a perceived "breakdown" through to implementation of a solution. This problem-solving model originated in Whitaker (1992) and has been subsequently applied to group decision support systems (Whitaker, 1994) and human factors aspects of group IT usage (Whitaker et al., 1995). More recently, the model has been integrated with Boyd's (1987) OODA (Observe-Orient-Decide-Act) construct from military strategic studies. The augmented model of Figure 6-1 is currently the basis for cognitive/instrumental analyses of mission-critical decision making and competitive leverage in the emerging area of *information warfare* (Whitaker, 1996). This model exhibits *scalability* and *self-similarity* as discussed in von Krogh and Roos (1995, pp. 69–93) because: (a) it is recursively (de-) composable and (b) it has proven viable across a range of organizational (e.g., team; department) and temporal (e.g., session; project) scopes.

During the course of this cycle, problem solvers' attention shifts between a *task venue* (the real world operational milieu) and a *depictive venue* (a repre-

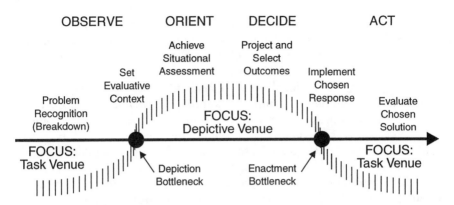

FIGURE 6-1 Informational Aspects of a Problem Solving Cycle (after Whitaker: 1992; 1994)

sentational milieu). The points at which these cross-venue shifts occur constitute problematical "bottlenecks" in the overall process. The first such transition—termed the *depiction bottleneck*—is the critical locus at which insufficiencies in recognizing task venue circumstances may become reified in working models within the depictive venue. The second such transition—the *enactment bottleneck*—is the locus at which deficiencies in working models may become reified in praxis. The depiction bottleneck is the critical failure point for knowledge building, and the enactment bottleneck is the critical failure point for knowledge application. Analyses of systems engineering failures consistently indicate suboptimal transitions at these two process bottlenecks. Of the two, the depiction bottleneck is the more critical. In addition to its being a failure point in and of itself, deficiencies in navigating through this bottleneck will likely propagate downstream, practically ensuring deficiency at the enactment bottleneck.

Most relevant to this discussion is the fact that the depiction bottleneck is the primary point at which "context" is formulated and applied. The context of the task venue should provide criteria for selecting and applying an adequate depictive model. The context established by a given depictive model will in turn circumscribe the manner in which the problem will be—and *can be*—addressed. In this sense, context delineates the epistemological "field" within which decision makers must operate, and from which they are by definition unable to escape. With respect to Boyd's OODA model, the depiction bottleneck occurs within the key "Orient" phase, where actors' correlation of data influences and is influenced by context defined as " . . . the interplay of genetic heritage, cultural tradition, previous experiences, and unfolding circumstances" (Boyd, 1987, p. 211). This corresponds to Ciborra and Lanzara's *formative context*—" . . . the set of the pre-existing institutional arrangements, cognitive frames, and imageries that actors bring and routinely enact in a situation of action" (1990, p. 151).

The transition from the task venue to the depictive venue entails the transformation of relevant task parametrics into a model suitable for analysis and deliberation. Because this model should adequately reflect the details of the task situation in a cohesive manner, the quality of the depiction bottleneck transition will be proportional to the quality in effecting the contextual functions of discrimination and coherence outlined above.

Unfortunately, conventional decision making models downplay or ignore contextual factors. Simonian cognitivistic approaches assume an objective situation to which the decision maker can (but admittedly does not) have complete access. This is why such approaches delimit deficiencies with respect to a "bounded rationality" of the decision maker rather than any "bounded interpretability" of the situation. This view is suspect in the light of results from empirical research demonstrating that the key to expert decision making performance is situation assessment (i.e., the contextualization of circumstances), not exhaustive reasoning (cf. Klein et al., 1993). It is further called into question by results from the CSCW (computer supported cooperative work) community showing that from 33 per cent to 80 per cent of time spent in management and design meetings is dedicated to explanatory cross-orientation (clarification of concepts and positions) among participants (Olson, 1995; Fuller, 1993). The reasonable conclusion is succinctly summarized by Winograd and Flores (1986, p. 146)—"The view of management as rational problem solving and decision making fails to deal with the question of background . . . The hard part is understanding how the alternatives relevant to a given context come into being. The critical part of problem solving lies in formulating the problem."

CONTEXT AS A "STATE OF THE ART" ISSUE

Active generation, maintenance, and exploitation of "organizational knowledge" is the hallmark of current "organizational learning" efforts. In following prescriptions for systemic approaches (e.g., Senge, 1990; Morgan, 1986), such efforts are subject to the state of the art in systems theory. In applying structured analyses and IT to facilitate such processes, these efforts are subject to the state of the art in modeling techniques. By involving enterprise members through interaction, the linguistic state of the art is relevant. In terms of these three key dimensions of enterprise (re-)engineering, context is a "state of the art" concern. The following sections briefly sketch the paths leading to this situation.

Context as an Issue in Systems Theory

Since the 1940s, reciprocal cross-pollination between engineering, management, and social scientists has fostered a view of the enterprise as a system—an ordered set of components whose synergistic operation constitutes more than merely "the sum of its parts." The value of systemic principles has been touted by technocratic "systems engineers," the "socio-technical" proponents who claimed to supersede them, and the "participatory re-engineering" proponents who claim to supersede both. During this past half-century, systems-theoretical constructs have become increasingly sophisticated in accordance with heightened awareness of the complexities of real-world enterprises. Early systems analyses concentrated on the relatively static "clockwork" of organizational structure. Later the focus shifted to function, as analysts began to treat enterprises as dynamic systems whose configuration and behavior evolve in the course of their operations. In the 1960s, there arose a *second-order cybernetics* which integrated the observer's viewpoint into the delineation of a given system. More recently, new systemic theories permit us to address enterprise systems as self-organizing, in the sense that the paths of their evolution are largely determined by the systems themselves (Whitaker, 1995). Useful theories must attend to the manner in which system structure and function are "meaningful" both synchronically and diachronically. From a second-order cybernetics perspective, this entails the "context of the observer." For self-organizing systems, this entails the subject system as providing and enacting its own "context of evaluation."

Context as an Issue in Systems Modeling

This evolution in systemic theories has required a parallel evolution of strategies for modeling enterprises. Straightforward logical representations sufficed for static clockworks, and (e.g.) series of differential equations helped to capture the character of interdependent dynamics. Unfortunately, these earlier approaches were predicated upon specifying atomic referents which were "objective" in two senses—(a) relatively fixed or immutable and (b) unambiguously meaningful to an external observer/analyst. Where system referents are subject to dynamic local definition and modification (as in self-organizing systems), such "objectivity" cannot be obtained. Modeling auto-determinative systems requires careful attention to those factors which provide or qualify (i.e., contextualize) the systems' persistent form, their dynamics, and the manner in which they can be known and (re-)engineered. Recent innovations in social/organizational analyses (e.g., action research, ethnomethodology and other qualitative approaches) have attempted to overcome these limitations by focusing on people and enterprises—who they are and how they are—on their own terms (i.e., "in context").

Context as an Issue in Linguistics

Schematism—an approach to language as a formal system of objectively specifiable entities related through objectively specifiable conventions (Whitaker, 1992)—dominated linguistics and influenced other social sciences from the 1930s until recently. This approach runs into trouble when the subject turns to meaning-formulation in discourse. Meaning cannot be easily divorced from either the circumstantial (e.g., social) context of interaction or the personal (e.g., cognitive) context of the interactors. During the last 50 years, linguistics has evolved from schematism's preoccupation with form toward issues of function. Wittgenstein's (1963) notion of "language games" shifted the focus of analysis from abstract coding to interpersonal activity. Austin's (1962) *speech acts* described the manner in which utterances are instrumental actions. In the 1970s empirical research labeled conversation analysis began to concentrate on *conversational activity* in practice, providing hard data on how people actually interact discursively. The work deriving from these and other sources illustrates three basic points. First, linguistic form (syntax) is only approximately determinant of function in actual discourse, which is filled with incomplete phrases, poor grammar, and non-verbal cues. Second, interactors use utterances not as containers of deterministically-meaningful units, but as cues for selecting conceptual frames ("possible worlds") in successively focusing on some topic. Third, this ongoing selection is guided by shared contextual elements. In other words, the emergent view is that discourse is an activity conducted over a shared contextual base and effecting shifts in orientations holding between its participants and their respective views of that contextual base.

FROM OBJECTIVISTIC "CONTEXT" TO SYSTEMIC "CONTEXTURE"

Although an information-processing perspective makes for efficient introductory explanations, its utility is limited in dealing with contextual issues in practice. In large part, this is a consequence of the way such an approach defines "context" itself. That which guides interpretation of new data is itself treated as a set of ordered data. This is a circular definition which begs the following questions:

- How can we "ground" or anchor any candidate contextual base for analysis?
- How can we generate a specification of "context" without relying on the very information whose interpretation it is subject to?

So long as one stays within an objectivistic information-processing framework, these questions will evade definitive answers. There is one and only one case in which these problematical issues can be avoided—the case in which an "objective" analytical context is given *a priori*. This in turn assumes that the observing system already has a viable knowledge encompassing the situations to be confronted, the implications of new data, and the range of responses. Such an attitude necessarily entails that either (a) the observing system has a functional "omniscience" or (b) the observing system has a functional "dogma." The first alternative is, of course, impossible. The second alternative is the very brittleness which "organizational learning" is intended to overcome.

From a systemic perspective, each of these questions must be answered with respect to the observing system itself. This requires a shift of referential focus from abstract, objective "information quanta" to the operations by which the observing system engages its milieu and responds to changes. The most comprehensive systemic treatment of these issues is found in *autopoietic theory,* developed by Chilean biologists Maturana and Varela (Maturana and Varela, 1980; 1987; Varela, 1979; Whitaker, 1995). As a biological phenomenon, cognition is viewed with respect to the actor(s) whose conduct realizes that phenomenon. In autopoietic theory, cognition is a consequence of circularity and complexity in the form of any system whose behavior includes maintenance of that selfsame form. This shifts the focus from discernment of active agencies and replicable actions through which "cognition" is conducted (e.g., the information-processing approach) to the discernment of those features of an actor's form which determine its engagement with its milieu.

This orientation led Maturana and Varela to develop a systematic description of organisms as self-producing units in the physical space. Deriving from this formal foundation a set of operational characteristics (e.g., self-regulation; self-reference), Maturana and Varela developed a systemic explanation of cognition and a descriptive phenomenology. This work has generated innovative implications for (among other things) epistemology, communication and social systems theory. Applications of autopoietic theory range across diverse fields such as software engineering, artificial intelligence, sociology, management studies, and psychotherapy. The general theoretical issues are summarized in Mingers (1994), and implications for organizational studies can be found in Morgan (1986), Whitaker (1995), and von Krogh and Roos (1995).

In an autopoietic framework, discourse is not a process of transferring discrete symbols back and forth between interactors as if through a "conduit." Autopoietic systems engage their milieu via structural coupling—the reciprocal interplay between their flexible structure and the medium which " . . . will determine, on the one hand, the state of the system and its domain of allowable perturbations . . . " (Varela, 1979, p. 33). When two such systems structurally couple with each other, they generate " . . . an interlocked history of structural transformations, selecting each other's trajectories" (Ibid.). Language is a venue for action toward the *mutual orientation* of conversants within the *consensual domain* that is thus realized. Maturana reinterprets language as the archetypal human consensual domain and labels all such interactional domains as linguistic. This permits the theory to address types of "communication" other than formal languages and affords autopoietic theory a means for addressing the full range of semiotic phenomena (i.e., all forms of signifying events). "[T]he 'universal grammar' of which linguists speak as the necessary set of underlying rules common to all human natural languages can refer only to the universality of the process of recursive structural coupling" (Maturana, 1978, p. 52).

Adopting Maturana's view means forfeiting the notion of absolutely objective meaning in any interactional behavior. The reason is simple: the ascription of such meaning lies unavoidably with an observer/interpreter of the interaction (perhaps one of the interactors themselves). There is no sense of meaning except in such a cognitive domain. It is important to note that Maturana is not removing anything from the fundamental repertoire of epistemology; he is adding the observer as the most fundamental element of all. What, then, of "knowledge"? Maturana and Varela assert that knowledge is not a quantum commodity (e.g., a set of facts or propositions); it is a projected evaluation by some observer of behavior which is deemed to be effective under some criteria. "We admit knowledge whenever we observe an effective (or adequate) behavior in a given context." (1987, p. 174). "To know is to be able to operate adequately in an individual or cooperative situations" (Maturana and Varela, 1980, p. 53).

This reformulation of "knowledge" requires that we reconsider what we mean by "learning." In the autopoietic account "intelligence," like "knowledge," is an explanatory device for effective action (Maturana and Guiloff, 1980). Any innovation in the capacity for such effective action becomes the basis for ascribing "learning," based on "[t]he change in the domain of possible states that the [system] can adopt" (Maturana and Varela, 1980, p. 132). The learning capability of the observing system " . . . does not lie in its production of 'engrams' or representations of things in the world; rather it lies in its continuous transformation in line with transformations of the environment as a result of how each interaction affects it. From the observer's standpoint, this is seen as proportionate learning" (Maturana and Varela, 1987, p. 170). From this vantage point, "organizational knowledge" is the capacity of the enterprise to effectively engage its operational milieu, and "organizational learning" is nothing more or less than a facilitated process of enterprise self-organization.

In this view, "context" is not some meta-level informational quantum. Instead, it is an explanation for the filtering and patterning by which the observing system (a) acknowledges or recognizes environmental perturbations and (b) processually mediates between these perturbations and potential responses. Context is not, then, a thing which determines the form of abstract "information," but an ascribed capacity for ordering responses with respect to perturbations. As such, it is more enlightening to speak not of a thing called "context," but of a process. Whitaker (1992) terms this process *contexture*—an interweaving of referentiality and signification. The term comes from the same Latin root as "context," which means "to weave together." Contexture denotes the ongoing specification of trajectories of orientational and instrumental possibilities within continual flux, invoked to describe shifting individual and mutual orientations within the course of interaction.

This shift preserves the operational features of "context" discussed above. Contexture is a filtering process because it restricts the amount, type, or character of the cues recognized by the system. This in turn is a function of the observing system's configuration. This configuration may be exhibited in a number of dimensions such as: system structure (e.g., sensor limitations); location (e.g., connectivity/proximity); functional capacity (e.g., throughput constraints); and engagement (e.g., attentional focus). Contexture is a patterning process because it transforms the amount, type, or character of the system's "knowledge base" in response to cues. This patterning process is also a function of the observing system's configuration. These two processes are the systemic analogues of the "observational discrimination" and "orientational coherence" functions I initially addressed in information-processing terms.

AN EXAMPLE OF FACILITATING CONTEXTURE IN ENTERPRISE KNOWLEDGE PROCESSES

The next question is how one may implement this revised approach. To illustrate, this section presents a case study of organizational re-engineering in a public sector research laboratory (XLab) with a global reputation for its human physical and performance research. The nature of the work is very information-intensive, and XLab's operations are increasingly dependent on computers and computerized equipment. The laboratory staff consists of government managers/researchers, a contractor team, and occasional visiting consultants. Unlike similar laboratory units at their location, XLab has become largely self-supporting. Approximately 75 per cent of the unit's budget requirements are covered by contracts from clients external to XLab's parent enterprise. Requests for contract work outstrip XLab's work capacities, with only approximately 50 per cent of external requests accepted. Project management and workflow are complicated by this high external demand, obligations to prioritize requests from the parent enterprise, and complexities in the work. Finally, XLab is shifting from primarily manual work with centralized mainframe IT over to primarily computerized work and decentralized LANs. To summarize, XLab is a professional team of "knowledge workers" reliant on outsourcing, going through tremendous structural and functional change under conditions of increasing duress. As such, XLab exhibits the "profile" most cited in analyses of modern competitive enterprises.

In 1994, XLab undertook a process of self-review and self-analysis. XLab managers wished to devise a model of themselves which could support eventual structural reorganization, functional reorganization, workload consolidation, and operational policy making. Two prior analyses by organizational consultants had prescribed acceptable changes, but did not address the fundamental issues of XLab's identity and role(s). In return for the use of a computer-supported meeting room, tools, methods, and facilitation support, XLab agreed to serve as subjects for CSCW research into human factor aspects of collaborative activity. Over a period of several months, XLab personnel participated in regular seasions employing brainstorming, open discussion, concept mapping, flowcharting, and other facilitation techniques. The output from this effort was extensive documentation of XLab's current operating structures, goals, resources, and workload.

These specific results did not satisfy the goal of modeling XLab's identity and role(s). The knowledge acquisition tools and techniques provided *systematically* descriptive models of XLab's situational status, but somehow fell short of describing XLab as a systemically unified object of analysis. Specific problems identified as contributing to this shortfall included (a) the bad fit between the tools' capacities for static, reductionist descriptions and the task's demand for processual, systemic explanations and (b) the cognitive burden of framing comments with respect to a given representational schema. Specific deficiencies included gaps in the knowledge elicitation results and a tendency for subjects to proceed with primary attention to the mechanics of constructing a common representation rather than to the subject matter to be represented (*depictional lock-on*—Whitaker et al., 1995). Depictional lock-on can be characterized as the counterproductive effect of subjects becoming so absorbed in the depictive venue (see Figure 6-1) that they lose sight of the task venue they are trying to discuss. Phrased another way, depictional lock-on occurs when subjects pay too much attention to the depictive context and too little to the task context. In light of these problems, continuation required a new technique for facilitating exploratory, constructivistic generation of XLab's "self-image." The resultant specification, construction, and execution of an innovative structured knowledge elicitation technique (labeled *nichepicking*—a pun on "nitpicking") is described in the remainder of this article.

The main goals in developing the nichepicking methodology were concerned with context—(1) generating specifications of Xlab's contexts of operation and (2) tracking knowledge development within the contexts thus defined. The nichepicking elicitation procedure and the presentational/depictional artifacts employed were designed to minimize the effects of this depictional lock-on by reducing cognitive burden and correcting the bad fit between prior elicitation schemata and the subject matter. Interactions were made as "conversational" as possible, formal structuring was delayed until the latter phases of the exercise, abstraction was minimized by reliance on unconstrained text, and primary attention was given to setting XLab's context(s) before attempting to positively and definitively specify the lab's identity.

The approach to facilitating XLab's self-definition was based on functional contextualization in terms of a "niche." Niche was a construct denoting XLab's functional identity within the context of its operational domains (e.g., budgeting, research, external contracting). This term was chosen because its usage in ecology connoted the same factors as those at issue in this case: (1) a sense of operational role rather than static categorization; (2) a focus on the reciprocal relationship between the unit and its subsuming system; and (3) the notion that a unit may realize multiple niches within diverse "systems" or "cycles of operation." These factors were also consistent with Maturana and Varela's (1980) general tenets and their specific discussion of an autopoietic system's "niche."

The procedure for delineating Xlab's niches was based on specifying "boundaries." In biological autopoietic systems realized in the physical space, boundaries are literally realized in the physical structure of the organism. For systems not constrained to the physical space, the boundary may be defined in terms of functional or relational extension rather than literal spatial extent. The specific mechanism for delimiting boundaries was the formulation of bipolar *distinctions*. This derived from Maturana and Varela's (1980) position that the most fundamental act of cognition was drawing distinctions in a phenomenological domain. The practical result of these points was that the new elicitation methodology would proceed with primary regard to the specification and elucidation of distinctions delineating Xlab's "boundaries" within each of its discernible operational domains. This required the methodology to be formulated so as to: (1) outline the client's relevant operational domains (i.e., establish context); (2) distinguish the client enterprise from other units within each of those domains (i.e., refine context); and (3) provide mechanisms allowing the clients to orient and navigate within the potentially large set of representations generated in the course of (1) and (2) (i.e., track and adhere to context).

The initial nichepicking exercise was configured in three stages, as illustrated in Figure 6-2. In the first stage—Structured Brainstorming—subjects repetitively completed the statement "XLab is a _____." The subjects were free to answer as they saw fit, with no restrictions on the form or tone of their comments. During the second stage—Contextual Layout—the facilitator/analyst "parsed" the answers as instances of the form "XLab is a (Qualifier) (Object)." The set of Objects [O] was sorted into related Object Families—e.g., memberships ("division," "branch") ordered by organizational hierarchy. The set of explicit and implicit Qualifiers [Q] for each Object Family provided a set of relevant factors termed Object Issues. Tabular displays were then generated for each Object Family/Object Issue intersection. In each display, the Object Family was listed as the general referential context, and a single Object Issue was listed as a specific perspective or subcontext. Blank areas were left for comments regarding XLab versus any other entities operating within the same contextual "space." The displays were designed to enforce consistent contextual indexicality by orienting subjects to specific issues within the specifically-delimited contexts. This structuring was

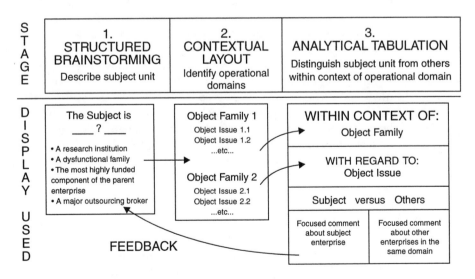

FIGURE 6-2 The 3-Stage Nichepicking Process

intended to organize comparative analysis and provide a framework for user orientation/navigation and consistency/completeness checking.

In the third stage of the process—Analytical Tabulation—the Objects and Object Issues were used to specify XLab's boundaries within each of the operational domains identified during Contextual Layout. In working with these displays, subjects compared XLab and others in each Object Family *vis à vis* the Object Issue, elucidating similarities and contrasts. As the subjects generated new insights, the results could be fed back through the process. This was accomplished in real-time during the Analytical Tabulation sessions. As it turned out, the Analytical Tabulation displays were sufficiently straightforward that they could be used as the sole tool for the nichepicking process. One manager asked to use this display format for the entirety of her participation. She managed to match her earlier relative productivity, and she reported no problems in using the tabular format for everything from initial brainstorming to final analysis. Nichepicking's concrete outputs were: (1) the compiled brainstorming listings; (2) the compiled Contextual Layout listings; (3) the database containing the Analytical Tabulation results; and (4) a summary report analyzing the results.

Nichepicking was uniformly judged a success in accomplishing its intended goals. Quantitatively, it surpassed prior techniques (mainly concept mapping) on volume of documented propositions (400% increase), productivity per unit time (at least 20% overall time savings), and percentage of utterances captured in real-time during brainstorming (98% versus an average 50%). In qualitative terms, the results were judged: (a) easy to comprehend; (b) easy to extend; and (c) easy to present and explain to others. Subjects deemed the nichepicking results to be more useful and "constructive" than products of the earlier techniques they'd used. They liked nichepicking's flexibility of expression and found Analytical Tabulation easy to do. Finally, the subjects judged (and review of earlier efforts confirmed) that nichepicking had detected and documented issues which had not been captured in prior self-specification attempts. The nichepicking results have become a key reference point for XLab's programmatic planning. The structured documentation serves as an evolving self-specification of policy, goals, and constraints. The niche specifications have been used to guide XLab's self-portrayal in briefings, program reviews, and publicity materials. Additionally, nichepicking has enabled the XLab management to clarify their self-explanations in support of their annual budget campaign and internal training. In all respects, nichepicking was successful in generating a comprehensive account of enterprise "self-knowledge."

CONCLUSIONS

This case illustrates that the points made earlier in this discussion can be reflected in concrete practices. The nichepicking procedure is consistent with the systems-theoretical, systems modeling, and interactional aspects of context's "state of the art" status. Because nichepicking began with formulation of "niches" within which details were subsequently framed, it prioritized context over specifics. Because the procedure allowed this formulation to be open-ended, the extent of detailed specification was limited only by the subjects' time constraints and motivation. The process realized through nichepicking achieved contexture in the sense of "weaving together" features and parameters to generate enterprise knowledge from the "outside inward." The procedure was expressly geared to support the client enterprise's systemic self-organization. Its participative nature allowed the enterprise's specification to be accomplished in its constituents' "own terms," and this in turn conformed to second-order cybernetics' focus on addressing systems only as they are delimited by a given observer. Finally, the material generated formed a "shared contextual base" about which subjects could mutually orient.

More generally, the nichepicking trial study demonstrated: (1) structured knowledge building strategies can facilitate enterprise self-organization; (2) contextual specification followed by (recursive, self-referential) elucidation is a viable process strategy; and (3) tabular displays for comparative analysis are very useful. From a human factors perspective, nichepicking succeeded in reducing cognitive burden early in the process and diminishing depictional lock-on during its course. In functional terms, nichepicking exceeded all prior facilitation practices with respect to productivity, time management, and ease of use. From a client perspective, nichepicking succeeded in producing a coherent enterprise self-image judged more useful and more amenable to elaboration than products of conventional procedures and depictive schemata.

REFERENCES

Austin, J. L., (1962), *How to Do Things with Words,* Cambridge MA: Harvard University Press.

Boyd, John R. (Col.), (1987), *A Discourse on Winning and Losing,* Air University Library, Maxwell AFB Report no. MU 43947 (unpublished briefing), August.

Ciborra, C., and G. Lanzara, (1990), Designing Dynamic Artifacts: Computer Systems as Formative Contexts, in Gagliardi, P. (ed.), *Symbols and Artifacts: Views of the Corporate Landscape,* Berlin: De Gruyter, pp. 147–165.

Dretske, F., (1981), *Knowledge and the Flow of Information,* Cambridge MA: MIT Press.

Fuller, M., (1993), Comments in Internet's GSS-L (Group Support System mailing list) *Discussion Forum,* Oct. 29.

Klein, G., J. Orasanu, R. Caldenwood, and C. Zsambok, (eds.), (1993), *Decision Making in Action: Models and Methods,* Norwood NJ: Ablex.

Maturana, H., (1978), Biology of Language: The Epistemology of Reality, in Miller, G., and E. Lenneberg (eds.), *Psychology and Biology of Language and Thought: Essays in Honor of Eric Lenneberg,* New York: Academic Press, pp. 27–64.

Maturana, H. and G. Guiloff, (1980), The Quest for the Intelligence of Intelligence, *Journal of Social and Biological Structures,* Vol. 3, pp. 135–148.

Maturana, H. and F. Varela, (1980), *Autopoiesis and Cognition: The Realization of the Living*, Dordrecht: D. Reidel.

Maturana, H. and F. Varela, (1987), *The Tree of Knowledge: The Biological Roots of Human Understanding*, Boston: Shambhala.

Mingers, J., (1994), *Self-Producing Systems: Implications and Applications of Autopoiesis*, New York: Plenum Publishing.

Morgan, G., (1986), *Images of Organization*, Newbury Park CA: Sage.

Olson, G., (1995), *Technology Support for Distributed Workgroups*, USAF Armstrong Laboratory Colloquium, Dayton OH, February.

Scharfstein, B., (1989), *The Dilemma of Context*, New York: New York University Press.

Senge, P., (1990), *The Fifth Discipline*, New York: Doubleday.

Varela, F., (1979), *Principles of Biological Autonomy*, New York: Elsevier (North-Holland).

von Krogh, G. and J. Roos, (1995), *Organizational Epistemology*, New York: St. Martin's Press.

Whitaker, R., (1992), *Venues for Contexture: A Critical Analysis and Enactive Reformulation of Group Decision Support Systems*, Umeå (Sweden): Umeå University Dept. of Informatics Research Report UMADP-RRIPCS 15.92, December.

Whitaker, R., (1993), Interactional Models for Collective Support Systems: An Application of Autopoietic Theory, in Glanville, R., and G. de Zeeuw (eds.), *Interactive Interfaces and Human Networks*, Amsterdam: Thesis Publishers, pp. 119–135.

Whitaker, R., (1994), GDSSi Formative Fundaments: An Interpretive Analysis, *Computer Supported Cooperative Work: An International Journal* (Dordrecht: Kluwer), Vol. 2, pp. 239–260.

Whitaker, R., (1995), Self-organization, Autopoiesis, and Enterprises, *ACM SIGOIS Illuminations*, Association for Computing Machinery, Organizational Information Systems SIG online journal, December. Available via WWW at: http://www.acm.org/sigois/auto/main.html

Whitaker, R., J. Selvaraj, C. Brown, and M. McNeese, (1995), *Collaborative Design Technology: Tools and Techniques for Improving Collaborative Design*, Dayton OH: USAF Armstrong Laboratory Technical Report AL/CF-TR-1995-0086.

Whitaker, R., (1996), Cognitive Engineering for Information Dominance, Dayton OH: USAF Armstrong Laboratory Technical Report.

Winograd, T., and F. Flores, (1986), *Understanding Computers and Cognition*, Norwood NJ: Ablex.

Wittgenstein, L., (1963), *Philosophical Investigations*, Oxford: Basil Blackwell.

7

Managing Professional Intellect: Making the Most of the Best

James Brian Quinn, Philip Anderson, Sydney Finkelstein

In the postindustrial era, the success of a corporation lies more in its intellectual and systems capabilities than in its physical assets. The capacity to manage human intellect—and to convert it into useful products and services—is fast becoming the critical executive skill of the age. As a result, there has been a flurry of interest in intellectual capital, creativity, innovation, and the learning organization, but surprisingly little attention has been given to managing professional intellect.

This oversight is especially surprising because professional intellect creates most of the value in the new economy. Its benefits are immediately visible in the large service industries, such as software, health care, financial services, communications, and consulting. But in manufacturing industries as well, professionals generate the preponderance of value—through activities like research and development, process design, product design, logistics, marketing, or systems management. Despite the growing importance of professional intellect, few managers have systematic answers to even these basic questions: What is professional intellect? How can we develop it? How can we leverage it?

WHAT IS PROFESSIONAL INTELLECT?

The true professional commands a body of knowledge—a discipline that must be updated constantly. The professional intellect of an organization operates on four levels, presented here in order of increasing importance:

Cognitive knowledge (or know-what) is the basic mastery of a discipline that professionals achieve through extensive training and certification. This knowledge is essential, but usually far from sufficient, for commercial success.

Advanced skills (know-how) translate "book learning" into effective execution. The ability to apply the rules of a discipline to complex real-world problems is the most widespread value-creating professional skill level.

Systems understanding (know-why) is deep knowledge of the web of cause-and-effect relationships underlying a discipline. It permits professionals to move beyond the execution of tasks to solve larger and more complex problems—and to create extraordinary value. Professionals with know-why can anticipate subtle interactions and unintended consequences. The ultimate expression of systems understanding is highly trained intuition—for example, the insight of a seasoned research director who knows instinctively which projects to fund and exactly when to do so.

Self-motivated creative (care-why) consists of will, motivation, and adaptability for success. Highly motivated and creative groups often outperform groups with greater physical or financial resources. Without self-motivated creativity, intellectual leaders can lose their knowledge advantage through complacency. They may fail to adapt aggressively to changing external conditions and particularly to innovations that obsolesce their earlier skills—just as the techniques of molecular design are superseding chemical screening in pharmaceuticals today. That is why the highest level of intellect is now so vital. Organizations that nurture care-why in their people can simultaneously thrive in the face of today's rapid changes and renew their cognitive knowledge, advanced skills, and systems understanding in order to compete in the next wave of advances.

Intellect clearly resides in the brains of professionals. The first three levels can also exist in the organization's systems, databases, or operating technologies, whereas the fourth is often found in its culture. The value of intellect increases markedly as one moves up the intellectual scale from cognitive knowledge to self-motivated creativity. Yet most enterprises focus virtually all their training attention on developing basic (rather than advanced) skills and little or none on systems or creative skills.

Most of a typical professional's activity is directed at perfection, not creativity. Customers primarily want professional knowledge delivered reliably and with the most advanced skill available. Although there is an occasional call for creativity, most of the work done by accounting units, hospitals, software companies, or financial service providers requires the repeated use of highly developed skills on relatively similar, though complex, problems. People rarely want surgeons, accountants, pilots, maintenance personnel, or nuclear plant operators to be very creative. Managers clearly must prepare their professionals for the few emergencies or other special circumstances that require creativity, but they should focus the bulk of their attention on delivering consistent, high-quality intellectual output.

Because professionals have specialized knowledge and have been trained as an elite, they often tend to regard their judgment in other realms as sacrosanct as well. Professionals generally hesitate to subordinate themselves to others or to support organizational goals not completely congruous with their special viewpoint. That is why most professional firms operate as partnerships and not as hierarchies, and why it is difficult for them to adopt a unified strategy.

Members of every profession tend to look to their peers to determine codes of behavior and acceptable standards of performance. They often refuse to accept evaluations by those outside their discipline. Many doctors, for example, resist the attempts of HMOs and insurance companies to tell them how to practice medicine. Such a posture is the source of many professional organizations' problems. Professionals tend to surround themselves with people who have similar backgrounds and values. Unless deliberately fractured, these discipline-based cocoons quickly become inward-looking bureaucracies that are resistant to change and detached from customers. Consider the many software or basic research organizations that become isolated inside larger organizations, creating conflicts with other professional groups such as marketing or manufacturing departments.

DEVELOPING PROFESSIONAL INTELLECT

At the heart of the most effective professional organizations we have observed are a handful of best practices for managing intellect that resemble successful coaching more than anything else.

Recruit the best. The leverage of intellect is so great that a few topflight professionals can create a successful organization or make a lesser one flourish. Marvin Bower essentially created McKinsey & Company; Robert Noyce and Gordon E. Moore spawned Intel; William H. Gates and Paul Allen built Microsoft; Herbert W. Boyer and Robert A. Swanson made Genentech; and Albert Einstein put Princeton's Institute for Advanced Study on the map. But even such organizations must find and attract extraordinary talent.

It is no accident that the leading management consultants devote enormous resources to recruiting and that they heavily screen the top graduates of the leading business schools. Microsoft interviews hundreds of highly recommended people for each key software designer it hires, and its grueling selection process tests not only cognitive knowledge but also the capacity to think about new problems under high pressure. The Four Seasons Hotels often interviews 50 candidates to make one hire. Venture capital firms, recognizing talent and commitment as the most critical elements for their success, spend as much time selecting and pursuing top people as they do making quantitative analyses of projects.

Because the most qualified professionals want to work with the best in their field, leading organizations can attract better talent than their lesser competitors. The best commercial programmers, for example, seek out and stay with Microsoft largely because they believe Microsoft will determine where the industry will move in the future and because they can share the excitement and rewards of being at that frontier. But second-tier organizations are not destined always to lag behind. Managers who understand the importance of the right kind of talent can pull a jujitsu reversal on industry leaders by acquiring such talent. When CEO Marshall N. Carter led State Street Bank's entry into the rapidly emerging custodials business, he hired world-class data processing managers to seed his new organization. Today State Street handles $1.7 trillion in custodial accounts, and virtually all its senior managers have data processing rather than traditional banking backgrounds.

Force intensive early development.   Professional know-how is developed most rapidly through repeated exposure to the complexity of real problems. Thus for most professionals, the learning curve depends heavily on interactions with customers. Accordingly, the best companies systematically put new professionals in contact with customers, where they work under the watchful eye of an experienced coach. Microsoft, for example, assigns new software developers to small teams of three to seven people. Under the guidance of mentors, the developers participate in the design of complex new software systems at the frontier of users' needs.

The legendary 80-hour weeks and all-nighters that give investment bankers and software developers their bragging rights serve a more serious developmental purpose: They enable the best talent to move up a learning curve that is steeper than anyone else's. On-the-job training, mentoring, and peer pressure can force professionals to the top of their knowledge ziggurat. Although burnout can be a problem if people are pushed too far, many studies show that intensity and repetition are critical to developing advanced skills in fields as diverse as the law and piloting aircraft.

People who go through these intensive experiences become noticeably more capable and valuable—compared with their counterparts in less intensively managed organizations—within six months to a year. If they are properly coached, they also develop a greater in-depth feel for systems interactions (know-why) and identify more with the company and its goals (care-why). The most successful organizations ensure such growth through constantly heightened (preferably customer-driven) complexity, thoroughly planned mentoring, substantial rewards for performance, and strong incentives to understand, systematize, and advance the discipline. The great intellectual organizations all seem to develop deeply ingrained cultures that emphasize these values. Most others do not.

Constantly increase professional challenges.   Intellect grows most when professionals buy into a serious challenge. Leaders of the best organizations tend to be demanding, visionary, and intolerant of halfhearted efforts. They often set almost impossible "stretch goals"—as did Hewlett-Packard's William R. Hewlett (improve performance by 50%), Intel's Gordon Moore (double the number of components per chip each year), and Motorola's Robert W. Galvin (achieve six sigma quality). Some professionals may drop out in response to such demands. Others will substitute their own even higher standards. The best organizations constantly push their professionals beyond the comfort of their book knowledge, simulation models, and controlled laboratories. They relentlessly drive associates to deal with the more complex intellectual realms of live customers, real operating systems, and highly differentiated external environments and cultural differences. Mediocre organizations do not.

Evaluate and weed. Professionals like to be evaluated, to compete, to know they have excelled against their peers. But they want to be evaluated objectively and by people at the top of their field. Hence, heavy internal competition and frequent performance appraisal and feedback are common in outstanding organizations. As a result, there is a progressive winnowing of talent. For example, at Andersen Consulting, only 10% of the carefully selected professional recruits move on to partnerships—a process that takes 9 to 12 years. Microsoft tries to force out the lowest-performing 5% of its highly screened talent each year. Great organizations are unabashed meritocracies; great organizations that fail are often those that forget the importance of objective praise and selective weeding.

LEVERAGING PROFESSIONAL INTELLECT

Conventional wisdom has long held that there are few opportunities for leverage in professional activities. A pilot can handle only one aircraft at a time; a chef can cook only so many different dishes at once; a researcher can conduct only so many unique experiments; a doctor can diagnose only one patient's illness at a time. In such situations, adding professionals at the very least multiplies costs at the same rate as benefits. In the past, growth most often brought diseconomies of scale as the bureaucracies coordinating, monitoring, or supporting the professionals expanded faster than the professional base. Universities, hospitals, research firms, accounting groups, and consultancies all seemed to pay the price.

For years, there were only two ways in which many organizations could create leverage: by pushing their people through more intensive training or work schedules than their competitors or by increasing the number of "associates" supporting each professional. The latter practice even became the accepted meaning of the term *leverage* in the fields of law, accounting, and consulting.

But new technologies and management approaches are changing the traditional economics of managing professional intellect. Organizations as diverse as Merrill Lynch, Andersen Worldwide, and NovaCare have found effective ways to link new software tools, incentive systems, and organizational designs in order to leverage professional intellect to much higher levels. Although each organization has developed solutions tailored to the specific needs of its business, there are a handful of common underlying principles.

Boost professionals' problem-solving abilities by capturing knowledge in systems and software. The core intellectual competence of many financial organizations—such as Merrill Lynch and State Street Bank—lies in the human experts and the systems software that collect and analyze the data that are relevant to investment decisions. A few financial specialists working at headquarters leverage their own high-level analytical skills through close interactions with other specialists and "rocket scientist" modelers, and through access to massive amounts of data about transactions. Proprietary software models and databases leverage the intellect of those professionals, allowing them to analyze markets, securities, and economic trends in ways that otherwise would be beyond their reach. Software systems then distribute the resulting investment recommendations to brokers at retail outlets who create further value by customizing the center's advice in order to meet the needs of individual clients. If one thinks about this organization as a center connected to customers at multiple points of contact, or nodes, leverage equals the value of the knowledge multiplied by the number of nodes using it. Value creation is enhanced if experimentation at the center increases know-why and incentive structures stimulate care-why.

Merrill Lynch's retail brokerage business follows the basic structure outlined above. Roughly 18,000 Merrill Lynch brokers operate out of more than 500 geographically dispersed offices to create custom investment solutions for clients. The typical retail broker is not a highly skilled financial professional with years of advanced training. Yet the firm's brokers serve millions of clients worldwide with sophisticated investment advice and detailed, up-to-date information on thousands of complex financial instruments. Information systems make this extraordinary leverage possible.

Electronic systems capture Merrill Lynch's aggregate experience curve, quickly enabling less trained people to achieve performance levels ordinarily associated with much more experienced personnel. The firm's computer network ensures that the retail brokers' cognitive knowledge is current and accurate. Merrill Lynch's information technologies allow the center to capture and distribute to the brokerage offices information about transactions, trading rules, yields, securities features, availability, tax considerations, and new offerings. Proprietary software, available on-line, serves as an instant training vehicle. It ensures that all brokers adhere to current regulations, make no arithmetic or clerical errors, and can provide customers with the latest market information. Capturing and distributing the firm's knowledge base through software allows Merrill Lynch to leverage the professional intellect at its core.

Information technology allows a large modern brokerage to be both efficient and flexible. At the center, it can achieve the full information power and economies of scale available only to a major enterprise. Yet local brokers can manage their own small units and accounts as independently as if they alone provided the service on a local basis. Their reward system is that of local entrepreneurs. The center functions primarily as an information source, a communications coordinator, or a reference desk for unusual inquiries. Field personnel connect with the center to obtain information to improve their performance, rather than to ask for instructions or specific guidance. At the same time, the center can electronically monitor local operations for quality and consistency. Most operating rules are programmed into the system and changed automatically by software. Electronic systems replace human command-and-control procedures. They also can eliminate most of the routine in jobs, free up employees for more personalized or skilled work, and allow tasks to be more decentralized, challenging, and rewarding.

Overcome professionals' reluctance to share information.   Information sharing is critical because intellectual assets, unlike physical assets, increase in value with use. Properly stimulated, knowledge and intellect grow exponentially when shared. All learning and experience curves have this characteristic. A basic tenet of communication theory states that a network's potential benefits grow exponentially as the nodes it can successfully interconnect expand numerically. It is not difficult to see how this growth occurs. If two people exchange knowledge with each other, both gain information and experience linear growth. But if both then share their new knowledge with others—each of whom feeds back questions, amplifications, and modifications—the benefits become exponential. Companies that learn from outsiders—especially from customers, suppliers, and specialists such as advanced design or software firms—can reap even greater benefits. The strategic consequences of exploiting this exponential growth are profound. Once a company gains a knowledge-based competitive edge, it becomes ever easier for it to maintain its lead and ever harder for its competitors to catch up.

Overcoming professionals' natural reluctance to share their most precious asset, knowledge, presents some common and difficult challenges. Competition among professionals often inhibits sharing, and assigning credit for intellectual contributions is difficult. When professionals are asked to collaborate as equals in problem solving, slow response is common as specialists try to refine their particular solutions to perfection. Because professionals' knowledge is their power base, strong inducements to share are necessary. Even then, the tendency of each profession to regard itself as an elite with special cultural values may get in the way of cross-disciplinary sharing. Many professionals have little respect for those outside their field, even when all parties are supposedly seeking the same goal. Often, in manufacturing companies, researchers disdain product designers, who disdain engineers. In health care, basic researchers disdain physicians (because "they don't understand causation"). Physicians disdain both researchers (who "don't understand practical variations among real patients") and nurses (who "don't understand the discipline"). Nurses disdain both doctors and researchers (who "lack true compassion"). And all three groups disdain administrators (who are " nonproductive bureaucrats").

To facilitate sharing, Andersen Worldwide has developed an electronic system linking its 82,000 people operating in 360 offices in 76 countries. Known as ANet, the T1 and frame-relay network connects more than 85% of Andersen's professionals through data, voice, and video interlinks. ANet allows Andersen specialists—by posting problems on electronic bulletin boards and following up with visual and data contacts—to self-organize instantly around a customer's problem anywhere in the world. ANet thus taps into otherwise dormant capabilities and expands the energies and solution sets available to customers. Problem-solving capacity is further enhanced through centrally collected and carefully indexed subject, customer-reference and resource files accessible directly through ANet or from CD-ROMs distributed to all offices.

Initially, Andersen spent large sums on hardware, travel, and professional training to encourage people not only to follow up on network exchanges but also to meet personally to discuss important problems—with disappointing results. Major changes in incentives and culture were needed to make the system work. Most important, participation in ANet began to be considered in all promotion and compensation reviews. To stimulate a cultural shift toward wider use of ANet, senior partners deliberately posed questions on employees' E-mail files each morning "to be answered by 10." Until those cultural changes were in place, ANet was less than successful despite its technological elegance.

Organize around intellect. In the past, most companies aimed to enhance returns from investments in physical assets: property, plant, and equipment. Command-and-control structures made sense when management's primary task was to leverage such physical assets. For example, the productivity of a manufacturing facility is determined largely by senior managers' decisions about capital equipment, adherence to standardized practices, the breadth of the product line, and capacity utilization. With intellectual assets, on the other hand, individual professionals typically provide customized solutions to an endless stream of new problems.

INVERTING ORGANIZATIONS

Many successful enterprises we have studied have abandoned hierarchical structures, organizing themselves in patterns specifically tailored to the particular way their professional intellect creates value. Such reorganization often involves breaking away from traditional thinking about the role of the center as a directing force.

Consider NovaCare, the largest provider of rehabilitation care and one of the fastest-growing health-care companies in the United States. Its critical professional intellect resides in its more than 5,000 occupational, speech, and physical therapists. As professionals, they work alone to customize their expertise for individual patients at 2,090 locations in 40 states. To be of greatest value, they must be highly trained and constantly updated on the best practices in their fields.

By organizing around the work of its therapists, NovaCare achieves considerable leverage. To focus their time on serving patients' needs, the organization frees the therapists from administrative and business responsibilities by, for example, arranging and managing their contracts with care facilities, scheduling and reporting on treatments they give, handling their accounting and credit activities, providing them with training updates, and increasing their earnings through the company's marketing capabilities.

NovaCare's software system, NovaNet, captures and enhances much of the organization's systems knowledge, such as the rules with which therapists must comply and the information they need about customers, schedules, and billing; it highlights for executives those trends or problem areas most pertinent to future operations. NovaNet collects information from all therapists about, for example, their costs and services, techniques that have worked well, and changing care patterns in different regions. This information is vital for recruiting, training, motivating, and updating therapists.

To facilitate the collection and analysis of knowledge, NovaCare records its therapeutic care activities in ten-minute blocks. This detailed information creates a database that can be used by a diverse group of stakeholders: caregivers, hospitals, clinics, payers, government agencies, executives, and outside financial and regulatory bodies. NovaCare utilizes extensive peer and customer reviews in evaluating its therapists' work and (based on the time units captured in NovaNet) rewards them on the amount and quality of the care they deliver.

NovaCare's professionals are highly self-sufficient; they have tremendous autonomy on questions involving patient care. Therapists can give orders to all intermediate line organizations. The company's regional and functional specialists in accounting, marketing, purchasing, and logistics exist primarily to support the therapists. Even CEO John H. Foster refers to the therapists as "my bosses." The leverage of NovaCare's organizational structure is "distributive"—that is, the support organization efficiently distributes logistics, analysis, and administrative support to the professionals. But it does not give them orders.

NovaCare has thus inverted the traditional organization. The former line hierarchy becomes a support structure, intervening only in extreme emergencies—as might the CEO of a hospital or the chief pilot of an airline. The function of former line managers changes: Instead of giving orders, they are now removing barriers, expediting resources, conducting studies, and acting as consultants. They support and help articulate the new culture. In effect, line managers evolve into staff people.

Inverted organizations like NovaCare make sense when individual experts embody most of the organization's knowledge, when they do not have to interact with one another to solve problems, and when they customize their knowledge at the point of contact with customers. The software behind inverted systems must serve two somewhat conflicting goals: rules enforcement and professional empowerment. First, because professionals often resist regimentation, the software forces Nova Care's therapists to provide information in a consistent format, to comply with corporate rules and external regulations, and to originate the information necessary to monitor quality, costs, and trends for the organization's overall operation. Second, the software captures and distributes to professionals all the knowledge the company has built up over time so they can do their jobs better or more efficiently. That knowledge includes information about customers, professional databases, analytical models, successful solutions to problems, and access to specialized sources of knowledge.

Inverted organizations pose some unique managerial challenges. The apparent loss of formal authority can be traumatic for former line managers. And field people who are granted formal power may tend to act more and more like specialists with strictly "professional" outlooks and to resist any set of organizational rules or business norms. Given those tendencies and without a disciplining software, field people often don't stay current with details about their organization's own complex internal systems. And their empowerment without adequate information and controls embedded in the company's technology systems can be dangerous. A classic example is the rapid decline of People Express, which consciously inverted its organization and enjoyed highly empowered and motivated point people but lacked the systems or the computer infrastructures to enable them to adapt as the organization grew.

If such organizations fail, it is usually because—despite much rhetoric about inversion—their senior managers did not support the concept with thoroughly overhauled performance-measurement and reward systems. Inverted systems rarely work until field people largely determine their "support people's" wages, promotions, and organizational progress. Former line people are reluctant to take this last crucial step. In our studies of more than 100 major structural changes in 60 large service organizations, less than 20% of the organizations had changed their performance-measurement systems significantly, and only about 5% had changed their reward systems (*Information Technology in the Service Society,* National Academy Press, 1993). Without such changes, the complications were predictable: People continued to perform according to the traditional measures.

CREATING INTELLECTUAL WEBS

In NovaCare's business, the professional therapists who create value are largely self-sufficient individual contributors. The inverted organization, coupled with the right software and incentives, allows NovaCare to enhance its therapists' productivity while giving them the operating autonomy they need. In other businesses, professional intellect is called on to create value by solving problems that exceed the capabilities of any solo practitioner. When problems become much more complex or less well defined, no one person or organization may know exactly what their full dimensions are, where key issues will ultimately reside, or who may have potential new solutions.

To tackle such problems—and to leverage their own intellectual assets to the maximum—a number of companies are using a form of self-organizing network that we call a *spider's web*. We use this term to avoid confusion with other, more traditional networklike forms more akin to holding companies or matrix organizations. Typically, a spider's web brings people together quickly to solve a particular problem and then disbands just as quickly once the job is done. The power of such interconnections is so great that even with a modest number of collaborating independent professionals (8 to 10), a spider's web can leverage knowledge capabilities by hundreds of times.

Consider Merrill Lynch's mergers and acquisitions group. At the firm's center, specialists work primarily with others in their own disciplines—for example, acquisitions, high-yield financings, or equity markets. But when a large financing opportunity emerges, the project becomes an intellectual focal point and a team of specialists from different locations forms to pursue each individual deal. Such projects are so complex that, as one executive says, "no one can be a know-everything banker. You can't have only specialists doing their own thing, and the client is not interested in dealing with multiple specialists." The key problem is focusing Merrill Lynch's rich but dispersed talents on a single customer's problem for a short time. Client-relationship managers, who best understand the customer's integrated needs, usually coordinate these teams, but they don't have direct, hierarchical control over team members.

Despite the current popularity of virtual organizations and of networks, few companies understand when and how to use networked forms to leverage professional intellect. As the Merrill Lynch example shows, networks can flexibly combine high specialization in many different disciplines with multiple geographic contact points and a sharp focus on a single problem or customer set. But without the firm's specifically tailored promotion and compensation evaluation processes, the system probably would not work.

At Merrill Lynch, individuals work with many different colleagues on a variety of projects over the course of a year. All of them submit a confidential evaluation on everyone with whom they have worked closely. People are willing to share knowledge and cooperate because their compensation is attached to this mosaic of peer relationships, and compensation is a major motivating factor in this business. There are enough close personal team contacts to allow a truly multifaceted picture of an individual's performance. According to one vice president of the mergers and acquisitions group, "In addition to profits generated, people are evaluated on how well they throw themselves into various projects, work with different groups to meet priorities, and meet clients' needs. The culture penalizes those who fail to be team players or to meet clients' needs. Under these rules, spider's webs have worked well in our relationship world. In our transactional world, however, we generally win by having the best specialists for that transaction."

Because each spider's web is unique in its purpose, patterns, and organizational power relationships, there is no single "best way" to manage all of them. For many projects, there may not be a single authority center. Often if the goal, problem, or solution is sufficiently clear, decisions may occur through informal processes if the parties agree. When the various centers of excellence need to operate in a highly coordinated fashion, they may delegate temporary authority to a project leader—as when widely dispersed researchers present a contract proposal. In other cases, the organization may designate one person as the lead in order to force decisions or to make final commitments—as when an insurance or investment banking consortium faces a deadline. How groups communicate and what they voluntarily communicate are as important as the advanced knowledge each center of excellence may have. For virtually all purposes, however, encouraging shared interests, common values, and mutually satisfying solutions is essential for leveraging knowledge in these structures. Research suggests that to accomplish this goal, network managers should force members to overlap on different teams in order to increase continuity of contact, joint learning, and informal information sharing; purposely keep hierarchical relations ill defined; constantly update and reinforce project goals; avoid overly elaborate rules for allocating profits to individual nodes; develop continuous mechanisms for updating information about the external environment (for example, tax code changes, customer needs, or scientific results); involve both clients and peers in performance evaluations; and provide node members with both individual and team rewards for participation. Such consciously structured management interactions can mitigate the most common failures and frustrations.

The other key leverage factor in most spider's webs is technology. Electronics allow many more highly diverse, geographically dispersed, intellectually specialized talents to be brought to bear on a single project than ever before. Because public telecommunications networks allow interconnection almost anywhere, the key to effective network systems generally lies in software that provides a common language and database for communications, captures critical factual data about external environments, helps players find knowledge sources (usually through electronic menus, Web browsers like Netscape, or bulletin boards), and allows interactive sharing and problem solving. Each node will of course have its own specialized analytical software. But networking, groupware, and interactive software—along with a culture of and incentives for sharing—are the keys to success in these systems.

Much can be done to leverage professional intellect through extraordinary recruitment, training, and motivational measures. But, increasingly, managing human intellect alone is not enough. More radical organizational structures, supported by specifically designed software systems, are essential to capture, focus, and leverage capabilities to the fullest. Such systems have become the glue that both joins together highly dispersed service-delivery centers and leverages the critical knowledge bases, intellectual skills, and accumulated experience in professional organizations. They also bond professionals to the organization by providing them with databases, analytical models, and communication power that they cannot find elsewhere. These tools enable professionals to extend their performance beyond their personal limits, allowing them to achieve more inside the organization than they could on their own.

No organizational form is a panacea. In fact, many different forms often coexist successfully in the same company. Properly used, each helps a company attract, harness, leverage, and deploy intellect for a quite different purpose. Consequently, each requires a carefully developed set of cultural norms supported by software and by performance-measurement and reward systems tailored to the organization's specific purposes.

Part Three

Creating a Culture That
Encourages Intellectual
Capital Formation and
Investment

8
Information Politics

Thomas H. Davenport, Robert G. Eccles,
Laurence Prusak

Information is not innocent.

—James March[1]

During the past decade, many firms have concluded that information is one of their most critical business resources and that broadening information access and usage and enhancing its quality are key to improving business performance. The "information-based organization," the "knowledge-based enterprise," and the "learning organization," forecasted by management experts, all require a free flow of information around the firm.[2] The computers and communications networks that manipulate and transmit information become more powerful each year. Yet the rhetoric and technology of information management have far outpaced the ability of people to understand and agree on what information they need and then to share it.

Today, in fact, the information-based organization is largely a fantasy. All of the writers on information-based organizations must speak hypothetically, in the abstract, or in the future tense. Despite forty years of the Information Revolution in business, most managers still tell us that they cannot get the information they need to run their own units or functions. As a recent article by the CEO of a shoe company put it: "On one of my first days on the job, I asked for a copy of every report used in management. The next day, twenty-three of them appeared on my desk. I didn't understand them. . . . Each area's reports were Greek to the other areas, and all of them were Greek to me."[3] A more accurate metaphor might be that these reports each came from a different city-state—Athens, Sparta, Corinth, Thebes, and Peloponnesus—each part of the organization but a separate political domain with its own culture, leaders, and even vocabulary.

We have studied information management approaches in more than twenty-five companies over the past two years. Many of their efforts to create information-based organizations—or even to implement significant information management initiatives—have failed or are on the path to failure. The primary reason is that the companies did not manage the politics of information. Either the initiative was inappropriate for the firm's overall political culture, or politics were treated as peripheral rather than integral to the initiative. Only when information politics are viewed as a natural aspect of organizational life and consciously managed will true information-based organizations emerge.

Furthermore, a good argument can be made—and there is increasing evidence for it—that as information becomes the basis for organizational structure and function, politics will increasingly come into play. In the most information-oriented companies we studied, people were least likely to share information freely, as perceived by these companies' managers. As people's jobs and roles become defined by the unique information they hold, they may be less likely to share that information—viewing it as a source of power and indispensability—rather than more so. When information is the primary unit of organizational currency, we should not expect its owners to give it away.[4]

This assertion directly contradicts several academic and popular concepts about how widespread information and information technology will affect organizations. These thinkers have hypothesized that as organizations make widespread use of information technology, information will flow freely and quickly eliminate hierarchy. Mention is rarely made in such accounts of the specter of information politics.[5] Although this optimistic view has widespread appeal, it is not what we see today in companies.

When owners of key information resist sharing it either outright or, more commonly, through bureaucratic maneuvers, they are often dismissed as unfair or opportunistic. Yet they may have quite legitimate reasons for withholding the information. Political behavior regarding information should be viewed not as irrational or inappropriate but as a normal response to certain organizational situations. Valid differences in interpretation of information, for example, may lead to apparently intransigent behavior. At an electronics company we once worked with, the marketing organizations for direct and indirect channels could never agree on what constituted a sale. Getting the product to the end-customer was direct marketing's sale; getting it to the distributor, even though it might return eventually, was how the indirect group wanted to measure its success. When the indirect channel was the dominant one for the company, this group's view of sales prevailed. Later, as more product moved directly to buyers, end-customer sales became the official definition. In information politics, might makes right. As a result of losing influence, however, the indirect group wanted to create its own sales databases and reports. Political disputes of this type will often arise when there is no consensus around the business's information needs.

One reason the stakes are so high in information politics is that more than information is at stake. In order to arrive at a common definition of information requirements, organizations must often address not just the information they use, but the business practices and processes that generate the information. Most firms have not recognized the linkage between processes and information, but there are a few exceptions. At a fast-growing specialty manufacturer, CEO-appointed information "czars" are responsible for ensuring consistency in the information-generating activities of their areas. For example, the order-processing czar mandated common companywide practices for assigning customer and product numbers, recognizing revenue, and determining contract prices. At IBM, eighteen key business processes (e.g., "customer fulfillment") are being redesigned to build a new information infrastructure. Out of each new process will come information on its performance—how long it takes, how much it costs, how satisfied the customer is with it—as well as the more traditional results-oriented information such as sales and profitability. At Dow Chemical, managers believe there must be common financial processes around the world in order to create common measures of financial performance.

The overall organizational climate is also a powerful influence on information politics.[6] Unfortunately, the very factors that make free information flow most desirable and necessary also make it less likely. An organization that is highly unstable and operating in an uncertain business, in which employees are uncertain about their job security and place in the hierarchy, needs as much information as possible about the environment and its own performance. Yet this type of organization is most likely to engender information politics that inhibit sharing.

Our purpose is to help companies understand information politics and manage them. In the next section, we classify the major models of information politics we have seen in client companies and firms we have studied. Following that, we present a set of approaches to managing information politics at both a strategic and a day-to-day level.

MODELS OF INFORMATION POLITICS

We have identified five information models (or, to continue the political metaphor, "states") that are representative of the practices we have observed (see Table 8-1). Three of these, technocratic utopianism, anarchy, and feudalism, are less effective than the other two, monarchy and federalism.[7] After we define each model, we will evaluate their relative effectiveness along the dimensions of information quality, efficiency, commonality, and access.

Any organization is likely to have proponents for more than one of these models. Sometimes the models conflict, and sometimes one model predominates. Table 8-2 shows the distribution of models among the companies we studied. The first step in managing information more effectively and realistically is explicitly recognizing these existing models and then choosing a single desired state. Maintaining multiple models is confusing and consumes scarce resources. Once a model has been selected, an organization can manage the daily politics of information, just as an alderman manages a ward.

TABLE 8-1   Models of Information Politics

Technocratic Utopianism	A heavily technical approach to information management stressing categorization and modeling of an organization's full information assets, with heavy reliance on emerging technologies.
Anarchy	The absence of any overall information management policy, leaving individuals to obtain and manage their own information.
Feudalism	The management of information by individual business units or functions, which define their own information needs and report only limited information to the overall corporation.
Monarchy	The definition of information categories and reporting structures by the firm's leaders, who may or may not share the information willingly after collecting it.
Federalism	An approach to information management based on consensus and negotiation on the organization's key information elements and reporting structures.

Technocratic Utopianism

Many companies have a strong bias toward approaching information management from a technological perspective. This approach eschews information politics, assuming that politics are an aberrant form of behavior. It is usually driven by a firm's information systems (IS) professionals, who see themselves as the custodians, if not the owners, of the firm's information. Their technological efforts to alleviate information problems often involve a considerable amount of detailed planning and revolve around modeling and efficient use of corporate data. Their goal is to plan a technology infrastructure that can deliver information to each individual's desktop and then to build databases with the correct structure to store this information without redundancy. Some technical efforts around information management are reasonable; however, when the technological approach to information predominates, the company's model of information management can be described as technocratic utopianism.

Although neither the IS professionals nor the users may be consciously creating a technocratic utopia, there is an underlying assumption that technology will resolve all problems and that organizational and political issues are nonexistent or unmanageable. In fact, information itself—its content, use, and implications for managing—receives little attention in this model. The focus is instead on the technologies used to manipulate the information.

We found technocratic utopianism, either by itself or alongside another model, in almost a third of the firms we analyzed. The model usually coexists,

TABLE 8-2   Models Observed in Research Sites

25 Companies Studied	Federalism	Monarchy	Technocratic Utopianism	Anarchy	Feudalism
Chemicals					
Company A			✔		✔
Company B	✔	✔			
Company C	✔		✔		
Computers					
Company A	✔			✔	✔
Company B	✔		✔		
Consumer Goods					
Company A			✔		✔
Company B					✔
Direct Marketing		✔			
Electronics					
Company A					✔
Company B					✔
Entertainment					✔
Financial Services		✔		✔	✔
Gas Transmission		✔			
Information Services					
Company A			✔		
Company B	✔				✔
Insurance					
Company A		✔	✔		
Company B	✔				✔
Company C					✔
Medical Supplies					
Company A			✔		
Company B	✔				✔
Office Products	✔		✔		
European Office Products			✔		
Software					
Company A		✔		✔	
Company B				✔	
Specialty Manufacturing		✔			
Total	8	7	9	4	12

however uneasily, with other models; in fact, the technocratic utopian model is often held by a small group of technologists supported by many technical journals, consultants, and technology vendors. While the technologists plan a utopia around the free flow of information, the senior executives for whom they work usually ignore, or are ignorant of, their efforts. Because these technical models are difficult for nontechnologists to understand, managers outside the IS function are rarely active participants. If a technocratic utopia is the only political model, it is probably because senior managers have abdicated their roles in selecting and managing information.

Technocratic utopians often have three factors in common: they focus heavily on information modeling and categorization; they highly value emerging hardware and software technologies; and they attempt to address an organization's entire information inventory.

A key emphasis in most technocratic utopias is information modeling and categorization. Once a unit of information is represented in an "entity-relationship model" or a "data-flow diagram," all problems in managing it have been solved, according to the extreme utopians. They consider such modeling and categorization a key aspect of the engineering of information (indeed, "information engineering" is an established discipline within the IS profession). In this ideal world, information flows like water, and the only task is to construct appropriate canals, aqueducts, and dams in order for information to flow freely to those who need it. Information sometimes feels as common in organizations as water; since it is so plentiful, there is a natural instinct to try to channel it rather than drown in it.

Information engineering is important, of course, but the political aspects cannot be neglected. Information may flow like water, but in the real world even water doesn't flow without political assistance. Those knowledgeable about the back-room politics involved in bringing water to Los Angeles or about Robert Moses's political steamrolling in New York's water management will understand the role of politics in managing a "natural" resource like information.[8]

Technologists also frequently assert that new forms of hardware and software are the keys to information success. Executives often hear that they will get the information they need "when our new relational database system is installed" or "when our new network is complete." The coming panacea for many organizations is object-oriented technologies, in which information is combined with application functions in reusable modules. Too often, however, when the silver bullet arrives it does not have the intended effect. No technology has yet been invented to convince unwilling managers to share information or even to use it. In fact, we would argue that technology vendors suffer from the same political forces as do data modelers. The failure of the "diskless workstation" to thrive in the marketplace may well be due to individuals' reluctance to lose control of their information.

Finally, utopians focus on all information throughout the corporation—at least all that can be captured by a computer. A common example is the creation of an "enterprise model"—a structured inventory and categorization of all data elements used throughout the firm. Such modeling exercises often take years and yield vast amounts of detail. Although their purpose is often to eliminate redundant data storage, they often yield little real business value. Several MIT researchers have chronicled their failure.[9] Like most utopias, they lead to nowhere (or, in Samuel Butler's famous utopian novel, *Erewhon*—nowhere almost backwards).

Technocratic utopians assume that managing information is an exercise without passion. Their rallying cry is an uninspiring, "Data is a corporate asset." They believe, consciously or unconsciously, that information's value for business decisions is not only very high but also self-evident. They assume that employees who possess information useful to others will share it willingly. They assume that information itself is valueless, or at least that its value is the same to all organizational members. If they are conscious of the relationship between information access and hierarchy, they assume that those high in the hierarchy would not restrict the free flow of information for any reason other than corporate security. These assumptions resemble human behavior found only in utopias.

Anarchy

Some firms have no prevailing political information model and exist in a state of anarchy. Rarely do organizations consciously choose this state, in which individuals fend for their own information needs. Information anarchy usually emerges when more centralized approaches to information management break down or when no key executive realizes the importance of common information. Information anarchy was made possible—and much more dangerous—by the introduction and rapid growth of the personal computer. Suddenly individuals and small departments could manage their own databases, tailoring their own reports to their own needs at any time and at minimal cost.

Although several firms we researched have allowed anarchy to survive, we found only one firm that had consciously chosen it. This software firm had previously tried to develop an overall information management structure by asking key managers what information they needed to run the business. When the firm could not achieve consensus, it determined that a bottom-up structured exchange of documents across its network, using a new software technology developed for this purpose, would yield all of the required information. Even here, however, an alternative information model flourished in some quarters; as one senior executive put it, "I get all the information I need in breakfast meetings with the CEO."

The long-term shortcomings of information anarchy are obvious. Technologists might worry that so much redundant information processing and storage is inefficient, but anarchy has more serious shortcomings. When everyone has his or her own database, the numbers for revenues, costs, customer order levels, and so on will diverge in databases throughout the company. Although anarchy is seldom chosen consciously, its effects are not uncommon; we know of several firms in which it was the source of late or inaccurate quarterly earnings reports. A firm cannot survive for long with such information discrepancies. The desire for information that leads to anarchy should quickly be harnessed into a more organized political model.

Feudalism

The political model we most often encountered was feudalism. In a feudal model, individual executives and their departments generally control information acquisition, storage, distribution, and analysis.[10] These powerful executives determine what information will be collected within their realms, how it will be interpreted, and in what format it will be reported to the "king" or CEO. They can also decide what measures are used to understand performance as well as what "language," by which we mean a common vocabulary, is used within the realm. Different realms often end up with different languages, and the subsequent fragmenting of information authority diminishes the power of the entire enterprise—just as the growth of powerful noblemen and their entourages inhibited the king's power in medieval times.

Feudal actions diminish the central authority's power to make informed decisions for the common good. Key measures of the enterprise's health often are not collected, reported, or even considered beyond roll-up of financial outcomes, further diminishing the central authority's power. Corporatewide performance is of interest only to those within corporate headquarters, and its indicators may poorly reflect what is actually happening around the firm.

Feudalism flourishes, of course, in environments of strong divisional autonomy. When divisions have their own strategies, products, and customers, it is almost inevitable that their information needs will differ. Furthermore, they may also be reluctant to fully disclose potentially negative information at the corporate level.

At a major consumer electronics firm's U.S. subsidiary, the feudalism was quite overt. The firm was organized along product lines; product division heads were informally referred to as "barons." Each had his or her own financial reporting system, with only the most limited amounts of data shared with the subsidiary head. The latter executive eventually brought in consultants to give a seminar on the value of common data and systems—all, the last we heard, to no avail.

At a large consumer goods firm organized by distribution channel, each channel had its own measures of performance that it thought were important. This information autonomy had prevailed for years and was tolerated because the firm had long been profitable using any set of measures. A new CEO arrived at a time when profits were down, and he felt he had no way to manage across the entire firm. He mandated the development of a common information architecture. Unfortunately, the IS group charged with this initiative began to create a technocratic utopia. We suspect that the feudal culture will eventually prevail.

We have also seen a few examples of functional feudalism, in which financial and operational functions have their own information architectures and cannot achieve consensus on what should be monitored and how. In one high-technology manufacturing firm, for example, the quality function head created an executive information system that reported on operational performance and quality data. The IS director, and the CFO to whom he reported, strenuously opposed the system, arguing that the firm's traditional financially oriented reporting approach should be the only one. The quality-oriented system was building adherents (and product quality) until the quality director left for a summer vacation. When he returned, he found that the IS head and CFO had enlisted sufficient support from other executives to shut down the system. The battle over which type of system will eventually predominate is still raging.

Despite these battles in feudal environments, some degree of cooperation can emerge. Powerful executives can create strategic alliances to share information or establish a common network or architecture, just as feudal lords banded together to build a road or common defense wall, go to war, or plan a marriage for mutual enrichment—although such communal efforts rarely include all of the lords. It is also possible that, as in Renaissance times, the proliferation of patrons will encourage innovation and creativity within each realm—for example, the development of a particularly useful quality information system by one division.

Monarchy

The most practical solution to the problems inherent in the feudal model is to impose an information monarchy. The CEO, or someone empowered by the chief executive, dictates the rules for how information will be managed. Power is centralized, and departments and divisions have substantially less autonomy regarding information policies.

Much depends on the approach the "monarch" takes to managing the realm's information. A more benign monarch (or enlightened despot, as they were called in the eighteenth century) will tilt toward freer access and distribution of key information and may attempt to rationalize and standardize the parameters used to measure the state's health and wealth. This top-down model may be most appropriate for firms that have difficulty achieving consensus across business units.

The rapidly growing specialty manufacturer mentioned above is an example. The CEO, who felt that information flow was critical to developing a flexible organization, decreed a policy of "common information" to bring about access to consistent information by all who needed it. His appointment of czars to define and implement common information policies reflected his belief in the importance of information management issues. Currently efforts are underway to embed this decree into a set of business practices and a technical architecture. This top-down approach is an example of enlightened monarchy at its best, since the action was taken not in response to a specific crisis but as a well-considered response to a broad organizational objective.

A progressive further step is a constitutional monarchy. Constitutional monarchy can evolve directly from feudalism or from the more despotic forms of monarchy. It is established by a document that states the monarch's limitations, the subjects' rights, and the law's authority. As a model for information management, this means that dominion is established over what information is collected, in what form, by whom, and for what ends. The chart of accounts becomes the realm's Magna Carta ("great charter"), a document establishing rules that will be enforced by processes and enabled by an information technology platform. A common vocabulary is developed so that the information's meaning is consistent and has integrity throughout the firm. The financial functions at both Digital and Dow Chemical are establishing constitutional monarchies for financial information, with strong support from the CEOs.

We have seen several firms in which the installation of an executive information system (EIS) was the occasion for an attempt at constitutional monarchy. The CEO is usually considered the primary user of such a system, although some attempt is usually made to solicit the information requirements of other executives. The exercise of building consensus on the system's content can help to build a constitutional monarchy. However, the effort is not always successful. At one insurance company we studied, an EIS intended for the entire senior management team was never used seriously by anyone other than the CEO. Other executives were concerned about how their units would fare under close analysis, and they kept their own feudal information sources.

One drawback to any information monarchy is the simple fact of mortality. When a monarch dies or is overthrown, new governments can be imposed. Likewise, retirement or turnover of CEOs and senior executives can open the door to very different approaches to information, even in the most constitutional of monarchies. Cultures and traditions take years to solidify in an enterprise. In one high-tech manufacturing firm, the founder CEO's retirement led to information anarchy for many years; only now is the firm beginning to establish a more structured environment. The short reigns of most monarchs bodes poorly for the growth of persistent information traditions.

Federalism

The final information state, federalism, also has a number of desirable features, and in today's business environment, it is the preferred model in most circumstances. Its distinguishing feature is the use of negotiation to bring potentially competing and non-cooperating parties together. Federalism most explicitly recognizes the importance of politics, without casting it in pejorative terms. In contrast, technocratic utopianism ignores politics, anarchy is politics run amok, feudalism involves destructive politics, and monarchy attempts to eliminate politics through a strong central authority. Federalism treats politics as a necessary and legitimate activity by which people with different interests work out among themselves a collective purpose and means for achieving it.

Firms that adopt or evolve into this model typically have strong central leadership and a culture that encourages cooperation and learning. However, it takes tough negotiating and a politically astute information manager to make the federalist model work. Such an information manager needs to have the CEO's support (although not too much support, or a monarchy emerges) as well as the trust and support of the "lords and barons" who run the divisions. He or she needs to understand the value of information itself as well as of the technology that stores, manipulates, and distributes it. Such skills are not widely distributed throughout organizations, even (or perhaps especially) among IS executives.

An executive who has this perspective can then use cooperative information resources to create a shared information vision. Each realm contracts with the executive and with other realms to cede some of its information assets in return for helping to create a greater whole. This is a genuine leveraging of a firm's knowledge base.

At IBM, the former head of corporate information services, Larry Ford, concluded that the firm needed to manage information in a dramatically new way. Ford and his organization produced an information strategy that focused on the value that information can bring to all of IBM. The strategy was refined and ratified by all of the senior executives, and now Ford, his staff, and the divisional IS executives have gone out into the field to negotiate with senior managers about sharing their information with others in the company. "Would you share your product quality data with the service organization? How about sales?" Eventually all the important information will be in easy-to-access "data warehouses." Information management at IBM has become very personal politics, like the ward politician campaigning door to door.

Of course, the politician has only so much time to ring doorbells. A division may have hundreds of important data elements that need to be shared. IBM is finding that the time to educate and persuade information owners of their responsibilities is the biggest constraint to implementing a federalist model. Ford's departure from IBM to head a software firm may also place the federalist initiative at risk.

MANAGING INFORMATION POLITICS

Given these options for building an information polity, how do firms begin to effectively manage information? The first step is to select the preferred information model, as discussed in the next section. Following that, we present other principles of politically astute information management, including matching information politics to organizational culture, practicing technological realism, electing the right information politicians, and avoiding empire-building.

Select an Information State. The first step in managing information politics is figuring out which models people in the firm hold, which model currently predominates, which is most desirable, and how to achieve it. As we have noted, adopting multiple models will needlessly consume scarce resources and will confuse both information managers and users. Therefore, a firm should choose one model and move continually toward it, however long it takes.

We believe that there are only two viable choices among the five models: monarchy and federalism. In a business culture that celebrates empowerment and widespread participation, federalism is preferable, but it is harder to achieve and takes more time. Federalism requires managers to negotiate with each other in good faith while avoiding the temptation to use and withhold information destructively. Most firms we know of profess a desire to move toward a federalist model. But a firm that has difficulty getting consensus from its management team on other issues may find that federalism is impossible; a benevolent monarchy may be almost as effective and easier to implement.

Table 8-3 summarizes our assessments of the five political models along four dimensions: (1) commonality of vocabulary and meaning; (2) degree of access to important information; (3) quality of information—that is, its currency, relevance, and accuracy; and (4) efficiency of information management. These dimensions can be useful for evaluating a firm's current model and its effectiveness.

Commonality refers to having a set of terms, categories, and data elements that carry the same meaning throughout the enterprise. The desirability of common discourse may appear obvious, but in our experience it does not exist in many large firms. Even the definition of what a "sale" is can be variously interpreted by different divisions, to say nothing of more ambiguous terms such as "quality," "performance," and "improvement."[11]

The degree of information access is another good indicator of political culture. Many firms proclaim that all employees should have the information they need to do their work well. However, in making the choices about who actually needs what information, firms are making political decisions, whether or not they acknowledge it. The technocratic utopians focus less on what information is accessed by whom and more on the mechanisms of distribution.

TABLE 8-3   Ranking Alternative Models of Information Politics

	Federalism	Monarchy	Technocratic Utopianism	Anarchy	Feudalism
Commonality of Vocabulary	5	5	3	1	1
Access to Information	5	2	3	4	1
Quality of Information	3	2	1	2	2
Efficiency of Information Management	3	5	3	1	3
Total	16	14	10	8	7

Key: 5 = high 3 = moderate 1 = low

In many ways the quality of information is the most important of these indicators. Information quality is achieved through detailed attention to its integrity, accuracy, currency, interpretability, and overall value. As with other types of products, the quality of information is best judged by its customers. Even companies that declare themselves as firmly in the Information Age, however, rarely have measures or assessments of their information's quality.

Efficiency is often the objective of technologists who wish to minimize redundant data storage. The incredible improvements in price-performance ratios for data storage technologies have reduced this issue's importance somewhat. However, there is still the human factor. Multiple measures of the same item take time to analyze and synthesize. Effective management requires focusing on a few key performance indicators. Computers and disk drives may be able to handle information overload, but people still suffer from it.

Federalism has the potential to be effective on all four dimensions of information management. A common vocabulary emerges through negotiations between levels and units. This makes possible the widespread access and distribution of meaningful information, which is then used for the benefit of the whole enterprise. Federalism strikes a balance between the unintegrated independence of the feudal baronies and the undifferentiated units under monarchy. Although satisfying all constituencies may require gathering more information than is absolutely necessary (hence decreasing efficiency), and the necessary compromises may reduce quality, federalism scores higher in the minds of the managers we interviewed than any other model.

Because federalism explicitly acknowledges the important positive role that information politics can play, it is apt to be the most effective model for companies that rely on individual initiative for generating collective action. This is most likely to be the case for companies operating in complex and rapidly changing competitive environments, which create a high level of uncertainty. The federalist approach supports both autonomy and coordination. Accomplishing it, of course, requires negotiating skills and the willingness of managers to take the time to negotiate. Not all companies have executives with the ability or the commitment to do this. The temptation always exists to look to a strong monarch to resolve the endless negotiations by fiat, to fall prey once more to the alluring utopian vision painted by the technologists, to fall back into a nasty and brutish condition of feudal conflict, or to dissolve into the chaos of anarchy. Firms may want to pursue alternative models, in case federalism fails. In fact, as Table 8-2 shows, many of the firms pursuing federalism were also pursuing other models, either consciously or implicitly as a backup strategy. Sooner or later it is obviously best to settle on one model, though most firms find this difficult.

An information monarchy solves some of the problems of managing information throughout the enterprise. A strong, top-down approach ensures that a common language—in both vocabulary and meaning—underlies the information generated. Little unnecessary information is collected or distributed, guaranteeing a high level of efficiency. The monarch and his or her ministers mandate and oversee the right processes to generate the right information to be used in the right way—all enhancing information quality, at least as they perceive it. These advantages, however, are often gained at the expense of information access. It is the rare monarch who has enough democratic ideals to make information as broadly available as in a federalist state.

Technocratic utopianism focuses on using information technology to dramatically improve data distribution. Efficiency is high, at least in terms of a lack of data redundancy. Information access is also relatively high, at least for technologically oriented users. Because technocratic utopians do not concern themselves with the processes that produce information, the quality of information remains low. Further, the quality of information usage is inhibited by technocratic efforts such as complex data modeling that are often not understood or appreciated by line managers. As a result, the information produced by computer systems and the information actually used to manage the company are decoupled. Although this model scores high in principle, many of these initiatives fail. Commonality, access, and efficiency in a failed utopian scheme may actually be as low as in feudalism or even lower.

Although few executives would consciously adopt anarchy, it is not the lowest-scoring model. Commonality and efficiency are the lowest possible, of course, but at least individuals have easy access to the data they need. The customer controls information, thus its quality is likely to be high—unless the customer is an executive trying to take an organizationwide perspective.

Feudalism is the least effective political model along these dimensions. The existence of strong, independent, and often warring fiefdoms prevents the development of a common vocabulary and shared meaning. The feudal lords restrict access to and distribution of information under their authority. Feudalism gets only middling marks for quality; it may be high for individual divisions, but it is low from the corporate perspective. Finally, because some information is duplicated around the organization, efficiency is also only moderate. Feudalism is the least desirable yet the most common state in the organizations we researched; when more difficult and effective models fail, it is easy to fall back into the feudal state.

The key in managing information politics is to know which political model is currently in ascendance within the firm and to which the organization should be moving. Most firms we know of profess a desire to move toward a federalist model, while currently operating in a feudal or technocratic utopian environment. But a firm that has difficulty getting consensus from its management team on other issues may find that information federalism is impossible; a benevolent monarchy may be almost as effective.

Match Information Politics to Your Organizational Culture. It is no accident that democracy emerged in eighteenth-century America, a sprawling continent with vast resources and an ethic of independence and self-sufficiency. Similarly, a firm's culture must be conducive to participative information management and free information flow before they will happen. Put another way, information flow does not make an organizational culture less hierarchical and more open; rather, democratic cultures make possible democratic information flows. When faxes were flying to and from pre-Tiananmen China, some observers argued that the free flow of information was leading to a more open society; now that the faxes and those who faxed are silent, we know that the causal relationship was in the other direction.

Information policies, we have found, are among the last things to change in an organization changing its culture. We have never seen increased information flow leading to elimination of a management layer or a greater willingness to share information. When these latter changes happen, they happen for reasons unrelated to information: restructurings, tighter cost control, external events (e.g., the 1970s' oil shocks or the current banking crisis), and so forth. Several companies, however, state that their new organization could not have survived without new information policies. Phillips Petroleum, for example, radically reduced its management ranks after a raider-forced restructuring. A new information policy was the key to its functioning.[12]

We observed this relationship between organizational culture and information politics in two computer companies. One firm was a fast-growing personal computer (PC) manufacturer when we studied it; since then, its growth has slackened. The other firm was a large manufacturer of several types of computers that was experiencing financial problems when we visited it. Their cultures seemed similar at first glance; they both had tried to develop cultures in which information was shared freely throughout their organizations with little regard to level or function. However, two key aspects of their cultures—their organizational structures and their relative financial success—had led to radically different information politics.

The PC firm had a traditional functional structure. According to the executives and employees we interviewed, information flowed relatively freely in the company. The firm had an explicit ethic of open communications, stressing early notification of problems and a "don't shoot the messenger" response. As a key U.S. executive stated, "Someone in international can request any piece of data and ask us to explain it. Allowing others access to information requires a lot of trust, but that trust seems to exist here." However, the firm is beginning to face more difficult competitive conditions, as PCs increasingly become commoditized. In more difficult times, with new management, the open information environment may not persist.

The other firm had a "networked" organization, with ad hoc teams assembling to address specific tasks. This structure, which made the firm flexible and responsive, also seemed to hinder the flow of important information. Several managers we interviewed reported that hoarding of valuable information was common. The ad hoc teams often resisted sharing their unique information. The managers we interviewed speculated that this was because a team that shares its information fully may lose its reason to exist. This is particularly true during the economically difficult times now facing the company. If an organizational structure is defined by information nodes, then those who freely surrender information may lose their place in the structure. Put more broadly, in the information-based organization, information becomes the primary medium of value and exchange, and who would give it away for free?

How do you know when your culture is right for more democratic information politics? There are a number of indicators. We have noticed, for example, that companies that successfully implement quality programs have to deal with many of the same issues affecting information flow. They have to empower front-line workers to make decisions, work cross-functionally to improve processes, and remove as much as possible the use of fear as a motivator. Similarly, companies highly attuned to customer satisfaction must be able to deal with negative results in a positive fashion—a trait highly necessary in an information democracy.

Not surprisingly, in an era of mergers, acquisitions, and global management, most large organizations have multiple political cultures. A newly acquired firm may resist adopting the information-sharing norms of its acquirer (or even, as seen in *Barbarians at the Gate,* of its potential acquirers attempting to perform due diligence).[13] Poorly performing divisions will rarely be as enthusiastic about new information reporting initiatives as long-term strong performers. And geographic differences affecting the willingness to share information are legendary; how many times has it been uttered, "We're having problems getting data from our French subsidiary."

Practice Technological Realism.   Although technology will not lead us to an information utopia, there are still important technological factors to consider. Information engineering should be highly focused, information should be in units that managers can understand and negotiate with, and technology platforms should be as common as possible.

Previously we pointed out the folly of trying to engineer an organization's entire information inventory. We (and other researchers) believe that focused, less ambitious information management objectives are more likely to succeed, given that the volume of information in corporations is too great to be rigorously categorized and engineered.[14] This is particularly true in a federalist environment, in which each key information element will require substantial negotiations. Information management efforts must be directed at only those information elements that are essential to implementing strategy and to running the business day to day. At IBM, for example, the firm's internal information strategy focuses primarily on customer and market information and secondarily on process quality information.[15] Although this approach includes a great deal of data, it also excludes a considerable amount.

It is also important to acknowledge that not all information will be managed through technological means, just as most of the water around us does not run through our water meters. Only about 5 percent to 10 percent of the information in most firms is in electronic form. According to a recent study of information use by managers, even computer-based data are often preceded by word-of-mouth renditions of the same information.[16] The verbal and visual information that informs all of us is not totally unmanageable, but it cannot be modeled and categorized through technological means.

Companies may also find it useful in negotiating on information to use a larger unit of information than the data element. Most managers do not think in such narrow terms; as one executive said, "Don't give me all the molecules; tell me the key compounds they can form." A more relevant unit of information may be the document—form, report, or memo. Technologists must concern themselves with the data elements that appear on documents, but managers will normally be happy not to delve below the document level in developing a common information language. Xerox, having designated itself "The Document Company," is beginning to explore how business processes can be supported through documents.[17]

A key aspect of making information more widely available, ineffective technocratic utopias to the contrary, is the nature of the information technology platform. Specifically, technology for widespread information use must be common, easily used, and interconnectible.[18] Technological realists recognize that their computers may not be best for all applications, but they meet basic needs. Common, standardized technology is essential if the same information is to be presented in the same way all around the company. Aetna Life & Casualty, American Airlines, Du Pont, IBM, and a large consumer products firm are all initiating efforts to build and operate a common platform for information distribution. This may seem obvious, but few companies can send a piece of data to all their workstations without considerable machinations to address different products, protocols, and other technical particulars. These companies are discovering that the same federalist approach required for achieving consensus on information meaning is also required to achieve consensus on a standard technology platform.[19]

Elect the Right Information Politicians. Along with having a suitable political culture and technology environment, companies desiring to change their information politics must elect (or otherwise get into office) the right information politicians. We find that the information politician role—not the owner of information but the manager with primary responsibility for facilitating its effective use—is still up for grabs in many companies, despite some pretenders to the throne. In one fast-growing software company, for example, problems with information flow were widespread, but no one below the CEO took any ownership of the problem.[20] One would assume that CIOs would own this domain, but until now they have not necessarily been the best choice.

Until recently, most CIOs were selected for technical acumen rather than political skills. Few would have embarked on initiatives to improve the way information—not just information technology—is used and managed. Only a few IS function heads have the political clout to persuade powerful barons to share their information for the good of the entire kingdom. Still, this is changing. At companies such as IBM, Xerox, Kodak, and Merrill Lynch, recent CIOs have been fast-track executives with records of managing important nontechnology aspects of the business. If these nontechnical managers can master the considerable technical challenges in creating an information infrastructure, they will likely have the skills and influence to bring about a political environment in which the information can be shared and used.

The CFO is another candidate for information politician. Most CFOs, however, are solely associated with financial information. In order to take on broader responsibility for information management, they must at a minimum convince operational executives of their ability to understand and manage operational performance information. We have found a few CFOs with the sincere desire to do this but have seen no examples of a CFO becoming a successful information politician.

The CEO is perhaps best positioned to lobby for a particular information environment; indeed, in an information monarchy, the CEO is the only politician who counts. In more democratic environments, such as federalism, the CEO must appreciate the importance of information and communicate it throughout the firm. The time demands of day-to-day information negotiation may require that the CEO delegate political authority to other managers.

Like real politicians, information politicians must be good at both charismatics and organization. They must be able to persuade both individuals and the masses of the importance of information management and the correctness of the chosen political model. They must also organize collections of "advance agents" and "ward heelers" to work every day at building coalitions, influencing opinion leaders, and swaying recalcitrant members of the electorate.

Avoid Building Information Empires.   Because information is such a powerful tool, federalist organizations will inherently resist or distrust managers who try to build an empire by controlling information. Concentration of all responsibility for collecting, maintaining, and interpreting information in one person, regardless of position, is too much power in any organization with democratic leanings. In fact, the concept of information ownership is antithetical to federalist information management. Rather, companies should institute the concept of information stewardship—responsibility for ensuring data quality—with ownership by the corporation at large. Stewardship of information, again perhaps at the document level rather than for individual data elements, should be assigned widely throughout the organization.

The IS organization should be particularly careful to avoid building an information empire. It may already wield considerable power by virtue of its technical custody of information. We have observed organizations that cede control over information to this "independent" third party, assuming that it will not use information for political gain. But the IS function may have its own interests to advance, its own kingdom to build.

For example, at a major direct marketing firm, nontechnical executives were intimidated by technology, and control over the firm's sixty-million-name database was ceded to IS. As a result, access to the database had to be on terms acceptable to IS. This often meant denial and delay to managers wishing to exploit the database for valid business purposes. IS built a proprietary database management system, further reinforcing the walls around the database. When the CEO himself was denied a report, the IS head was deposed and replaced by a trusted nontechnical associate of the CEO. Yet because he could not understand the technology, he could not dismantle the walls around the data. A new IS vice president was brought in from outside the company with an explicit mandate to open up the empire.

CONCLUSION

Explicitly recognizing the politics of information and managing them constructively is a difficult, complex, and time-consuming task. It will not happen by itself, nor will the problem go away. Effectively managing information politics requires a shift in organizational culture; new technology and even new executives alone are not enough to make this happen. Information management must become something that all managers care about and most managers participate in. They must view information as important to their success and be willing to spend time and energy negotiating to meet their information needs. As in real democracies, democratic information models like federalism require informed participation of all organizational citizens.

Unless the politics of information are identified and managed, companies will not move into the Information Age. Information will not be shared freely nor used effectively by decision makers. No amount of data modeling, no number of relational databases, and no invocation of "the information-based organization" will bring about a new political order of information. Rather, it will take what politics always take: negotiation, influence-exercising, back-room deals, coalition-building, and occasionally even war. If information is truly to become the most valued commodity in the businesses of the future, we cannot expect to acquire it without an occasional struggle.

NOTES

1. J.G. March, *Decisions and Organizations* (Cambridge, Massachusetts: Basil Blackwell, 1988).
2. For example: M.S. Scott Morton, *The Corporation of the 1990s: Information Technology and Organizational Transformation* (New York: Oxford University Press, 1991); P.G.W. Keen, *Shaping the Future: Business Design through Information Technology* (Boston: Harvard Business School Press, 1991); and D.R. Vincent, *The Information-Based Corporation: Stakeholder Economics and the Technology Investment* (Homewood, Illinois: Dow Jones-Irwin, 1990).
3. J. Thorbeck, "The Turnaround Value of Values," *Harvard Business Review,* January–February 1991, pp. 52–62.
4. J. Pfeffer, *Power in Organizations* (New York: HarperBusiness, 1986).
5. See articles in W.G. McGowan, ed., *Revolution in Real-Time: Managing Information Technology in the 1990s* (Boston: Harvard Business School Press, 1991). A notable exception to the apolitical perspective is found in M.L. Markus, "Power, Politics, and MIS Implementation," *Communications of the ACM* 26:6 (June 1983): 434–444.

6. J.G. March, "The Business Firm as a Political Coalition," in J.G. March (1988).

7. A term similar to "technocratic utopianism" has been defined, without reference to information management, by Howard P. Segal. See: H.P. Segal, *Technological Utopianism in American Culture* (Chicago: University of Chicago Press, 1985).

8. See R.A. Caro, *The Power Broker: Robert Moses and the Fall of New York* (New York: Random House, 1975); and *Chinatown,* the film.

9. See D.L. Goodhue, J.A. Quillard, and J. F. Rockart, "Managing the Data Resource: A Contingency Perspective," *MIS Quarterly* (September 1988), 373–392; and D.L. Goodhue, L. Kirsch, J.A. Quillard, and M. Wybo, "Strategic Data Planning: Lessons from the Field" (Cambridge, Massachusetts: MIT Sloan School of Management, Center for Information Systems Research, Working Paper No. 215, October 1990).

10. Some interesting examples of feudalism, again largely outside the information management context, are described in: J. Pfeffer, *Managing with Power* (Boston: Harvard Business School Press, 1991).

11. Some of the reasons for these discrepancies are described in: S.M. McKinnon and W.J. Bruns, Jr., *The Information Mosaic* (Boston: Harvard Business School Press, 1992).

12. L.M. Applegate and C.S. Osborn, "Phillips 66 Company: Executive Information System," 9-189-006 (Boston: Harvard Business School, 1988).

13. B. Burrough and J. Helyar, *Barbarians at the Gate* (New York: Harper & Row, 1990).

14. See Goodhue et al. (1988) and Goodhue et al. (1990).

15. "Using Information Strategically: A Road Map for the 90s," Information and Telecommunications Systems, IBM Corporation, 15 November 1990.

16. McKinnon and Bruns (1992).

17. See the proceedings volume from the Xerox Document Symposium, March 10–11, 1992, Xerox Corporation, Stamford, Connecticut.

18. L. Sproull and S. Kiesler, *Connections: New Ways of Working in the Networked Organization* (Cambridge, Massachusetts: MIT Press, 1991).

19. See J. Linder and D. Stoddard, "Aetna Life & Casualty: Corporate Technology Planning," 9-187-037 (Boston: Harvard Business School, 1986).

20. J. Gladstone and N. Nohria, "Symantec," N9-491-010 (Boston: Harvard Business School, 1990, revised 4 February 1991).

9

Understanding Organizations as Learning Systems

Edwin C. Nevis, Anthony J. DiBella,
Janet M. Gould

With the decline of some well-established firms, the diminishing competitive power of many companies in a burgeoning world market, and the need for organizational renewal and transformation, interest in organizational learning has grown. Senior managers in many organizations are convinced of the importance of improving learning in their organizations. This growth in awareness has raised many unanswered questions: What is a learning organization? What determines the characteristics of a good learning organization (or are all learning organizations good by definition)? How can organizations improve their learning? In the literature in this area, authors have used different definitions or models of organizational learning or have not defined their terms.[1] Executives have frequently greeted us with comments like these:

- "How would I know a learning organization if I stumbled over it?"
- "You academics have some great ideas, but what do I do with a mature, large organization on Monday morning?"
- "I'm not sure what a good learning organization is, but you should not study us because we are a bad learning organization."

Our research is dedicated to helping organizations become better learning systems. We define organizational learning as the capacity or processes within an organization to maintain or improve performance based on experience. Learning is a systems-level phenomenon because it stays within the organization, even if individuals change. One of our assumptions is that organizations learn as they produce. Learning is as much a task as the production and delivery of goods and services. We do not imply that organizations should sacrifice the speed and quality

Reprinted from "Understanding Organizations as Learning Systems" by Edwin C. Nevis et al., *Sloan Management Review*, Winter 1995, pp. 73–84 by permission of the publisher. Copyright © 1995 Sloan Management Review Association. All rights reserved.

of production in order to learn, but, rather, that production systems be viewed as learning systems. While companies do not usually regard learning as a function of production, our research on successful firms indicates that three learning-related factors are important for their success:

1. Well-developed core competencies that serve as launch points for new products and services. (Canon has made significant investments over time in developing knowledge in eight core competencies applied in the creation of more than thirty products.)
2. An attitude that supports continuous improvement in the business's value-added chain. (Wal-Mart conducts ongoing experiments in its stores.)
3. The ability to fundamentally renew or revitalize. (Motorola has a long history of renewing itself through its products by periodically exiting old lines and entering new ones.)

These factors identify some of the qualities of an effective learning organization that diligently pursues a constantly enhanced knowledge base. This knowledge allows for the development of competencies and incremental or transformational change. In these instances, there is assimilation and utilization of knowledge and some kind of integrated learning system to support such "actionable learning." Indeed, an organization's ability to survive and grow is based on advantages that stem from core competencies that represent collective learning.[2]

As a corollary to this assumption, we assume that all organizations engage in some form of collective learning as part of their development.[3] The creation of culture and the socialization of members in the culture rely on learning processes to ensure an institutionalized reality.[4] In this sense, it may be redundant to talk of "learning organizations." On the other hand, all learning is not the same; some learning is dysfunctional, and some insights or skills that might lead to useful new actions are often hard to attain. The current concern with the learning organization focuses on the gaps in organizational learning capacity and does not negate the usefulness of those learning processes that organizations may do well, even though they have a learning disability. Thus Argyris and Schön emphasize double-loop learning (generative) as an important, often missing, level of learning in contrast with single-loop learning (corrective), which they have found to be more common.[5] Similarly, Senge makes a highly persuasive case for generative learning, "as contrasted with adaptive learning," which he sees as more prevalent.[6] The focus for these theorists is on the learning required to make transformational changes—changes in basic assumptions—that organizations need in today's fast-moving, often chaotic environment. Their approach does not negate the value of everyday incremental "fixes"; it provides a more complete model for observing and developing organizational learning. After periods of significant discontinuous change, incremental, adaptive learning may be just the thing to help consolidate transformational or generative learning.

Another assumption we make is that the value chain of any organization is a domain of integrated learning. To think of the value chain as an integrated learning system is to think of the work in each major step, beginning with strategic decisions through to customer service, as a subsystem for learning experiments. Structures and processes to achieve outcomes can be seen simultaneously as operational tasks and learning exercises; this holds for discrete functions and for cross-functional activities, such as new product development. The organization encompasses each value-added stage as a step in doing business, not as a fixed classification scheme. Most organizations do not think this way, but it is useful for handling complexity. With this "chunking," we are able to study learning better and to see how integration is achieved at the macro-organizational level. This viewpoint is consistent with a definition of organizations as *complex arrangements of people in which learning takes place.*

While we have not looked at organizations' full value-added chains, we selected our research sites so that we could examine learning in different organizational subsets. In addition, we gathered data indicating preferences or biases in investments in learning at different points of the chain and to understand how learning builds, maintains, improves, or shifts core competencies. Do organizations see certain stages of the chain where significant investment is more desirable than at others?

Our last assumption is that the learning process has identifiable stages. Following Huber, whose comprehensive review of the literature presented four steps in an organizational learning process, we arrived at a three-stage model:

1. Knowledge acquisition—The development or creation of skills, insights, relationships.
2. Knowledge sharing—The dissemination of what has been learned.
3. Knowledge utilization—The integration of learning so it is broadly available and can be generalized to new situations.[7]

Most studies of organizational learning have been concerned with the acquisition of knowledge and, to a lesser extent, with the sharing or dissemination of the acquired knowledge (knowledge transfer). Less is known about the assimilation process, the stage in which knowledge becomes institutionally available, as opposed to being the property of select individuals or groups. Huber refers to the assimilation and utilization process as "organizational memory." While this is an important aspect of knowledge utilization, it is limited and works better when discussing information, as distinct from knowledge. True knowledge is more than information; it includes the meaning or interpretation of the information, and a lot of intangibles such as the tacit knowledge of experienced people that is not well articulated but often determines collective organizational competence. Studies of organizational learning must be concerned with all three stages in the process.

Early in our research, it became clear that organizational learning does not always occur in the linear fashion implied by any stage model. Learning may take place in planned or informal, often unintended, ways. Moreover, knowledge and skill acquisition takes place in the sharing and utilization stages. It is not something that occurs simply by organizing an "acquisition effort." With this in mind, we shifted our emphasis to look for a more fluid and chaotic learning environment, seeking less-defined, more subtle embodiments.

The first phase of our research was based on intensive field observations in four companies, Motorola Corporation, Mutual Investment Corporation (MIC), Electricité de France (EDF); and Fiat Auto Company.[8] We wanted to have both service and manufacturing settings in U.S. and European environments. We chose two sites where we had access to very senior management and two where we were able to study lower levels. We selected Motorola as an example of a good learning organization; we were able to observe organizational learning during its fourteen-year quality improvement effort.

We did not attempt to study entire firms or to concentrate on any single work units in these four organizations. For example, at Motorola, we began by studying two senior management teams of twenty to twenty-five executives each from all parts of the corporation. Each team focuses on a critical issue defined by the CEO and COO, to whom the groups report. The teams' structures were designed as executive education interventions and vehicles for "real-time" problem solving. Our objective was to see how these teams reflected and utilized organizational learning at Motorola.

From our interview data, we identified what organizational members claimed they had learned and why. We wrote case descriptions of the learning processes in their organizations, which we shared with the organizations to ensure their accuracy. Using a grounded analysis, we identified categories that reflected learning orientations and then constructed a two-part model of the critical factors that describe organizations as learning systems.[9] We have since tested this model in data-gathering workshops with personnel from more than twenty *Fortune* "500" companies. Our testing led us to revise some of the model's components, while retaining its overall framework.

CORE THEMES

Next we discuss the core themes that emerged from our research and provided a basis for our model.

All Organizations Are Learning Systems

All the sites we studied function as learning systems. All have formal and informal processes and structures for the acquisition, sharing, and utilization of knowledge and skills. Members communicated broadly and assimilated values, norms, procedures, and outcome data, starting with early socialization and continuing through group communications, both formal and informal. We talked with staff people in some firms who claimed that their companies were not good learning organizations, but, in each, we were able to identify one or more core competencies that could exist only if there were learning investments in those areas. Some type of structure or process would have to support the informed experience and formal educational interventions required for knowledge acquisition, sharing, and utilization. We found this in both our field sites and other firms. For example, one firm that considers itself to be a poor learning organization because of its difficulty in changing some dysfunction has a reputation in its industry for superior field marketing. It is clear that this group has well-developed recruiting, socialization, training and development, and rotating assignment policies that support its cadre of respected marketing people. Obviously, some learning has been assimilated at a fairly deep level.

Learning Conforms to Culture

The nature of learning and the way in which it occurs are determined by the organization's culture or subcultures. For example, the entrepreneurial style of MIC's investment funds group results in a learning approach in which information is made available to fund managers and analysts, but its use is at the managers' discretion. In addition, there is a good deal of leeway in how fund managers make their investments; some are intuitive, some rely heavily on past performance, and a few use sophisticated computer programs. Thus the fund managers' use or application of learning is largely informal, not dictated by formal, firmwide programs. Meanwhile, the culture of MIC's marketing groups is more collaborative; learning is derived more from interaction within and between cross-functional work groups and from improved communication.

In contrast, there is no question that a great deal of organizational learning about quality has occurred at Motorola, but its emphasis on engineering and technical concerns resulted in an earlier, complete embrace of total quality by product manufacturing groups. In a culture that heavily rewards product group performance, total quality in products and processes that require integrated, intergroup action lags behind, particularly in the marketing of systems that cut across divisions.

Style Varies between Learning Systems

There are a variety of ways in which organizations create and maximize their learning. Basic assumptions about the culture lead to learning values and investments that produce a different learning style from a culture with another pattern of values and investments. These style variations are based on a series of learning orientations (dimensions of learning) that members of the organization may not see. We have identified seven learning orientations, which we see as bipolar variables.

For example, each of two distinct groups at both Motorola and MIC had different approaches to the way it accrued and utilized knowledge and skills. One Motorola group had great concern for specifying the metrics to define and measure the targeted learning. The other group was less concerned with very specific measures but, instead, stressed broad objectives. In the two groups at MIC, the methods for sharing and utilizing knowledge were very different; one was informal, and the other more formal and collaborative. From these variations, we concluded that the pattern of the learning orientations largely makes up an organizational learning system. The pattern may not tell us how *well* learning is promoted but tells a lot about what is learned and where it occurs.

Generic Processes Facilitate Learning

How well an organization maximizes learning within its chosen style does not occur haphazardly. Our data suggest that talking about "the learning organization" is partially effective; some policies, structures, and processes do seem to make a difference. The difference is in how easy or hard it is for useful learning to happen, and in how effective the organization is in "working its style." By analyzing why learning took place in the companies we studied, we identified ten facilitating factors that induced or supported learning. While we did not observe all the factors at each site, we saw most of them and at other sites as well. Thus we view them as generic factors that any organization can benefit from, regardless of its learning style. For example, scanning, in which benchmarking plays an important role, was so central to learning at Motorola that it is now an integral, ongoing aspect of every important initiative in the company. Although MIC tends to create knowledge and skill internally, it maintains an ongoing vigilance toward its external environment. On the negative side, the absence of solid, ongoing external scanning in other organizations is an important factor in their economic difficulties.

A MODEL OF ORGANIZATIONS AS LEARNING SYSTEMS

Our two-part model describes organizations as learning systems (see Figure 9-1). First, *learning orientations* are the values and practices that reflect where learning takes place and the nature of what is learned. These orientations form a pattern that defines a given organization's "learning style." In this sense, they are descriptive factors that help us to understand without making value judgments. Second, *facilitating factors* are the structures and processes that affect how easy or hard it is for learning to occur and the amount of effective learning that takes place. These are standards based on best practice in dealing with generic issues.

Both parts of the model are required to understand an organization as a learning system; one without the other provides an incomplete picture. In addi-

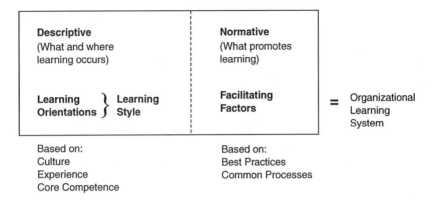

FIGURE 9-1 A Model of Organizations as Learning Systems

tion, separating the parts enables organizations to see that they do indeed function as learning systems of some kind, and that their task is to understand better what they do well or poorly. (The idea of assessing what exists is more useful than the pejorative notion that there is only one good way to be a learning organization.) Finally, a refined, detailed list of factors related to organizational learning may help companies select areas for learning improvement that do not demand drastic culture change but, rather, can lead to incremental change over time.

Learning Orientations

In the next section, we expand on the definitions of the seven learning orientations and provide examples of each.

1. Knowledge Source. To what extent does the organization develop new knowledge internally or seek inspiration in external ideas? This distinction is seen as the difference between innovation and adaptation—or imitation. In the United States, there is a tendency to value innovativeness more highly and look down on "copiers." American critiques of Japanese businesses often mention that the Japanese are good imitators but not good innovators. In our opinion, both of these approaches have great merit as opposing styles rather than as normative or negative behaviors.

Although our data show a tendency in organizations to prefer one mode over the other, the distinction is not clear-cut. While MIC does scan its environment, it prefers to innovate in responding to customer needs and problems and has been a leader in developing new financial products and services. EDF modeled its nuclear power plants on U.S. technology. Motorola appears to be equally vigorous in innovation and in reflective imitation; it has been innovative in developing new products and adroit at adapting others' processes, such as benchmarking and TQM procedures. Among firms not in this study, American Airlines, Wal-Mart, Merck, and Rubbermaid appear to be innovative in producing knowledge. And American Home Products is a good example of a highly successful, reflective imitator, as are AT&T's Universal Credit Card, Tyco Toys (a Lego "copier"), and Lexus and Infiniti automobiles.

2. Product-Process Focus.   Does the organization prefer to accumulate knowledge about product and service outcomes or about the basic processes underlying various products? Many observers have stated that one reason Japanese companies are so competitive is that they make considerably more investments in process technologies in comparison to U.S. companies. The difference is between interest in "getting product out the door" and curiosity about the steps in the processes. All organizations give some attention to each side; the issue is to organize for learning in both domains.

Motorola makes learning investments on both sides. The executives we observed spent roughly equal amounts of time in collaborative learning about processes and outcomes. They paid less attention to "people processes" than to "hard" or technical processes, but many of them accepted the importance of process issues. MIC, EDF, and Fiat have traditionally focused almost exclusively on product issues but are now making greater learning investments in process issues.

3. Documentation Mode.   Do attitudes vary as to what constitutes knowledge and where knowledge resides? At one pole, knowledge is seen in personal terms, as something an individual possesses by virtue of education or experience. This kind of knowledge is lost when a longtime employee leaves an organization; processes and insights evaporate because they were not shared or made a part of collective memory. At the other pole, knowledge is defined in more objective, social terms, as being a consensually supported result of information processing. This attitude emphasizes organizational memory or a publicly documented body of knowledge.

MIC's investment funds group focuses on a personal documentation style, eschewing policy statements and procedure manuals. In keeping with its entrepreneurial orientation, MIC makes it possible for individuals to learn a great deal, but there is little pressure to codify this. Though engaged in a business that values "hard data," the group supports subjective, tacit knowledge in decision-making processes. And at Fiat's Direzione Technica, where the individual has historically been the repository of knowledge, efforts are being made to establish a *memoria technica,* or engineering knowledge bank. Motorola shows evidence of both approaches but works hard to make knowledge explicit and broadly available.

4. Dissemination Mode.   Has the organization established an atmosphere in which learning evolves or in which a more structured, controlled approach induces learning? In the more structured approach, the company decides that valuable insights or methods should be shared and used by others across the organization. It uses written communication and formal educational methods or certifies learning through writing the procedures down. In the more informal approach, learning is spread through encounters between role models and gatekeepers who compellingly reinforce learning. In another approach, learning occurs when members of an occupational group or work team share their experiences in ongoing dialogue.[10]

MIC's investment funds group clearly prefers informal dissemination in which learning develops and is shared in loosely organized interactions. This method occurs in other MIC areas, although the marketing groups are becoming more structured in their dissemination. Motorola supports both approaches, though it invests heavily in structured, firmwide programs when senior management wants a basic value or method institutionalized. It considered quality so critical that it now includes vendors and customers in its dissemination. (Recently, some vendors were told that they had to compete for the Malcolm Baldrige Quality Award in order to be on the company's approved vendor list.) EDF prefers formal modes, emphasizing documented procedures that all share. Fiat's Direzione Technica formally spreads knowledge by accumulating it in specialist departments and then disseminating it to cross-functional design teams.

5. **Learning Focus.** Is learning concentrated on methods and tools to improve what is already being done or on testing the assumptions underlying what is being done? Argyris and Schön call the former "single-loop learning" and the latter "double-loop learning."[11] They have rightfully argued that organizational performance problems are more likely due to a lack of awareness and inability to articulate and check underlying assumptions than to a function of poor efficiency. In our opinion, these learning capabilities reinforce each other. Organizations may have a preference for one mode over the other, but a sound learning system can benefit from good work in both areas.

Our research sites displayed a range of behavior. EDF is primarily focused on incremental issues and does not question its basic assumptions. It prides itself on being the world's major nuclear power utility and devotes significant resources to being the most efficient, safe operator through small improvements rather than transformations. Though similar, Fiat's Direzione Technica is beginning to question assumptions about its new product development process. Since 1987, MIC has been in a transformational mode, particularly in the way that its marketing groups have focused on a questioning learning style. Motorola is fairly well balanced in its orientation; the founding family has historically accepted the concept of organizational renewal, which has led to far-reaching changes in the company's product lines through the years and to an inquisitive style. On the other hand, its strong dedication to efficiency learning often precludes questioning basic assumptions.

6. **Value-Chain Focus.** Which core competencies and learning investments does the organization value and support? By learning investments, we mean all allocations of personnel and money to develop knowledge and skill over time, in-

cluding training and education, pilot projects, developmental assignments, available resources, and so on. If a particular organization is "engineering focused" or "marketing driven," it is biased in favor of substantial learning investments in those areas. We divided the value chain into two categories: internally directed activities of a "design and make" nature, and those more externally focused of a "sell and deliver" nature. The former include R&D, engineering, and manufacturing. The latter are sales, distribution, and service activities. Although this does some disservice to the value chain concept, the breakdown easily accounts for our observations.

At MIC, the investment funds group focuses on the design and make side. While this is balanced by learning investments on the deliver side in the MIC marketing groups, there is a strong boundary between these groups, and the fund management side is regarded as the organization's core. Motorola's total quality effort clearly recognizes the importance of value-added at both sides, but "design and make" is significantly ahead of "deliver" in learning investments in quality. Fiat's Direzione Technica is clearly oriented toward design and make, although its new system of simultaneous engineering is balancing its approach with increased sensitivity to the deliver side. EDF nuclear operations focuses squarely on efficient production. While not in our study, Digital Equipment Corporation's learning investments traditionally were much more heavily focused on "design and make" than on "deliver."

7. **Skill Development Focus.**   Does the organization develop both individual and group skills? We believe it helps to view this as a stylistic choice, as opposed to seeing it in normative terms. In this way, an organization can assess how it is doing and improve either one. It can also develop better ways of integrating individual learning programs with team needs by taking a harder look at the value of group development.

MIC designed the investment funds group to promote individual learning, which seems to fit with its culture and reward system. Heavy investment in team learning would probably improve its performance. On the other hand, MIC's marketing groups, more supportive of collective learning, are now investing in team development as one way to improve its total effectiveness. Fiat's Direzione Technica has been oriented toward more individual development, but, with its new reliance on cross-functional work teams, group development is increasingly more important. Recently, Motorola has become more team oriented and is making heavier investments in collaborative learning. It designed the two executive groups we observed to foster collective learning on two strategic issues affecting the entire company. EDF develops both individual and group skills, especially in control-room teams. All EDF employees follow individual training programs for certification or promotion. Control-room teams also learn, in groups, by using plant simulators. Some other firms that emphasize team learning are Federal Express, which invests heavily in teams for its quality effort, and Herman Miller, which stresses participative management and the Scanlon plan.

We view the seven learning orientations as a matrix. An organizational unit can be described by the pattern of its orientations in the matrix, which in turn provides a way to identify its learning style. Given the characteristics of the sites we studied and other sites we are familiar with, we believe it is possible to identify learning styles that represent a distinct pattern of orientations. Such styles may reflect the industry, size, or age of an organization, or the nature of its technology.

Facilitating Factors

The second part of our model is the facilitating factors that expedite learning.

1. Scanning Imperative. Does the organization understand or comprehend the environment in which it functions? In recent years, researchers have emphasized the importance of environmental scanning and agreed that many organizations were in trouble because of limited or poor scanning efforts. Thus many firms have increased their scanning capacity. Five years into Motorola's quality program a significant scanning effort showed it what others, particularly the Japanese, were doing. In reaction, Motorola substantially changed its approach and won the first Baldrige Award four years later. By contrast, the mainframe computer manufacturers (Cray, Unisys, IBM) and the U.S. auto companies in the 1970s failed to respond to developing changes that sound investigative work would have made painfully visible. Recent changes at Fiat result from a concerted scanning effort in which fifty senior managers visited the manufacturing facilities of world-class auto and other durable goods companies.

2. Performance Gap. First, how do managers, familiar with looking at the differences between targeted outcomes and actual performance, analyze variances? When feedback shows a gap, particularly if it implies failure, their analysis often leads to experimenting and developing new insights and skills. One reason that well-established long-successful organizations are often not good learning systems is that they experience lengthy periods in which feedback is almost entirely positive; the lack of disconfirming evidence is a barrier to learning.

Secondly, is there a potential new vision that is not simply a quantitative extension of the old or goes well beyond the performance level seen as achievable in the old vision? One or more firm members may visualize something not previously noted. Awareness of a performance gap is important because it often leads the organization to recognize that learning needs to occur or that something already known may not be working. Even if a group cannot articulate exactly what that need might be, its awareness of ignorance can motivate learning, as occurred at Motorola after its 1984 benchmarking. Currently, this "humility" is driving Fiat's Direzione Technica to make a major study of what it needs to know.

In our findings, EDF provides perhaps the best instance of a performance gap leading to adaptive learning. Due to the nature of the nuclear power business, performance variations became the catalyst for a learning effort to again achieve the prescribed standard. We also found that future-oriented CEOs encouraged performance-gap considerations related to generative learning at Motorola and MIC (parent company).

3. **Concern for Measurement.** Does the organization develop and use metrics that support learning? Are measures internally or externally focused, specific, and custom-built or standard measures? The importance of metrics in total quality programs has been well documented and is used in target-setting programs such as management by objectives.[12] Our interest is in how the discourse about measurements, and the search for the most appropriate ones, is a critical aspect of learning, almost as much as learning that evolves from responding to the feedback that metrics provide.

Motorola executives believe that concern for measurement was one of the most critical reasons for their quality program's success. At three or four critical junctures, reexamination of measurement issues helped propel a move to a new level of learning. They are applying this factor to new initiatives, a major concern of the executive groups we observed. At EDF, the value of metrics is clearly associated with the performance gap. Its nuclear power plants are authorized to operate at certain specifications that, if not met, may suggest or predict an unplanned event leading to shutdown. Each occasion becomes an opportunity for learning to take place.

4. **Experimental Mind-set.** Does the organization emphasize experimentation on an ongoing basis? If learning comes through experience, it follows that the more one can plan guided experiences, the more one will learn. Until managers see organizing for production at any stage of the value chain as a learning experiment as well as a production activity, learning will come slowly. Managers need to learn to act like applied research scientists at the same time they deliver goods and services.[13]

We did not see significant evidence of experimental mind-sets at our research sites, with some notable exceptions at Motorola. At its paging products operation, we observed the current production line for one product, a blueprint and preparation for the new setup to replace the line, and a "white room" laboratory in which research is now underway for the line that will replace the one currently being installed. Motorola University constantly tries new learning approaches; the two executive groups we observed at Motorola were also part of an experiment in executive education.

We have seen evidence of experimental mind-sets in reports about other firms. For example, on any given day, Wal-Mart conducts about 250 tests in its stores, concentrated on sales promotion, display, and customer service. Although a traditional firm in many ways, 3M's attitude toward new product development and operational unit size suggests a strong experimental mind-set.

5. **Climate of Openness.** Are the boundaries around information flow permeable so people can make their own observations? Much informal learning is a function of daily, often unplanned interactions among people. In addition, the opportunity to meet with other groups and see higher levels of management in operation promotes learning.[14] People need freedom to express their views through legitimate disagreement and debate. Another critical aspect is the extent to which errors are shared and not hidden.[15]

Perhaps the most dramatic example of openness in our findings is EDF, where abnormalities or deviations are publicly reported throughout the entire system of fifty-seven nuclear power plants. The company treats such incidents as researchable events to see if the problem exists anywhere else and follows up with a learning-driven investigation to eliminate it. It then disseminates this knowledge throughout the company. While this openness may be explained by the critical nature of problems in a nuclear power plant, we can only speculate as to what would be gained if any organization functioned as though a mistake is potentially disastrous and also an opportunity to learn.

6. **Continuous Education.** Is there a commitment to lifelong education at all levels of the organization? This includes formal programs but goes well beyond that to more pervasive support of any kind of developmental experience. The mere presence of traditional training and development activities is not sufficient; it must be accompanied by a palpable sense that one is never finished learning and practicing (something akin to the Samurai tradition). The extent to which this commitment permeates the entire organization, and not just the training and development groups, is another indicator. In many ways, this factor is another way of expressing what Senge calls "personal mastery."

MIC does an excellent job of exposing its young analysts to developmental experiences. Its chairman also seeks knowledge in many areas, not just direct financial matters. Motorola has a policy in which every employee has some educational experience every year; it has joint ventures with several community colleges around the country, joint programs with the state of Illinois for software competence development and training of school superintendents, and on-the-job and classroom experiences for managers up to the senior level. The company spends 3.6 percent of its revenues on education and plans to double this amount.[16] Among firms not in our study, General Electric, Unilever, and Digital Equipment Corporation have valued continuous education at all levels for many years.

7. **Operational Variety.** Is there more than one way to accomplish work goals? An organization that supports variation in strategy, policy, process, structure, and personnel is more adaptable when unforeseen problems arise. It provides more options and, perhaps even more important, allows for rich stimulation and interpretation for all its members. This factor helps enhance future learning in a way not possible with a singular approach.

We did not see a great deal of variety at our sites. EDF, perhaps due to the importance of total control over operations, shows little variation. Fiat's Direzione Technica follows similar response routines, although the change to a new structure should lead to greater variation because of its independent design teams. An exception is MIC investment funds group, where we identified at least three different methods that fund managers used in making investment decisions. Senior management, although a bit skeptical about one of the methods, seemed willing to support all three as legitimate approaches.

8. **Multiple Advocates.**   Along with involved leadership, is there more than one "champion" who sets the stage for learning? This is particularly necessary in learning that is related to changing a basic value or a long-cherished method. The greater the number of advocates who promote a new idea, the more rapidly and extensively the learning will take place. Moreover, in an effective system, any member should be able to act as an awareness-enhancing agent or an advocate for new competence development. In this way, both top-down and bottom-up initiatives are possible.

One of the authors participated in two significant change efforts that failed, largely because there was only one champion in each case. One highly frustrated CEO said, "It doesn't do me or the company any good if I'm the only champion of this new way of doing business." At Motorola, we found that a major factor in the quality effort's success was the early identification, empowerment, and encouragement of a significant number of advocates. In a current initiative we observed, Motorola is enlisting a minimum of 300 champions in strategic parts of the company. Digital Equipment Corporation has had learning initiators throughout the company since its early days. Digital's problem has been in assimilating and integrating the lessons of its myriad educational and experimental efforts, rather than in creating an environment that enables broad-scale initiation. MIC's investment funds group encourages many individuals to initiate their own learning but not to proselytize.

9. **Involved Leadership.**   Is leadership at every organizational level engaged in hands-on implementation of the vision? This includes eliminating management layers, being visible in the bowels of the organization, and being an active, early participant in any learning effort. Only through direct involvement that reflects coordination, vision, and integration can leaders obtain important data and provide powerful role models.

At Motorola, CEO Bob Galvin not only drove the quality vision, he was a student in the first seminars on quality and made it the first item on the agenda at monthly meetings with his division executives. Much-admired Wal-Mart CEO David Glass spends two or three days each week at stores and warehouses; employees can call him at home and are often transferred to his hotel when he is in the field. Mike Walsh of Tenneco (formerly of Union Pacific Railroad) meets with groups of employees at all levels in what Tom Peters calls "conversation."[17]

10. **Systems Perspective.**   Do the key actors think broadly about the interdependency of organizational variables? This involves the degree to which manag-

ers can look at their internal systems as a source of their difficulties, as opposed to blaming external factors. Research in the field of systems dynamics has demonstrated how managers elicit unintended consequences by taking action in one area without seeing its dynamic relationship to its effects.[18]

Despite its importance, this factor was relatively lacking at our research sites. MIC and Motorola are structured so that there are strong boundaries between groups and functions. Both have changed their perspectives recently, MIC as a consequence of unexpected internal problems related to the October 1987 stock market crash, and Motorola after experiencing difficulties in selling large-scale systems (as opposed to discrete products). In a 1992 survey of 3,000 Motorola employees that asked them to evaluate their unit based on Senge's five factors, they rated systems thinking the lowest and the one that required the most work to improve organizational learning. In contrast, Fiat's Direzione Technica took a systems approach to understanding the consequences of its structure on new product development. As a result, it changed the structure to establish mechanisms for simultaneous engineering. To reduce the new products' time to market, functions now work in parallel rather than sequentially.

GENERAL DIRECTIONS FOR ENHANCING LEARNING

We have divided the seven learning orientations and ten facilitating factors into three stages—knowledge acquisition, dissemination, and utilization. Figure 9-2 shows the orientations and factors within this framework. Within our two-part model, there are two general directions for enhancing learning in an organizational unit. One is to embrace the existing style and improve its effectiveness. This strategy develops a fundamental part of the culture to its fullest extent. For example, a firm that is a reflective imitator more that an innovator could adopt this strategy with heightened awareness of its value. A company that has benefited from heavy learning investments on the "make" side of the value chain would see the value of those investments and decide to build further on them. This approach builds on the notion that full acceptance of what has been accomplished is validating and energizing for those involved. It is similar to the appreciative inquiry numerous organizational change consultants advocate.[19] The task is to select two or three facilitating factors to improve on.

The second direction is to change learning orientations. The organizational group would make more learning investments at a different part of the value chain, try to be an innovator if it is now more of an imitator, and so on. These are different changes from those involved in enhancing the facilitative factors, and the tactics will be different. Some changes will be seen as an attack on the organization's basic values, and it may be possible to avoid this by moving toward balance between the two poles, so members of the organization will support the existing style and advocate the "new look" as a supplementary measure.

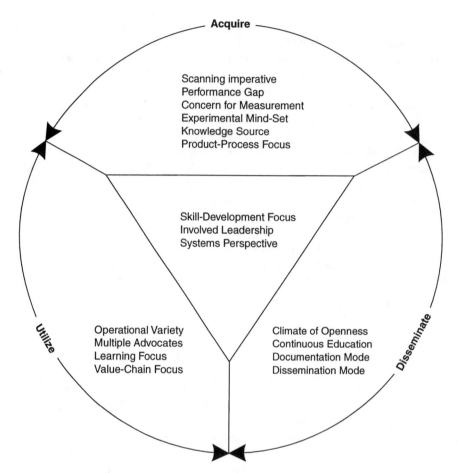

FIGURE 9-2   Elements of an Organizational Learning System

Supporting the Learning Orientations

In the second phase of our research, in which we worked closely with personnel from more than thirty *Fortune* "500" companies to identify their learning orientations, we validated our notion that organizations learn in varied ways. The singular "learning organization" should be a pluralistic model.

Looking at "what is" in a descriptive rather than normative way has another advantage in that you see better what you are *not* by examining better what you *are*. In the gestalt approach to dealing with resistance to organizational change, it has been well documented that change comes more readily if the targets of change first become more aware of and more accepting of their resistance.[20] In other words, it is important to gain full knowledge and appreciation of your organizational assumptions about learning whether you want to build on them or alter them.

This model may also be used to identify the complementarity of styles between coordinating organizations and to recognize that circumstances may dictate conditions and orientations in particular settings. For example, EDF's nuclear operations are constrained from transforming real-time operations due to the potentially dire consequences (e.g., the Chernobyl disaster) of operating under novel assumptions. However, at EDF, testing system assumptions is characteristic of its R&D division, which uses new technologies in the design of new plants. Thus changing one's style needs to be considered from a systems perspective; it may also be associated with the stage of organizational development.[21]

Strategies for Improving Organizational Learning Capability

When starting to improve its learning capabilities, an organization may decide to focus on any stage of the learning cycle—knowledge acquisition, dissemination, or utilization. While it maybe possible or necessary to look at all three phases simultaneously, focusing on a single area is more manageable. The next task is to select an option for focus:

1. Improve on learning orientations. There are two reasons for selecting this option. First, the organization may decide to shift its position on one or more learning orientations. Second, the current pattern of learning orientations has resulted in identifiable strong competencies, so improving or expanding them may be the best way to enhance the unit's learning capabilities. This focus assumes that facilitating factors meet an acceptable standard and that more can be accomplished by adding to the strong base established by the learning orientations.

2. Improve on facilitating factors. In this option, the organization accepts its pattern of learning orientations as adequate or appropriate to its culture and decides that improving the systems and structures of the facilitating factors is the most useful course. This option assumes that maximizing the facilitating factors would add more to the organization's learning capabilities than enhancing or changing the current learning orientations.

3. Change both learning orientations and facilitating factors. An organization should select this option when it sees the other variables as inadequate. This option assumes that large-scale change is necessary and that changing one group of variables without changing the other will be only partially successful.

Each organizational unit or firm must make the decision to pursue one strategy or another for itself. While there are no rules for making this decision, the three options are incrementally more difficult to implement (i.e., one is the easiest to implement; three is the hardest). From the first to the third options, the resistance to change within the organization increases significantly. It is one thing to develop a plan for improving what is already done reasonably well; it is another to engage in nothing less than near-total transformation. It is one thing to stay within accepted, assimilated paradigms; it is another to replace institutionalized models.

Whatever the organization's choice, we offer three guidelines for developing and implementing a chosen strategy:

1. Before deciding to become something new, study and evaluate what you are now. Without full awareness and appreciation of current assumptions about management, organization, and learning, it is not possible to grasp what is being done well and what might be improved or changed.

2. Though the systemic issues and relationships in organizational life require that change be approached from multiple directions and at several points, organizations can change in major ways if people experience success with more modest, focused, and specific changes. As with many skills, there is a learning curve for the skill of managing and surviving transitions. Large-scale change requires that many initiatives be put into place in a carefully designed, integrated sequence.

3. Organizations must consider cultural factors in choosing and implementing any strategy, particularly when considering how it does specific things. For example, in a highly individualistic society like the United States or the United Kingdom, skill development focuses on individual skills; in comparison, more communitarian societies such as Japan or Korea have traditionally focused on group skill development. Moving from one pole to the other is a major cultural change; to simply improve on the existing orientation is much easier.

To help managers better understand the learning capabilities in their own organizations, we have developed and are testing an "organizational learning inventory." This diagnostic tool will enable an organization's members to produce a learning profile based on our model. The profile can guide managers to their choices for improving learning capability. Through further research, we intend to show how learning profiles vary within and across different companies and industries.

NOTES

1. C. Argyris, "Double Loop Learning in Organizations," *Harvard Business Review,* September–October 1977, pp. 115–124; K. Weick, *The Social Psychology of Organizing* (Reading, Massachusetts: Addison-Wesley, 1979); B. Leavitt and J.G. March, "Organizational Learning," *Annual Review of Sociology* 14 (1988): 319–340; P.M. Senge, *The Fifth Discipline* (New York: Doubleday, 1990); and E.H. Schein, "How Can Organizations Learn Faster? The Challenge of Entering the Green Room," *Sloan Management Review,* Winter 1993, pp. 85–92.

2. C.K. Prahalad and G. Hamel, "The Core Competence of the Corporation," *Harvard Business Review,* May–June 1990, pp. 79–91.

3. J. Child and A. Kieser, "Development of Organizations over Time," in N.C. Nystrom and W.H. Starbuck, eds., *Handbook of Organizational Design* (Oxford: Oxford University Press, 1981), pp. 28–64; and E.H. Schein, *Organizational Culture and Leadership* (San Francisco: Jossey-Bass, 1992).

4. J. Van Maanen and E.H. Schein, "Toward a Theory of Organizational Socialization," *Research in Organizational Behavior* 1 (1979): 1–37.

5. C. Argyris and D.A. Schön, *Organizational Learning: A Theory of Action Perspective* (Reading, Massachusetts: Addison-Wesley, 1978).

6. Senge (1990).

7. Huber identifies four constructs linked to organizational learning that he labels knowledge acquisition, information distribution, information interpretation, and organizational memory. Implicit in this formulation is that learning progresses through a series of stages. Our framework makes this sequence explicit and connects it to organizational action. Huber does not make this connection since to him learning alters the range of potential, rather than actual, behaviors. See: G. Huber, "Organizational Learning: The Contributing Processes and Literature," *Organization Science* 2 (1991): 88–115.

8. At Motorola, we observed and interviewed fifty senior managers, visited the paging products operations, and had access to about twenty-five internal documents. At Mutual Investment Corporation (a pseudonym for a large financial services company based in the United States), we observed and interviewed corporation employees in the investment funds group and the marketing groups. At Electricité de France, we observed and interviewed employees in the nuclear power operations. At Fiat, we observed and interviewed employees in the Direzione Technica (engineering division) in Torino, Italy.

9. A. Strauss, *Qualitative Analysis for Social Scientists* (Cambridge: Cambridge University Press, 1987).

10. For a discussion of "communities of practice" see: J.S. Brown and P. Puguid, "Organizational Learning and Communities of Practice," *Organization Science* 2 (1991): 40–57.

11. Argyris and Schön (1978).

12. W.H. Schmidt and J.P. Finnegan, *The Race Without a Finish Line: America's Quest for Total Quality* (San Francisco: Jossey-Bass, 1992).

13. For the idea of the factory as a learning laboratory, see: D. Leonard-Barton, "The Factory as a Learning Laboratory," *Sloan Management Review,* Fall 1992, pp. 39–52.

14. This skill has been referred to as "legitimate peripheral participation." See: J. Lave and E. Wenger, *Situated Learning: Legitimate Peripheral Participation* (Palo Alto, California: Institute for Research on Learning, IRL Report 90-0013, 1990).

15. C. Argyris, *Strategy, Change, and Defensive Routines* (Boston: Putman, 1985).

16. See "Companies That Train Best," *Fortune,* 8 February 1993, pp. 44–48; and "Motorola: Training for the Millennium," *Business Week,* 28 March 1994, pp. 158–163.

17. T. Peters, *Liberation Management* (New York: Knopf, 1992).

18. Jay W. Forrester is considered to be the founder of the field of systems thinking.

19. S. Srivastra and D.L. Cooperrider and Associates, *Appreciative Management and Leadership* (San Francisco: Jossey-Bass, 1990).

20. E. Nevis, *Organizational Consulting: A Gestalt Approach* (Cleveland: Gestalt Institute of Cleveland Press, 1987).

21. W.R. Torbert, *Managing the Corporate Dream* (New York: Dow Jones-Irwin, 1987).

10

Rebuilding Behavioral Context: A Blueprint for Corporate Renewal

Sumantra Ghoshal and Christopher A. Bartlett

Few companies around the world have not tried to reinvent themselves—some more than once—during the past decade. Yet, for every successful corporate transformation, there is at least one equally prominent failure. GE's dramatic performance improvement starkly contrasts with the string of disappointments and crises that have plagued Westinghouse. ABB's ascendance to global leadership in power equipment only emphasizes Hitachi's inability to reverse its declining fortunes in that business. And Philips's successful revitalization since 1990 only highlights its own agonizingly slow turnaround in the preceding ten years.

What accounts for the success of some corporations and the failure of so many others? How did some organizations turn around transformation processes that had clearly stalled? In the course of five years of research into the nature and implications of the radically different organization and management models that have begun to emerge during the past decade, we studied more than a dozen companies as they implemented a succession of programs designed to rationalize their inefficient operations, revitalize their ineffective strategies, and renew their tired organizations. In the process, we have gained some insight into the reasons that some made recognizable progress in their transformational change process while others only replaced the dead weight of their bureaucracies with change program overload.

In observing how the successful corporate transformation processes have differed from those that struggled or failed outright, we were struck by two distinctions. First, successful transformation processes almost always followed a carefully phased approach that focused on developing particular organizational capabilities in appropriate sequence. Second, the managers of the successful com-

Reprinted from "Rebuilding Behavioral Context: A Blueprint for Corporate Renewal" by Sumantra Ghoshal and Christopher A. Bartlett, *Sloan Management Review*, Winter 1996, pp. 23–36 by permission of publisher. Copyright © 1996 Sloan Management Review Association. All rights reserved.

panies recognized that transformation is as much a function of individuals' behaviors as it is of the strategies, structures, and systems that top management introduces. As a result, rather than becoming preoccupied with downsizing and reengineering programs, they focused much attention on the changes required to fundamentally reshape what we described in our previous article as a company's behavioral context.[1]

A PHASED SEQUENCE OF CHANGE

The problem with most companies that have failed in their transformation efforts is not that they tried to change too little, but that they tried to change too much. Faced with the extraordinary demands of their highly competitive, rapidly changing operating environments, managers have eagerly embraced the flood of prescriptive advice that consultants and academics have offered as solutions— typically in the random sequence of a supply-driven market for management fads. According to a recent survey, between 1990 and 1994, the average company had committed itself to 11.8 of 25 such currently popular management tools and techniques—from corporate visioning and TQM programs to empowerment and reengineering processes.[2] Despite this widespread frenzy of activity, the study found no correlation between the number of tools a company used and its satisfaction with its financial performance. The authors did conclude, however, that most tools could be helpful "if the right ones were chosen at the right time and implemented in the right way."[3]

While such a generalization borders on the self-evident, we would endorse the importance that the conclusion gives to sequencing and implementing activities in a change process. In many companies, we have seen front-line managers bewildered when faced with multiple, inconsistent priorities. In contrast, we observed that the companies that were most successful in transforming themselves into more flexible, responsive organizations pursued a much simpler, more focused sequence of actions.

One widely recognized phased transformation process has been Jack Welch's revitalization of General Electric. From his emphasis on downsizing, delayering, and portfolio pruning in the early and mid-1980s, Welch shifted his focus to more developmental, integrative activities in the late 1980s. By the early 1990s, he had begun to create what he called a "boundaryless and self-renewing organization." Although he has faulted himself for not moving faster, Welch has remained firmly convinced of the logic in the sequence of his actions and of the need to make substantial progress at each stage before moving to the next.[4]

Our study results suggest that, as a model for corporate transformation, the GE example has broad applicability. It rests on the simple recognition that any company's performance depends on two core capabilities: the strength of each of its component units and the effectiveness of their integration. This is true of the integration of individually strong functional groups along an organization's value chain as well as of the synergistic linking of a company's portfolio of business units or the global networking of its different national subsidiaries. This assumption defines the two axes of the corporate renewal model represented in Figure 10-1.

As they face the renewal challenge, most companies find themselves with a portfolio of operations (represented by the circles in Figure 10-1): a few strong but independent units and activities (the tightly defined but separate circles in quadrant 2), another cluster of better integrated operations that, despite their better integration, are not performing well individually (the looser, overlapping circles in quadrant 3), and a group of business units, country subsidiaries, or functional entities that don't perform well individually and are also ineffective in linking and leveraging each others' resources and capabilities (the ill-defined, unconnected circles in quadrant 1).

The overall objective of the transformation process is to move the entire portfolio into quadrant 4 and find ways to prevent the units from returning to their old modes of operation. But while the goal of developing an organization built on well-integrated, efficient operating entities is clear, the path to this organizational nirvana is not well defined. Yet it matters immensely.

Some companies—General Motors during the 1980s, for instance—tried to take the direct route represented by the diagonal path A in the figure. While intellectually and emotionally appealing, this bold approach of trying to improve performance on both dimensions simultaneously has typically ended in failure due to the complex, often contradictory demands that overload the organization. GM discovered this during the 1980s when it pressured its five auto divisions to boost their individual market share and profitability while simultaneously improving

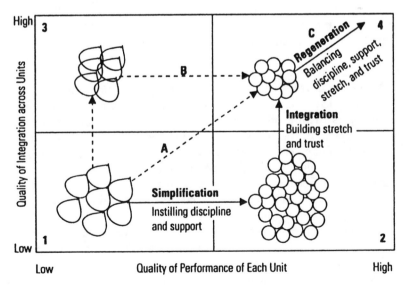

FIGURE 10-1 The Phased Process of Corporate Renewal

cross-unit synergies. It turned out that the demands of coordinating body styling and chassis design often conflicted with each division's ability to respond to the needs and opportunities of its own particular market segment. Like GM, IBM's attempt in the late 1980s to improve both unit performance and corporate integration also caused that company's transformation program to stumble.

Other companies—Philips in the late 1980s, for example—followed a more focused path, pushing first for integration on the assumption that better synergies among units would help each improve its individual performance. However, this change model, represented by path B, has also proved unsuccessful. In a bold reorganization, company president Cor van der Klugt declared Philips's consumer electronics, professional electronics, components, and lighting businesses the company's "core interdependent" operations and tried to create structures and processes that would help them manage their perceived interdependencies. As the company soon discovered, however, it was extremely difficult to integrate operations that were themselves struggling with enormous internal difficulties. And even where they succeeded, the linkages connecting uncompetitive individual businesses served mostly to emphasize and reinforce the liabilities of each. As corporate performance continued to decline and a new CEO was appointed to try another approach, Philips managers concluded, with classic gallows humor, that "four drunks do not make an effective team." It was a lesson that unfortunately was lost on Daimler Benz, which continued its efforts to integrate its diverse, overstaffed operations until a new top management team signaled a change in direction for the struggling transformation program in 1995.

The third option, path C in our model, defines the most effective sequence of transformational change processes. This is the path Jack Welch followed as he steered GE through an ongoing series of change processes that he initiated in the early 1980s. As we reviewed this much-admired transformation of one of the world's largest corporations, three distinct phases of activity were evident— phases we define as simplification, integration, and regeneration. In the simplification phase, Welch focused on strengthening the performance of each of the company's businesses, attempting to make each "number one or number two in its industry." During the next five years, he sold or closed operations valued at almost $10 billion and acquired new businesses worth $18 billion. He stripped away the heavy superstructure of sectors and groups that had long burdened front-line units and made drastic cuts in the size and responsibilities of corporate staffs. While this streamlining cost the company some ability to integrate and coordinate activities across units, Welch's primary concern was to give the managers of the core businesses the freedom to develop new strategies and to control their operations. By creating a sense of organizational clarity and managerial simplicity, he felt more able to hold them accountable for the results.

By the mid-1980s, with most of the acquisitions and divestitures completed, Welch evolved into a second phase, which we call integration. With thirteen businesses running strongly at the company's core, he began to look for ways he could link them to exploit potential scale economies, leverage their individual resources, and capture opportunities for cross-unit learning. Beginning with his top-level corporate executive committee meetings, he worked to develop an environment for interunit collaboration that would demonstrate the concrete benefits of cooperation. He urged his senior executives to accept some high-visibility, symbolic proposals—putting sixteen pounds of GE plastics into every GE refrigerator, for example, or having the engineers from the locomotive division resolve a serious design problem in the appliance business. During the next several years, he pushed collaboration deeper into the organization through programs designed to open minds, clear communications channels, and eliminate the parochial attitudes that had insulated functions, isolated businesses, and separated operating units from each other.

A decade after he began, Welch had simplified GE's organization and integrated its businesses, but he realized he had not yet created the kind of organization that he hoped to leave to his successor—one that continually replenished and renewed itself. So he initiated actions that moved GE into the third transformation phase, one that would imbue GE with a capability that we call self-regeneration. As he challenges employees with notions of "boundarylessness," Welch is trying to develop an organization with the ability to balance the tensions and management paradoxes implicit in the drive to achieve superior unit performance while simultaneously collaborating with other units to leverage the organization-wide benefits of integration. Like the first two phases, this one is also demanding profound behavioral change among the people who make up General Electric.

A NEW BEHAVIORAL CONTEXT

The major constraint in any corporate transformational process—and the explanation behind the need for the carefully sequenced stages—lies in people's capacity to accommodate change. Indeed, the most successful companies in our study were those that recognized behavioral change as not just an outcome of the transformation but as its driving engine. As a result, they focused their attention beyond the conventional concern about restructuring the hierarchy and reengineering its processes, and devoted most of their attention to the more subtle, demanding task of changing individual attitudes, assumptions, and behaviors.

This realization struck Jack Welch in the mid-1980s, a few years after he had initiated his bold, effective delayering and downsizing program that had eliminated several layers of GE's hierarchy and reduced its payroll by 70,000 employees. Although he had been extraordinarily successful at meeting his initial objectives, Welch understood that he could not achieve his long-term goals unless he won the minds and changed the behaviors of many front-line employees who were suspicious and even cynical about the motivations of a man they had begun to call "Neutron Jack." In 1985, he acknowledged to a group of employees, "A company can boost productivity by restructuring, removing bureaucracy, and downsizing, but it cannot sustain high productivity without cultural change."[5]

Successful corporate transformation, as Welch recognized, could not simply be imposed from the top through macro change programs. It also had to be built from the bottom through activities designed to ensure that everyone understood and supported the change. An effective change process needs to focus simultaneously on the company's "hardware"—its business configuration and organization structure—and on its "software"—the motivations, values, and commitments of the company's employees. In other words, together with the changes in structure and systems, managers also need to change what we described in our previous article as the behavioral context of the company.[6]

As we observed GE and other companies evolve through the long, painful process of transforming bureaucratic hierarchies into self-renewing organizations, we became aware of the importance not only of the sequencing of macro processes—simplification, integration, and regeneration—but also of the changes to individuals' behaviors that supported those broader initiatives. The performance-driven actions implicit in Welch's call for speed, simplicity, and self-confidence, for example, were different from the more collaborative behaviors he was trying to elicit in his subsequent emphasis on "a boundaryless organization." Our observations suggest that discipline, support, stretch, and trust—the four vital elements of the transformational behavioral context—were most effectively developed sequentially in a way that supported the three stages of renewal. Instilling discipline and support, for example, is crucial to managing the company through the simplification phase; instilling stretch and trust is essential to effective cross-unit integration; and balancing all four dimensions is the key to moving to a state of continuous regeneration.

SIMPLIFICATION: BUILDING FRONT-LINE INITIATIVE

Of all the companies we studied, the one that faced the most daunting transformation challenge was AT&T. Forced to divest 70 percent of its assets in an antitrust settlement, compelled to confront formidable global competitors in a suddenly deregulated business, and confronted with an industry fundamentally restructured by the converging technologies of computers and telecommunications, AT&T was a dinosaur on the brink of extinction for the first few years after the company's 1984 breakup. Within four years, its near monopoly of long distance service had been reduced to a 68 percent share, its once highly profitable equipment business was staggering under the attack of aggressive competition, and its computer business was floundering in a struggling partnership with Olivetti. At this time, Bob Allen became CEO and initiated a series of initiatives that illustrate the actions most effective in the first stage of transforming a classic bureaucracy into a self-renewing organization.

In a series of early moves, Allen signaled a radical departure from the previous integrative activities that management described as AT&T's "single enterprise" strategy. By deemphasizing cross-unit coordination, he was able to focus attention on simplifying the company's large, unwieldy organization, breaking it into twenty-one business units, each responsible for developing its own business model and for delivering its own results. To reinforce this message, he implemented a rigorous economic value-added (EVA) system that recorded and reported the return on capital employed for the newly created business units, each of which was required to manage not only its profit and loss account but also its own balance sheet. The business unit managers, in turn, created more than 100 focused product groups, each with its own profit and loss account, thereby fragmenting AT&T into more than 100 distinct management units. According to Allen, the dramatic improvement in AT&T's performance during the next five years, reflected in the 200 percent increase in the company's market value, would not have been possible without the restructuring that allowed front-line managers to simplify their tasks and focus their attention.

But simplifying the structure and systems was not enough to change the behavior of individuals who had spent their whole careers in an environment driven by directives, policies, and constraints. In an organization demotivated by several years of competitive defeats, operating losses, and personnel cuts, Allen saw his main objective as "helping our people learn how to win again." This required him to replace the context of imposed compliance and control with a more internalized model of behavior. While stripping out structural overhead, AT&T's top management was also focused on the huge task of establishing strong norms of self-discipline and building a context of support and encouragement.

Building Discipline

Over several years, Allen and his top management team designed numerous initiatives to shift the internal cultural norm of compliance to a context that encouraged self-discipline. Among these, the three that seemed the most influential—and common to other successful change processes we observed—were their attention to unambiguous performance standards, their commitment to feedback, and their process of clear, consistently applied rewards and sanctions.[7]

From his first day, one of Allen's strongest and most consistent messages was that financial success could no longer be negotiated in Washington in discussions among lobbyists, lawyers, and regulators, but instead would have to be won in the marketplace through the actions of front-line managers. Central to this communication effort was his introduction of the EVA concept. As a result of management's relentless insistence that each business prove its economic viability and strategic potential, business heads were motivated to translate their broad EVA objectives into a much richer set of internal performance benchmarks that, in turn, were reflected in clearly defined individual targets right down to the front lines of their operations. Supported by intense communication that helped managers understand the performance impact of their business decisions, EVA became more than just a mechanical control system; it became the basis of a behavioral context that resulted in a norm of fulfilling commitments and meeting tough standards—a discipline not widely observed in the predivestiture AT&T.

After focusing the organization on unambiguous performance standards, Allen and his top team worked on developing an effective feedback process so that individuals could see exactly how they were measuring up to the standards. AT&T accomplished this with a new accounting system that provided frequent, detailed, and disaggregated feedback to each unit and was designed to "ruthlessly expose the truth about performance." Again, it was not so much the system as the way senior management used it that was key to shaping the desired behavioral context. Through their practice of conducting open reviews within each unit and between business units and corporate staff, Allen and his top team did more than just define standards and clarify expectations. They used these exchanges to educate management to a new way of thinking and to provide honest, timely performance evaluations against the new expectations. The intensity and quality of this review process greatly contributed to the institutionalization of discipline as an established behavioral norm.

The third common contextual element in organizations that develop a strong sense of individual discipline is a consistently applied set of rewards and sanctions, clearly linked to the performance standards. At AT&T, the EVA system had a strong, direct linkage to the compensation system, a characteristic that gave it credibility and teeth. Equally important, the linkage was reinforced by the way senior managers implemented the system, not only awarding performance-based bonuses of up to 50 percent of base salary but also replacing managers and even selling or merging units unable to meet their EVA targets. The replacement of a number of key nonperforming managers with outsiders from high-discipline organizations strongly reinforced the emerging norm that managers deliver on their commitments—a centerpiece in AT&T's gradual shift in behavioral context from imposed compliance to internalized self-discipline.

Embedding Support

Over time, however, such unalloyed emphasis on results can become corrosive. In the course of our study, we found that the radical restructuring called for in the simplification stage was less likely to result in individual burnout or organizationwide rejection if the hard-edged tools of discipline were counterbalanced and complemented by management's nurturing and support of those spurred to action by the rigorous demands of the discipline-based context.[8] As AT&T discovered, a commitment to legitimate empowerment, access to resources, and a management style based on coaching and guidance proved most effective in creating such an environment of support.

One of Allen's first objectives was to break the sense of control and dependence that often characterized the relationships between superiors and subordinates. While he was holding business units accountable for their performance, for example, he was also radically decentralizing responsibility by giving unit leaders the authority to fundamentally change their businesses' strategy and operations. The new accounting system proved to be very important in this effort. Instead of being designed primarily around senior management's control needs, reports were explicitly developed to provide disaggregated information to support the operating level managers' activities and decisions. At the same time, however, the system provided AT&T senior managers an effective early warning tool that gave them confidence to loosen their control, knowing they had timely, reliable information so they could intervene before major problems developed.

Allen's huge commitment to train new managers to use the data and accept the responsibilities they were given reinforced this systems change. Furthermore, Allen took personal responsibility for appointments to all key positions and ensured that his selections were individuals with reputations as delegators and developers. But his own personal management style provided the most powerful empowerment message. He described his philosophy: "I have never thought that I could be so knowledgeable about our businesses and markets that I could make the decisions. I have always been an advocate of shared decision making. In fact, I believe this is one of the reasons I am CEO."

As most companies soon realize, empowerment is legitimized only when those given responsibility are also given access to the resources they need to implement their newly delegated decisions. Again, Allen initiated radical change by decentralizing many assets and resources traditionally controlled at the corporate level. In a major restructuring of Bell Labs, for example, he gave business units the authority to control the budgets of more than 80 percent of the lab's employees, thereby giving them direct access to and influence over AT&T's enormous technological resources. In middle-level managers' view, this increased access to financial and technological resources was key to the company's rapid transition from a highly centralized bureaucracy to a more flexible organization in which those deep in operations could initiate and drive action rather than just write proposals and await approvals.

To give substance to the norms of empowerment and to validate the redeployment of assets and resources, senior managers must be willing to move one stage further. They must retreat from their historic roles as chief planners and controllers and redefine their core responsibilities in more supportive terms. In the new environment of radically decentralized responsibility and authority, they must provide the coaching and guidance that separates legitimate empowerment from the knee-jerk version that often ends up as abdication. This third element of a supportive behavioral context has probably given Allen his most critical challenge. Starting with his own actions and those of his colleagues on the executive committee, he has tried to become a role model for the desired coaching and supporting relationship. When managers try to escalate issues for his decision, he is likely to tell them that his opinion is irrelevant and encourage them to solve the problem themselves.

To spread this management model, he has broadened the evaluation criteria for all senior managers to include a development measure that AT&T calls "people value-added" (PVA), which has the same weight as the well-established EVA measure. PVA is supported by a 360 degree assessment process in which each manager is evaluated not only by his or her boss but also by peers and subordinates. In typical fashion, Allen first applied the new process to himself and his top management team before introducing it to the company.

Through a broad array of such tools, programs, and individual actions, AT&T's management team created a supportive environment that smoothed the hard edges of the highly discipline-oriented demands that they had placed on the organization. Indeed, it was this finely balanced change in the company's behavioral context that management felt was central to AT&T's turnaround from a loss of $1.2 billion in 1988 to a $4.6 billion profit in 1994.

INTEGRATION: REALIGNING CROSS-UNIT RELATIONSHIPS

For most companies, the initial tightening of ongoing operating performance is only the first stage in a long transformation process toward becoming a self-renewing organization. While this simplification phase can improve the productivity of a company's resources, some very different efforts and abilities are required to restart its growth engine. For example, although AT&T's fragmentation into disciplined business units allowed it to reduce waste and cut expense, it also led to the creation of twenty-one highly autonomous units run by what one manager described as "a bunch of independent business-unit cowboys." Yet, to grow—whether by expansion into the dynamic new infocom business at the intersection of the computer, communications, consumer electronics, and entertainment industries or by exploiting the fabulous potential of the emerging Chinese market—the twenty-one entities would have to operate as one AT&T.

Between 1993 and 1995, AT&T struggled to turn around the momentum of its highly successful simplification process by creating the necessary coordinating mechanisms for the integration phase. Management initiated a number of structural measures, from building a new regional management group to coordinate the disparate international initiatives of the twenty-one business units, to creating project teams to address the emerging multimedia, data communication, and other cross-business-unit opportunities. To support the integrative behaviors required by these structural changes, the company made a huge effort to embed a shared vision that focused on how the different parts of AT&T could collectively allow people to communicate with one another "anytime, anywhere," and to articulate shared values as a "common bond" to tie the whole organization together. Yet, after two years, the company was finally forced to abandon this effort and break up into three separate entities, demonstrating the enormous difficulties of managing the transition from the simplification process to the integration phase.

In contrast to AT&T's difficulties in integrating the company by leveraging the interdependencies across its different businesses, ABB Asea Brown Boveri, the Swedish-Swiss electrotechnical giant, is quite far along this path and illustrates some important requirements for managing the second phase of renewal. Within three months of his appointment as CEO of the $17 billion company formed through the merger of Asea and Brown Boveri, Percy Barnevik expressed his vision for the new organization as three dualities: "global and local, big and small, radically decentralized with central reporting and control." For the first few years, however, Barnevik focused on only one part of each duality: he wanted to build the new company on a solid foundation of small, local, radically decentralized units. To break the back of the old bureaucracies and strip excess resources, Barnevik radically restructured the company into 1,300 legally separate companies, giving them control over most of ABB's assets and resources. At the same time, he slashed the old hierarchies from eight or nine levels to a structure that had only three management levels between him and the front line. Although somewhat more radical, these early actions were very similar to those Allen took at AT&T.

By the early 1990s, however, Barnevik and his team began to pay more attention to the challenge of ensuring ABB's long-term growth. This task needed the revitalization of activities in a mature set of business operations through the integration of the independent units and numerous acquisitions into a single company. At this stage, ABB's managers began to focus on the other half of the dualities as they worked to capture the benefits of the company's size and reach. By more effectively linking and leveraging the resources of the 1,300 local companies, ABB used its global scale and scope to build new capabilities in existing power-related businesses, to develop new business opportunities in areas like environmental engineering, and to enter new markets such as Eastern Europe, India, and China.

Just as the behavioral change in the simplification phase is facilitated through certain changes in structure and process—fragmenting the organization into smaller units and developing simple, rigorous, and transparent systems, for example—the behavioral context that supports integration also requires some changes in the organizational hardware. At ABB, the organizational structure designed to create the tension that drives cross-unit collaboration is provided by a carefully managed global matrix with a complementary overlay of boards, committees, and task forces at all organizational levels.

Beyond changes in the organizational hardware, just as the simplification phase needs the behavioral software of discipline and support for effective implementation, the integration phase needs a behavioral context of stretch and trust to motivate the vital cross-unit collaboration. ABB's experiences are a good example of how these two attributes of behavioral context can be shaped to drive an organization through this second phase of corporate transformation.

Creating Stretch

Stretch is an attribute of an organization's context that enhances people's expectations of themselves and the company. Stretch is the antithesis of timidity and incrementalism and results in the boldness to strive for ambitious goals rather than settle for the safety of achievable targets. In observing the integration efforts at companies like General Electric, Intel, and ABB, we identified three elements at the core of the most successful efforts to create an environment of raised personal aspirations and extraordinary collaborative efforts. First was development of shared ambitions that energized the organization; second was the need to establish unifying values to reinforce an individual's commitment to the organization; and third was an ability to give employees a sense of personal fulfillment by linking their individual contributions directly to the larger corporatewide agenda.[9]

To decouple individuals from the parochial interests that drive performance in the simplification stage, companies need to motivate them to collaborate. In most organizations, this implies creating a shared ambition that exceeds the company's ability to achieve without cooperation: to stretch the organization's collective reach beyond each unit's individual grasp. At the broadest level, Barnevik did this by building a corporatewide commitment to making ABB "a global leader— the most competitive, competent, technologically advanced, and quality-minded electrical engineering company in our fields of activity." But rather than leave this broadly framed vision statement unconnected to the organization's day-to-day operations, he and his top team traveled 200 days a year to communicate and translate it so that each operating unit began to share the ambition and understand its implications for their own particular objectives.

While ambition can be highly energizing, only when the organization's objectives connect with an individual's basic belief system is the required personal commitment likely to endure. It takes a deeply embedded set of unifying values to create such an individual-level commitment to its corporate ambition. For example, ABB has a stated objective "to contribute to environmentally sound sustainable growth and make improved living standards a reality for all nations around the world." Depending on management's actions, such a statement has the potential to become a source either of unifying personal commitment or of organizational cynicism. At ABB, Barnevik ensured that the stated values were not just displayed in the annual report but were part of documented commitments in the company's "Mission, Values, and Policies" book, which insiders referred to as "the policy bible." More important, the values became the basis for face-to-face discussion between top management and employees at every level and, over the years, were confirmed by corporate leaders' actions as they acquired environmental management capability and committed to massive investments in the developing world.

Finally, management must deal with the fact that modern societies in general and large corporations in particular provide individuals with few opportunities to feel they are making a difference. To create a sense of stretch, companies need to counteract the pervasive meaninglessness that people feel about their contributions and replace it with a sense of personal fulfillment in their work. To do this, they must be able to link the macro agenda to each individual's tasks and contributions. At ABB, a whole portfolio of new communication channels and decision-making forums was designed to give front-line managers access to and influence in the company's vital decisions. Through these overlaid devices, ABB's top managers were able to invite the heads of national companies to serve on the internal boards of other local units or even on their worldwide business boards. Similarly, local functional heads can serve on one of the many functional councils that the company uses to identify and transfer best practice worldwide. Through such service, these individuals can see firsthand how they fit into the larger objective and, more important, how their individual efforts contribute to a broader agenda. It has become a highly motivating characteristic of the company's behavioral context.

Developing Trust

The ability to link resources and leverage capabilities is central to the integration process, and this intensively collaborative behavior cannot be induced solely by stretching people's goals and expectations. Like discipline, stretch lends a hard edge to the behavioral context that gives rise to individual energy and enterprise but, in its raw form, can also lead to organizational exhaustion. In the second stage of the renewal process, the appropriate offsetting quality to stretch is trust, a contextual characteristic vital to the development and nurturing of the collaborative behavior that drives effective integration.[10]

Unfortunately, the level of trust in a company just emerging from the major restructuring implied by the simplification process is often quite low, with autonomous units intensely competing for scarce resources and once loyal employees feeling that their implicit contracts with the company have been violated by serial layoffs and cutbacks. Most of the companies we studied seemed to accept this erosion in individual and group relationships as an inevitable by-product of a necessary process. While they tried to minimize its impact during that phase, the task of rebuilding individual and intergroup trust was primarily left to the integration stage when frequent and spontaneous cooperation among individuals and across organizational units became vital. Clearly, trust is an organizational characteristic that is built only slowly, carefully, and with a great deal of time and effort. Among the most common behaviors exhibited by managers in organizations that succeeded in developing this vital contextual element were a bias toward inclusion and involvement, a sense of fairness and equity, and a belief in the competence of colleagues.

Involvement is a critical prerequisite of trust, allowing companies to build both organizational legitimacy and individual credibility. ABB's integrative forums provided the infrastructure for routinely bringing managers together to discuss and decide on important issues. As we described earlier, local company managers were appointed to their business area boards where they participated in decisions affecting their business's global strategy and operations, while their functional managers' membership on worldwide functional councils gave them a major role in deciding the policies and developing the practices that governed their area of expertise.

This bias toward inclusion and participation extended beyond the formal boards and committees, however, and ABB's senior managers made employee involvement integral to their daily operating style. For example, in one of ABB's business areas that we studied, the new global strategy was formulated not by the global business manager and his staff or even by the more inclusive business area board. It was developed by a group of managers drawn from deep in the worldwide operations who were asked to define the business's objectives, options, and priorities as perceived by those closest to the customers, the technologies, and competitive markets. The process of developing this strategy and top management's subsequent approval created a strong bond among those on the team and trust in their superiors. The new relationship was reflected in and confirmed by the informal contract that developed around the strategic blueprint they had developed together.

Such widespread involvement in the activities and decisions relating to issues beyond their direct control created a vital openness for creating fairness and equity, the second component in a trust-building context. The formal matrix organization—the core design element that management believed allowed ABB to manage the dilemmas in its objective to be "local and global, big and small, radically decentralized with central control"—required the development of such an organizational norm to resolve the tension implicit in the structural dualities and to manage the conflicting demands in the strategic paradoxes they reflected. The function of the numerous boards, teams, and councils was not only to allow widespread involvement but also to create the channels and forums in which often conflicting views and objectives could surface and be debated and resolved openly and reasonably.

But fairness cannot simply be designed into the structure; it must be reinforced by managers' words and actions, particularly at the most senior level. Backed by the "policy bible's" commitment to build employee relations on the basis of "fairness, openness, and respect," ABB's senior management conducted the constant stream of decisions surrounding ongoing plant closing, employee layoffs, and management reassignments in an environment of transparency and rationality rather than through backroom political maneuvering. The resulting perception of fairness protected and, indeed, enhanced feelings of trust, despite the inherent tensions and painfulness of the decisions.

Finally, trust requires people to believe in the competence of their colleagues and particularly their leaders, because it is in these people that individuals place their confidence as they relinquish the traditional safety of incrementalism to achieve new stretch targets. At ABB, Barnevik set the tone in selecting his senior management team. Recognizing that their drastically delayered, radically decentralized organization placed a huge premium on high-level competence, he personally interviewed more than 400 executives from both Asea and Brown Boveri to ensure that ability assessment rather than horse trading dominated the selection for the top positions in the newly merged companies. His actions not only provided a model that influenced the whole selection and promotion process but also signaled that the identification and development of human resources was a vital management responsibility.

This integration process, supported by greater cross-unit collaboration, has allowed ABB to leverage the one-time productivity gains from the massive simplification program that radically restructured the company between 1988 and 1990. It helped the company develop new products and enter new markets during a recession that caused almost all its competitors to retrench in the first three or four years of the 1990s. It was a critical stage of the renewal process that was made possible by managers' behavioral changes framed by an expectation of stretch and supported by a growing culture of trust.

REGENERATION: ENSURING CONTINUOUS LEARNING

The hardest challenge for companies that have reconfigured their structures and realigned behaviors through the simplification and integration processes is to maintain momentum in the ongoing transformation process. This is particularly difficult for companies that have been through two successive processes and are striving to maintain an internal context to support both the individual initiative for driving the ongoing performance of front-line operations and the collaborative team-based behaviors for supporting resource linkages and best-practice transfers across individual entities. The final stage of self-renewal is when organizations are able to free themselves from the embedded practices and conventional wisdom of their past and continually regenerate from within.

As in the earlier transformation stages, the challenge of the regeneration phase is not just in changing the structure or the processes but, rather, in fundamentally altering the way managers think and act. As ABB executive vice president Göran Lindahl saw it, this final stage would be achieved only when he had succeeded in a long, intense development process he described as "human engineering," through which he hoped to change engineers into capable managers, and capable managers into effective leaders. "When we have developed all our managers into leaders," he explained, "we will have a self-driven, self-renewing organization."

Top executives at GE and ABB would readily acknowledge, however, that they have not yet achieved this stage of self-generated continuous renewal. Indeed, of the many companies that have undertaken organizational transformation programs during the past decade, few have moved beyond the rationalization of the simplification stage, and even fewer have successfully revitalized their businesses in the manner we have described in the integration process. Nonetheless, in our study, we observed a handful of companies that had reached the stage of constantly regenerating themselves by developing new capabilities and creating new businesses on an ongoing basis.

In most of these companies, like 3M in the United States or ISS, the Danish cleaning-services company, this elusive self-regenerative capability is based on long-established, deeply embedded corporate values and organizational norms, often linking back to the influence of the founder or other early leaders. But we observed a few companies in which a more recent transformation process led to the creation of this impressive organizational capability. A good example is Kao, the Tokyo-based consumer packaged goods company.

For its first fifty years, Kao had been a family-run soap manufacturer, eventually expanding into detergents in the 1940s as the company modernized by unabashedly copying leading foreign companies (even Kao's corporate logo was amazingly similar to Procter & Gamble's famous moon and stars symbol). Only after Yashio Maruta took over as president in 1971 did the company gradually develop a self-regenerative capability. As Maruta stated, "Distinct creativity became a policy objective, supporting our determination to explore and develop our own fields of activity." By 1990, after it had expanded into personal care products, hygiene products, cosmetics, and even floppy disks, Kao was ranked by *Nikkei Business* as one of Japan's top ten companies along with Honda, Sony, and NEC, and ahead of such icons as Toyota, Fuji-Xerox, Nomura Securities, and Canon.

In our analysis of Kao and other successful self-regenerating companies like 3M, ISS, Intel, and Canon, we developed some notions about two management tasks that inevitably played a central role in the development of such capabilities. The first was an ability to integrate the entrepreneurial performance-driving behavior shaped by the contextual elements of discipline and support with the equally vital cross-unit integrative learning framed by the managerial characteristics of stretch and trust. The second was the somewhat counterintuitive task of ensuring that these basic contextual elements were kept in a state of dynamic disequilibrium to ensure that the system never became locked into a static mode of reinforcing and defending its past.

Integrating the Contextual Frame

Maruta always introduced himself first as a Buddhist scholar and second as president of Kao; he saw these two roles as inextricably linked. Over the years, he embedded two strong Buddhist values and beliefs into Kao as a basis for its self-regenerating capability. The first core principle is an absolute respect for and belief in the individual, a value supported by an explicit rejection of elitism and authoritarianism and an active encouragement of individual creativity and initiative. The other pervasive value is a commitment that the organization function as an educational institution in which everyone accepted dual roles as teacher and student. At this level of corporate philosophy and organizational values, the vital entrepreneurial and collaborative behaviors are legitimized and integrated.

Reflecting the strong belief that the ideas and initiatives of individual managers drove performance, Maruta created an organization in which all employees were encouraged to pursue their ideas and seek support for their proposals. Central to this environment was one of the most sophisticated corporate information systems in the world. Instead of designing it to support top management's need for control, as most such systems were, Maruta had spent more than twenty years ensuring that its primary purpose was to stimulate operating-level creativity and innovation. For example, one internal network linked the company directly with thousands of retail stores, allowing marketing managers not only to monitor market activity and trends in a direct way, but also to give those retailers analyses of store-level data. Kao also developed an artificial intelligence–based market research system that processed huge volumes of market, product, and segment data to generate clues about customer needs, media effectiveness, and various other marketing questions. A third information gathering process, based on Kao's consumer research laboratory, combined a traditional monitoring of product usage in a panel of households with an ongoing analysis of calls to customer service. Managers used the integrated output to define new product characteristics and fine-tune existing offerings.

In launching the company's new Sofina cosmetics, the new-product team members used these and other data resources and intelligence systems to define a product-market strategy that defied the industry's conventional wisdom. They developed a uniquely formulated product line based on technical data and scientific research rather than on new combinations of traditional ingredients; they positioned it as a skin care product, rather than on the more traditional image platform; they sold it through mass retail channels rather than through specialty outlets; and they priced it as a product for daily use rather than as a luxury item.

Although respect for individual initiative was central to Kao's philosophy, so too was the commitment to organizationwide collaboration, particularly as a way to transfer knowledge and leverage expertise. Collaboration was aimed at achieving what Maruta described as "the power of collective accumulation of individual wisdom" and relied on an organization "designed to run as a flowing system."

Throughout Kao, there was much evidence of this philosophy, but a most visible manifestation of its commitment to the sharing of knowledge and expertise was the open conference areas known as "decision spaces." From the tenth floor corporate executive offices down, important issues were discussed in the decision spaces, and anyone interested, even a passerby, could join the debate. Likewise, R&D priorities were developed in weekly open meetings, and projects were shaped by laboratories hosting monthly conferences to which researchers could invite anyone from any part of the company. In all the forums, information was freely transferred, nobody "owned" an idea, and decision making was transparent.

Through such processes, individual knowledge in particular units was transferred to others, with the process becoming embedded in policies, practices, and routines that institutionalized learning as "the company way." Similarly, isolated pockets of expertise were linked together and leveraged across other units, in the process developing into distinctive competencies and capabilities on which new strategies were developed.

The vital management role at this stage was to create and maintain an internal environment that not only stimulated the development of individual knowledge and expertise to drive the performance of each operating unit, but also supported the interunit interaction and group collaboration to embed knowledge and develop competencies through an organizational learning process. This demanded the creation of a delicately balanced behavioral context in which the hard-edged norms of stretch and discipline were counterbalanced by the softer values of trust and support to create an integrated system that Maruta likened to the functioning of the human body. In what he termed "biological self-control," he expected the organization he had created to react as the body does when one limb experiences pain or infection: attention and support immediately flows there without being requested or directed.

At this stage, the organization becomes highly effective at developing, diffusing, and institutionalizing knowledge and expertise. But, while a context shaped by discipline, support, stretch, and trust is necessary for organizational regeneration, it is not sufficient. It needs a second force to ensure that the contextual frame itself remains dynamic.

Maintaining a Dynamic Imbalance

Less obvious than the task of creating a behavioral context that supports both individual unit performance and cross-unit collaboration is the complementary management challenge of preventing such a system from developing a comfortable level of "fit" that leads toward gradual deterioration. The great risk in a finely balanced system of biological self-control such as the one Kao developed is that it can become too effective at embedding expertise and institutionalizing knowledge. This capability risks becoming a liability when unquestioned conventional wisdom and tightly focused capabilities constrain organizational flexibility and strategic responsiveness, leading the system to atrophy over time.

Recently, the popular business press has been full of stories about once great companies that fell victim to their own deeply embedded beliefs and finely honed resources—the so-called "failure of success" syndrome. Digital Equipment's early recognition of a market opportunity for minicomputers grew in its strong commitment to VAX computers that blinded managers to the fact that the segment they were serving was disappearing. There are similar stories in hundreds of other companies, from General Motors and Volkswagen to Philips and Matsushita. These stories underscore the role top managers must play to prevent the organizational context they create from settling into a static equilibrium. Despite the widely advocated notion of organizational fit, the top-level managers in the self-regenerating companies we studied were much more concerned about doing what one described as "putting a burr under the saddle of corporate self-satisfaction."

Contrary to their historically assumed role of reinforcing embedded knowledge through policy statements of "the company way" and reaffirming well-established capabilities as core competencies, top managers in dynamic, regenerating companies perceive their task to be almost the opposite. While creating a context in which front-line and middle managers can generate, transfer, and embed knowledge and expertise, they see their role as counterbalancing and constraining that powerful process. By challenging conventional wisdom, questioning the data behind accumulating knowledge, and recombining expertise to create new capabilities, top managers at companies like Kao, Intel, ISS, and 3M created a dynamic imbalance that proved critical in the process of continuous regeneration.

Maruta and his colleagues at Kao maintained this state of slight organizational disequilibrium through two major devices: a micro process aimed at providing continuous challenge to individual thinking, and a macro process based on regular realignment of the organizational focus and priorities. With regard to the former, Maruta was explicit about his willingness to counterbalance the strong unifying force of Kao's highly sophisticated knowledge-building process. He repeatedly told the organization, "Past wisdom must not be a constraint, but something to be challenged." One approach that Maruta adopted to prevent his management team from too readily accepting deeply ingrained knowledge as conventional wisdom was his practice of discouraging managers from referring to historical achievements or established practices in their discussion of future plans. As one senior manager reported, "If we talk about the past, the top management immediately becomes unpleasant." Instead, Maruta constantly challenged his managers to tell him what new learning they had acquired that would be valuable in the future. "Yesterday's success formula is often today's obsolete dogma," he said. "We must continually challenge the past so that we can renew ourselves each day."

At a more macro level, Maruta created a dynamic challenge by continually alternating his emphasis on simplification and integration. Soon after assuming Kao's presidency in 1971, he initiated the so-called CCR movement, a major corporate initiative to reduce work-force size through a widespread computerization of activities. This efficiency-driven initiative was followed in the mid-1970s by a TQM program that focused on organizationwide investments and cross-unit integration to improve long-term performance. By the early 1980s, an office automation thrust returned attention to the simplification agenda, which, by the mid-1980s, was broadened into a total cost reduction (TCR) program. By the late 1980s, however, top management was reemphasizing the integration agenda, and the company's TCR slogan was reinterpreted as "total creative revolution" requiring intensive cross-unit collaboration.

Through this constant shift between simplification and integration, Maruta created an organization that not only supported both capabilities but embedded them dynamically to ensure that no one mode of operation became the dominant model. This organizational context was vital for ongoing business regeneration.

LEADING THE RENEWAL PROCESS

Managers in many large companies recognize the need for the kind of radical change we have described. Yet, most shy away from it. The European head of a large U.S. company gave us perhaps the most plausible explanation for this gap between intellectual understanding and emotional commitment to action: "The tragedy of top management in large corporations is that it is so much more reassuring to stay as you are, even though you know the result will be certain failure, than to try to make a fundamental change when you cannot be certain that the effort will succeed."

Many of the recent books and articles on corporate transformation suggest that the process is inherently complex and messy. While that is true, many also ascribe a mystical characteristic to transformation by claiming that it is impossible to generalize it. That is not true. We have seen several companies that made effective, sustainable change toward the self-regenerative capability we have described. In all such cases—Motorola, GE, AT&T, ABB, Lufthansa, and several others—we observed the same sequential process, with distinct, though overlapping phases of simplification, integration, and regeneration. At the same time, others like IBM, Daimler Benz, DEC, Philips, and Hitachi that have tried alternative routes have made little progress until a change of top management led them to something closer to the model we have described. Similarly, when such a phased approach failed, as it did at Westinghouse, it was because changes in the organizational hardware were not matched with changes in the behavioral software. The model we have presented is general, and while we have inferred it from observations of practice, recent theoretical advances suggest that the particular sequence we have proposed is necessary to break down the forces of organizational inertia.[11]

We do not mean, however, that leading a company through such a renewal process will be easy, quick, or painless. The metaphor of a caterpillar transforming into a butterfly may be romantic, but the experience is an unpleasant one for the caterpillar. In the process of transformation, it goes blind, its legs fall off, and its body is torn apart, as beautiful wings emerge. Similarly, the transformation from a hierarchical bureaucracy to a flexible, self-regenerating company will be painful and requires the enormous courage of its leaders. We hope the road map we have provided will help instill this courage by removing some of the mysticism and uncertainty from the most daunting challenge of corporate leadership today.

NOTES

1. See C.A. Bartlett and S. Ghoshal, "Rebuilding Behavioral Context: Turn Process Reengineering into People Revitalization," *Sloan Management Review,* Fall 1995, pp. 11–23.

2. Results are from the Bain & Co./Planning Forum Survey reported in: D.K. Rigby, "Managing the Management Tools," *Planning Review,* September–October 1994, pp. 20–24.

3. Ibid.

4. Jack Welch described this logic in a presentation at the Harvard Business School in 1992. The logic can also be inferred from the detailed descriptions of the changes at GE. See: N.M. Tichy and S. Sherman, *Control Your Destiny or Someone Else Will* (New York: Doubleday, 1993).

5. "Competitiveness from Within," speech to GE employees, 1985.

6. Bartlett and Ghoshal (1995).

7. Past research on organizational climate has highlighted the importance of standards, feedback, and sanctions in building organizational discipline. See, for example: G.H. Litwin and R.A. Stringer, "Motivation and Organizational Climate" (Boston: Harvard Business School, Division of Research, 1968); R.T. Pascale, "The Paradox of Corporate Culture: Reconciling Ourselves to Socialization," *California Management Review*

13 (1985): 546–558; and G.G. Gordon and N. DiTomaso, "Predicting Corporate Performance from Organizational Culture," *Journal of Management Studies* 29 (1992): 783–798.

8. For the importance of support in enhancing corporate performance, see: R. Walton, "From Control to Commitment in the Workplace," *Harvard Business Review,* March–April 1985, pp. 76–84. For a more academically grounded analysis of the organizational requirements to create this attribute of behavioral context, see: R. Calori and P. Sarnnin, "Corporate Culture and Economic Performance: A French Study," *Organizational Studies* 12 (1991): 49–74.

9. Gordon and DiTomaso have shown the positive influence that ambitious goals can have on organizational climate. See Gordon and DiTomaso (1992). For the importance of values and personal meaning, see: J.R. Hackman and G.R. Oldham, *Work Redesign* (Reading, Massachusetts: Addison-Wesley, 1980); and K.W. Thomas and B.A Velthouse, "Cognitive Elements of Empowerment: An Interpretative Model of Intrinsic Task Motivation," *Academy of Management Review* 15 (1990): 666–681.

10. The importance of trust features prominently in the academic literature on organizational climate. See, for example: J.P. Campbell, M.D. Dunette, E.E. Lawler, and K.E. Weick, *Management Behavior, Performance, and Effectiveness* (New York: McGraw-Hill, 1970). For a more recent contribution on the effect of trust, see: R.D. Denison, *Corporate Culture and Organizational Effectiveness* (New York: John Wiley, 1990).

11. See, for example: R.P. Rumelt, "Inertia and Transformation," in C.M. Montgomery, ed., *Resource-Based and Evolutionary Theories of the Firm* (Boston: Kluwer Academic Publishers, 1995).

Part Four

Monitoring, Valuing, and Reporting Intellectual Capital

11

Knowledge and Competence as Strategic Assets

Sidney G. Winter

An *asset*, my dictionary says, may be defined as "a useful thing or quality." Among commentators on corporate strategy, it is widely accepted that knowledge and competence are useful things for a company to have. At times, particular approaches to the acquisition and profitable exploitation of productive knowledge—such as the experience curve—have been the central focus of strategic discussion. At other times, explicit attention to the place of knowledge considerations in the strategic picture has waned, perhaps to the point where such issues have "dropped through the cracks" of strategic analysis (see Peters 1984: 115). But they certainly cannot drop very far below the analytical surface because any discussion of innovation and indeed the activity of strategic analysis itself implicitly concedes their importance.

The dictionary offers an alternative definition of an asset as "a single item of property." In some cases, this second meaning may be applicable, along with the first, to knowledge held by a business firm. A basic patent, for example, may certainly be a useful thing for a company to have, and at the same time it may represent a discrete bundle of legally defined and enforceable property rights; such an item of property can be conveyed from one owner to another just as a stock certificate or a deed can. In general, however, it is decidedly problematic whether the realities denoted by such terms as *knowledge, competence, skills, know-how,* or *capability* are the sorts of things that can be adequately discussed as items of prop-

From "The Competitive Challenge" by David J. Teece. Copyright © 1987 by Center for Research in Management, School of Business Administration, University of California, Berkeley. Reprinted by permission of HarperCollins, Publishers, Inc.

I am indebted to seminar participants at the University of California, Berkeley, and the University of Pennsylvania for helpful comments and challenging questions. David Teece gets special thanks both for his suggestions and for his patient encouragement of the entire effort (without thereby incurring any responsibility for the result). Financial support from the National Science Foundation, Division of Policy Research and Analysis, and from the Sloan Foundation is gratefully acknowledged, as is the research assistance of Allen Presseller.

erty. The word *item* is suggestive of a discreteness, of a potential for severance from the prevailing context, that is frequently not characteristic of the skills of individuals and organizations. The term *intellectual property* is established in legal parlance, but there are nevertheless often profound ambiguities in both principle and practice regarding the scope and locus of the rights associated with the possession of knowledge.

Thus, of the two definitions of *assets*, one is plainly applicable to the knowledge and competence of a business firm, while the other is of uncertain applicability. This situation does not pose a problem for lexicographers, but it does pose a problem for analysts of strategy. The reason is that the disciplines of economics, accounting, and finance have developed and defined the asset concept in ways that are largely specializations of the second dictionary definition (which, of course, is itself a specialization of the first definition). Where the second definition does not apply, the tool kits of those important disciplines contain little that affords a useful analytical grip on strategic issues. Systematic analysis is crippled, and many important issues are addressed only with the general purpose tools of aphorism and anecdote.

This chapter attempts to bridge the gap between the two meanings of *asset* as they relate to the knowledge and competence of a business firm. The first section introduces a state description approach to strategy that borrows elements from optimal control theory and from evolutionary economics. The next two sections develop this approach, with particular emphasis on its relationship to the valuation of the firm's productive system, link the state description approach to the diverse set of organizational phenomena denoted by *knowledge, competence,* and kindred terms, and explore some distinctions among these phenomena that are of major importance for strategy. The next section draws on the Yale survey of corporate R&D managers to suggest the extent to which the key mechanisms affecting the creation and diffusion of productive knowledge differ from one branch of manufacturing industry to another. The final section briefly reviews the major themes of the chapter.

STRATEGIC STATE DESCRIPTION

An organizational strategy, I propose, is a summary account of the principal characteristics and relationships of the organization and its environment—an account developed for the purpose of informing decisions affecting the organization's success and survival. This formulation emphasizes the normative intent of strategic analysis and rejects the notion that there are strategies that have "evolved implicitly" (Porter 1980: xiii) or that strategy is a "non-rational concept" (Greiner 1983: 13). There may of course be strategies that are clearly formulated but then rejected or ignored, that are not written down but are nevertheless successfully pursued, or that lead to abject failure rather than to success. These realistic possibilities are consistent with a view of strategic analysis as a form of "intendedly rational" (Simon 1957: xxiv) behavior directed toward pragmatically useful understanding of the situation of the organization as a whole. By contrast, mere habits of thought or action, managerial or otherwise, are not strategies. Such habits may as easily be parts of an (unintended) problem as parts of an (intended) solution.

The propensity to perceive habits as strategies may well derive from the valid observation that much of the behavior of an organization is quasi-automatic and neither requires the attention of top management on a day-to-day basis nor, when it receives such attention, responds to it in a straightforward and constructive way. This phenomenon is most frequently noted in connection with organizational resistance to change—that is, as a problem facing change agents. But it is also cited as a factor on the bright side, contributing to excellence in organizational performance or as indicative of the positive results achievable when lower levels of the organization are successfully imbued with appropriate operational versions of organizational goals. Thus, as Peters (1984: 111) says:

> *Distinctive organizational performance, for good or ill, is almost entirely a function of deeply engrained repertoires. The organization, within its marketplace, is the way it* acts *from moment to moment—not the way it thinks it* might *act or* ought *to act.*

Peters's statement is quite consistent with the viewpoint on organizations that is basic to the evolutionary economic theory developed by Richard Nelson and myself (Nelson and Winter 1982: 134–36.) The same view is a fundamental constituent of the approach to strategy set forth in this chapter. Nevertheless, it should be clear that this view is potentially quite subversive of the whole undertaking of normative strategic analysis. The more deeply ingrained the organizational repertoires, the less clear it is what important decisions remain for an analyst to advise on or an executive to execute. When apparent choice situations of apparent strategic significance confront the organization, perhaps outcomes are fully determined by some combination of habit and impulse.[1]

This is exactly the way the organizational world is envisaged, for purposes of *descriptive* theorizing, in evolutionary economics. In that theoretical world, strategic analysis in the sense defined here has no place, although of course there is abundant scope for *ex post facto* discussion of which habits and impulses proved successful. As a response to a need for guidance in the real world, this fatalistic perspective has obvious and severe limitations.

A key step in strategic thinking is the identification of the attributes of the organization that are considered subject to directed change and the implicit or explicit acknowledgment that some attributes do not fall in that category. As the Alcoholics Anonymous serenity prayer puts it, "God grant me the serenity to accept the things I cannot change, courage to change the things I can, and wisdom to know the difference." Substitute for *courage* the words *managerial attention and related resources supporting strategic decisionmaking* and you have here the beginnings of a paradigm for strategic analysis, its role being to help with the wisdom part. Of course, the sort of wisdom contributed by an economist will include the observations that change *per se* is presumably not the goal, that change will often be a matter of degree, and that the trick is to allocate the available change capacity in the right way.

STATE DESCRIPTION AS A GENERALIZED ASSET PORTFOLIO

The concept of the state of a dynamic system has a long history in control theory and related subjects (Bellman 1957; Pontryagin *et al.* 1962; and a vast literature of applications). The distinction between the *state variables* of a system and the *control variables* is roughly the distinction between aspects of the system that are not subject to choice over a short time span and aspects that are. The values chosen for control variables, however, do affect the evolution of the state variables over larger time spans. As far as the internal logic of a control theory model is concerned, the list of state variables constitutes a way of describing the system that is sufficiently precise and comprehensive so that the motion of the system through time is determined, given the settings of the control variables and the state of the external environment at each point of time.

In general, a variety of alternative state descriptions provide formally equivalent approaches to a given problem. Also, the conceptual distinctions among state variables, control variables, and the environment can become blurred in the sense that particular considerations may be treated under different headings in formulations of two very closely related problems. There is, for example, little substantial difference between a given feature of the environment and a system state variable that is alterable only over a very narrow range.

In evolutionary economics, the notion of state description is extended to cover behavioral patterns that most economists or management scientists would instinctively place in the control variable category. Behavior is conceived as governed by *routines* (or alternatively, by "deeply ingrained repertoires") rather than deliberate choice. The object of a theoretical exercise is not to discover what is optimal for a firm, but to understand the major forces that shape the evolution of an industry (Nelson and Winter 1982: 18–19):

> *The core concern of evolutionary theory is with the dynamic process by which behavior patterns and market outcomes are jointly determined over time. The typical logic of these evolutionary processes is as follows: At each point of time, the current operating characteristics of firms, and the magnitudes of their capital stocks and other state variables, determine input and output levels. Together with market supply and demand conditions that are exogenous to the firms in question, these firm decisions determine market prices of inputs and outputs. The profitability of each individual firm is thus determined. Profitability operates, through firm investment rules, as one major determinant of rates of expansion and contraction of individual firms. With firm sizes thus altered, the same operating characteristics would yield different input and output levels, hence different prices and profitabil-*

ity signals, and so on. By this selection process, clearly, aggregate input and output and price levels for the industry would undergo dynamic change even if individual firm operating characteristics were constant. But operating characteristics, too, are subject to change, through the workings of the search rules of firms. Search and selection are simultaneous, interacting aspects of the evolutionary process: the same prices that provide selection feedback also influence the directions of search. Through the joint action of search and selection, the firms evolve over time, with the condition of the industry in each period bearing the seeds of its condition in the following period.

It is clear that *among* the things that are candidate variables inclusion for a state description of a business firm are the amounts of the firm's tangible and financial assets, the sorts of things that are reflected on the asset side of a balance sheet. It is equally clear that the conception of a firm state description in evolutionary theory goes well beyond the list of things conventionally recognized as assets. Theoretical studies employing control theory techniques, by economists and management scientists, have established characteristics of optimal behavior in problems in which state variables correspond closely to things recognizable as assets—for example, inventory or capacity levels—but also things that are not so recognized, at least in financial accounting—for example, stocks of customers, employees, and advertising or R&D capital. There is, therefore, a relationship but also a conceptual gap between the concepts of a *state description* and a collection (or *portfolio*) of assets. There is likewise a relationship but also a gap between evolutionary theory's notion of a state description for a *business firm,* a description that is comprehensive in principle, however limited or stylized it may be in a particular analytical application, and the descriptions that derive from the conventions of asset accounting or from the focused objectives that necessarily govern the construction of a control theory model, whether for theoretical or practical use. In particular, the state description concept in evolutionary theory, and the concept of a routine more specifically, direct attention to the problem of reflecting the knowledge and competence of a firm in a state description—but offer only minimal guidance as to how this might be done.

ORGANIZATIONAL GOALS

The bridges that are to be constructed across the gaps just referred to must be anchored, at least for the time being, in a strong commitment regarding the goals of the organizations whose strategic problems are to be analyzed. The discussion will relate only to organizations for which present value maximization, or expected present value maximization, adequately characterizes the organizational goal as perceived by the actor or actors for whose guidance the analysis is conducted. It is to be hoped that some of the illumination will extend well beyond the range of the assumptions adopted here, but how far that may be the case is an is-sue that must be left open.[2]

The assumption of a present-value goal for the organization places this analysis in a simple and orthodox tradition in economic theorizing. This tradition of viewing the firm as a unitary actor with well-defined preferences has long been challenged by organization theorists and social scientists outside of economics, and by a few economists of heretical bent (such as Cyert and March 1963). In-creasingly, this tradition has been abandoned by numerous theoretical economists of diverse points of view, and the assumption made here might well be regarded as a throwback.[3] There are indeed some key issues in the strategic management of knowledge assets that relate to whether the firm can hold together in the face of conflict among the diverse interests of the participants. Although these issues are touched on below, for the most part they remain on the agenda for future work. The assumption that the present value of the concern is maximized is maintained for the time being in the spirit of dividing the difficulties.

The major restrictions on the scope of this discussion having been duly noted, it is now time to emphasize its generality. The concept of a system state is highly flexible, yet within the confines established by a present value criterion it can easily be linked to the conventional (second definition) concept of an asset. A complete and accurate state description for a business firm is plainly an unattain-able goal outside the confines of a theoretical model. Yet the idea of seeking a nor-matively useful state description is realistic and familiar. When the normative purpose in view involves the direction of the entire organization, an attempt at strategic state description may be helpful.

Theories of strategy, accounting principles, and many other aspects of busi-ness practice can be understood as providing conceptual structures for state de-scriptions that are practical and often quantitative but clearly partial. The value of these schemes, at least regarding the strategic guidance they provide, is often lim-ited by the weakness of their connections to economically relevant conceptions of assets and returns on assets. Relatedly, and perhaps more significantly, they are but weakly connected to the most basic of all paradigms for making money—"buy low, sell high."[4] The strategic state description paradigm developed here does not suffer from these limitations, but, as emphasized below, it cannot escape the fact that any implementable state description scheme is necessarily partial.

STATE DESCRIPTION AND VALUATION

Full Imputation

The mathematics of optimal control theory reflects a long-familiar heuristic principle in economic thinking, the principle of *full imputation*. This principle states that a proper economic valuation of a collection of resources is one that precisely accounts for the returns the resources make possible.[5] For present pur-poses, the simplest relevant application of this principle is "an asset (def. 2) should be valued at time at T at the present value of the net returns it will yield from T onward." A more exact formulation, appropriate for present purposes, is that the owner(s) of an asset should value it at the present value of the net future returns it generates under present ownership, where the interest rate(s) employed in the discounting reflect the lending opportunities open to the owners. This is an owners' reservation price valuation; if more than this is offered for the asset, the owners should take it. In the optimal control theory context with a present value criterion, a more complex version of this same proposition attributes the maximized present value attainable from the system to its initial state together with features of the environment and the laws of change. Of course, the policy choices made affect the present value achieved—but since *optimal* control theory points the way to *optimal* choices of these policy variables, once these choices are made the policy followed is not explicitly a determinant of value.

The adoption of this valuation principle carries the direct implication that the notion that an excess return or (economic) profit can be earned by holding an asset is illusory. Properly valued assets yield only normal returns, where *properly valued* refers to the owner's reservation price defined above. If there is a gain or loss, the full imputation principle declares it to be a *capital* gain or loss associated with having acquired the asset at a price below or above its true value—that is, it is in the nature of a success or failure in speculation.

What sort of speculation is involved, and what are the sources of success in this activity? One clear possibility is blind luck in the making of decisions to buy or sell. Perhaps success also can be explained by superior knowledge, competence, insight, skill, or information.[6] But the guidance provided by the full imputation principle suggests that the words *can be explained by* might reasonably be replaced by *should be imputed to*—a conceptual maneuver that makes the full imputation fuller than it was before, restores blind chance as the sole source of net returns, and leaves us with a conception of the assets involved in the situation that is broader and more remote from financial accounting conventions than it was before. The subtleties of this imputation dialectic—full imputation for one process discloses unaccounted returns in a causally antecedent process, which then calls for a fuller imputation—must be confronted if strategic analysis is to have solid foundations in economic reasoning.

Whether confronted or not, they are key issues when the strategic options include acceptance or rejection of a bid to purchase the company, and in the wider range of cases involving transactions in functioning business units, large or small. Rational action in such situations demands attention to the question of what future earning power actually "comes with" the entity whose ownership is transferred. That question cannot be answered without inquiring deeply into the sources of earning power—that is, without confronting the imputation problem.

The subtleties are particularly fundamental to understanding the strategic role of knowledge and competence. For, as is discussed further in the next section, policies affecting the growth or decline of knowledge and competence assets can have major effects on earning power over time but may do so without posing the question "What is this worth?" with the clarity with which it is posed in a major transaction.

State Descriptions, Optimization, and Heuristic Frames

Strategic analysis would present no challenge if only two conditions were satisfied: (1) if it were easy to identify the real problem faced by the organization (that is, to correctly identify and assess the state variables, control variables, constraints, and laws of change affecting the organizational system) and (2) if the problem thus identified were easily solved. Once these easy steps were taken, any apparent superiority or inferiority in actual organizational performance over time would reflect the play of pure chance. In fact, because of the bounded rationality of individuals and organizations, neither of these conditions is remotely satisfied in the real world. It is therefore inevitable that real strategic analysis involve highly simplified and perhaps fragmented conceptualization of what the strategic problem is and that the solution to the identified problem involve a continuing process of situational analysis, decisionmaking, action taking, and evaluation of the results. Difficulties in implementation appear, which is to say that some of the things conceived as control variables do not have the anticipated effects on things conceived as state variables or that presumed control variables themselves turn out to be not so controllable after all. Surprises occur as environmental situations arise that were not conceived as possible or were regarded as of negligibly low probability. Failures to comprehend fully the internal logic of the strategic problem may become manifest in coordination failures and intraorganizational conflict.

Since strategic analysis is necessarily imperfect in the real world, there is always room for improvement. In general, there is room for improvement both at the stage of problem definition (since the real problem, nicely formulated, is not handed to the analyst on a platter) and at the stage of problem solution (since it is not necessarily a trivial matter to derive the policy implications of a statement of the strategic problem, however clearly formulated). Because bounded rationality limits achievement at both stages, the relations between the two are more subtle than the simple define problem/solve problem scheme might suggest. Stage one must be conducted with a view both to capturing the key features of the strategic situation and with a view to the available capabilities for deriving specific conclusions in stage two. As a result, there is a tension or tradeoff between flexibility and scope on the one hand versus problem-solving power on the other.

I will use the term *heuristic frame* to refer to a collection of possible approaches to a particular strategic problem whose members are related by the fact that they all rely on the same conception of the state variables and controls that are considered central to the problem. A heuristic frame corresponds to a degree of problem definition that occupies an intermediate position on the continuum between a long and indiscriminate list of things that might matter at one end and a fully formulated control-theoretic model of the problem at the other. Within a heuristic frame, there is room for a wide range of more specific formulations of the problem—but there is also enough structure provided by the frame itself to guide and focus discussion. On the other hand, a rich variety of different heuristic frames may represent plausible approaches to a given problem. Commitment to a particular frame is thus a highly consequential step in strategic analysis and one that deserves careful consideration.

Most of the approaches to strategic problems that are to be found in the literature do not involve explicit reference to state descriptions and heuristic frames or emphasize the possibility of translating the analysis into the language, if not the formalism, of control theory. (Therein lies, of course, the claim to novelty of the strategic state description approach presented here.) Many strategic perspectives can, however, be recast in this form without too much sacrifice of content and often with the benefit of revealing gaps, limitations, or vagueness in the particular perspective. The danger of neglecting alternative heuristic frames may also be highlighted.

Consider, for example, the classic BCG doctrine based on the experience curve. At the level of the individual line of business, this doctrine identifies unit cost and cumulative output to date as the key state variables and current output as the control. The connection from output to unit cost is mediated by cumulative output and the experience curve; an obvious identity relates current output and cumulative output to the new value of cumulative output. Market share can seemingly play alternative roles in the scheme, being sometimes a surrogate for output as the control variable (especially in situations in which multiple outputs are involved), sometimes a surrogate for cumulative output as a determinant of cost (where shares have been constant over an extended period), sometimes a control variable causally antecedent to current output (where the step between producing more output and getting it sold is itself strategically problematic), and sometimes a state variable subsequent to unit cost (low cost makes high share attainable, and high share makes high profits attainable). At the corporate level, the state description is the list of lines of business, with each line characterized by a market growth rate and a market share. Allocations of investment funds to the various lines of business are among the control variables. An allocation to a line of business relieves the cash constraint on the control variable for that line, making possible an increase of market through a capacity increase, advertising campaign, price cut, or whatever. Acquisitions and divestitures are also corporate-level controls, making possible direct changes in the corporate-level state variables.

The general character of the normative guidance that is loosely derived from this scheme presumably needs no review. One notable feature of most accounts of the BCG approach in the literature is the absence of discussion of the costs at which changes in state variables are affected, at either the line of business or corporate level; needless to say, there is also no discussion of balancing costs and benefits at the margin. A second feature is the sparsity of the description of the environment, which treats market share as the only significant characteristic of rivals and also does not address features of the market itself that, along with growth, might affect profitability—such as the price elasticity of demand. Spelling out the heuristic frame of the BCG analysis, and noting the character of the questions that would need to be answered to complete a control-theoretic formulation thus leads rather quickly to the identification of what seem to be important gaps; it is proposed that the same critical approach might be helpful more generally.

Applying the full imputation principle within the BCG heuristic frame tells us what the value of a company depends on. It depends on the unit cost and cumulative output levels in all the individual lines of business, considered in conjunction with the environmental facts of market sizes, market growth rates, and sizes of leading rivals—plus, of course, the net financial assets of the company. If the heuristic frame were fully and correctly expanded into an optimal control problem, and that problem were in turn correctly solved, then (for the purposes of strategic analysis) these considerations and net financial assets would be the *only* determinants of the company's value; nothing would be left of the strategic problem but to carry out the optimal policy. Actually, since problem formulations and solutions are the imperfect products of bounded rationality, there will almost certainly be room for influencing the value of the company through a different implementation of the strategic approach defined by a particular heuristic frame.

More central to the purposes of the present paper is the observation that a quite different heuristic frame might be adopted. An alternative frame provides a different list of things that influence profitability in the long run and of how these relate to things that are controllable in the short run. A different approach to valuation, and perhaps a very different result, is implied. Whether the new strategic valuation is lower or higher is not indicative of the merit of the change of frame; what matters is whether the guidance obtained from the new frame serves the company better or worse in obtaining actual returns than the guidance obtained from the old. In particular, a change of heuristic frame may be a response to recognition that the old frame embodies an overoptimistic view of the strategic situation and the present value it implies is unrealizable.

DESCRIBING KNOWLEDGE STATES

Simple descriptors of knowledge states, often involving a single variable, have played an important role both in the theory of economic growth and in empirical research on R&D, the determinants of profitability, and related topics.[7] Although considerable insight has been derived from these studies, both the theory and the evidence are generally at too aggregative a level to be more than the suggestive for the purposes of strategic analysis. The domain of strategic choice certainly includes, for example, the choice of a level of R&D expenditure, but such a choice ordinarily interacts with the details of project selection.

It is therefore necessary to confront the difficulties that arise from the complexity and diversity of the phenomena denoted by such terms as knowledge, competence, skill, and so forth. When we use such terms, we hardly ever know precisely what we are talking about (except when we are expert in the area under discussion), and there is sometimes a nagging concern that we are too far from the complex details to be making sense at all. The purpose of this discussion is to alleviate this situation in some degree—to introduce some distinctions that clarify the conceptual issues surrounding knowledge and competence as strategic assets.

Taxonomic Dimensions

Suppose that we have under discussion something that we tentatively think of as a knowledge or competence asset. Figure 11-1 below lays out some dimensions along which we could try to place this asset and thus come to a clearer understanding of what the thing is and what its strategic significance might be. In general, a position near the left end of any of the continua identified in the figure is an indicator that the knowledge may be difficult to transfer (thus calling into question its status as an asset in the second sense), whereas a position near the right end is indicative of ease of transfer. This interpretation is elaborated below.

The first of the continua listed in Figure 11-1 ranges from highly tacit to fully articulable knowledge. Individual skills are often highly tacit in the sense that *"the aim of a skillful performance is achieved by the observance of a set of rules which are not known as such to the person following them"* (Polanyi 1962: 49, emphasis in original). "Not known as such" here means that the person could not provide a useful explanation of the rules. Fully articulable knowledge, on the other hand, can be communicated from its possessor to another person in symbolic form, and the recipient of the communication becomes as much "in the know" as the originator.

The reality of the phenomenon of tacit knowing at the level of individual skills is obvious from introspective evidence; its sources and significance were explored in depth in Nelson and Winter (1982). An article in the *New York Times* (Blakeslee 1985) cited recent scientific evidence that different brain structures are involved in memory for the "procedural" knowledge underlying skills as opposed to memory for the "declarative knowledge" of facts, and provided a striking ex-

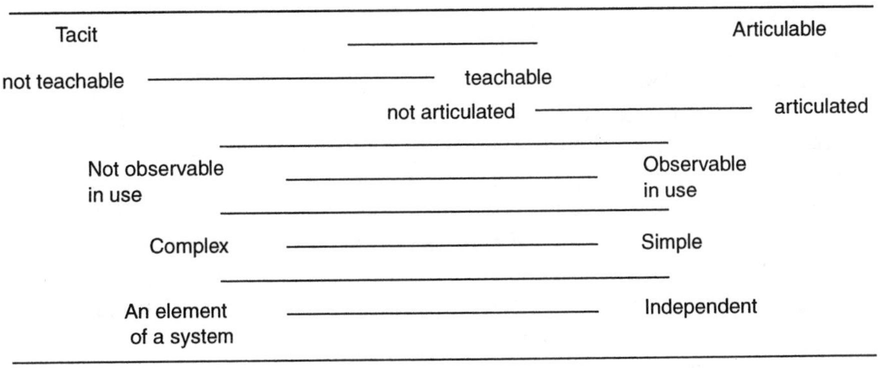

FIGURE 11-1 Taxonomic Dimensions of Knowledge Assets

ample of the distinction. A brain-damaged man retained his ability to play a good game of golf (something that he obviously could not transfer to another person by mere communication), but could not recall where the ball had just landed or keep track of his score (fully articulable knowledge that his damaged memory could not retain).

Knowledge possessed by an organization may be tacit knowledge in the sense, first, that the possession arises from the association with the organization of an individual for whom the knowledge in question is tacit. Related articulable knowledge may be possessed by other members of the organization, to the effect that "We have someone who knows about (or can do) that." Second, the fact that the myriads of relationships that enable the organization to function in a coordinated way are reasonably understood by (at most) the participants in the relationship and a few others means that the organization is certainly accomplishing its aims by following rules that are not known as such to most participants in the organization. Third, in a metaphorical sense an organization's knowledge is tacit to the extent that its top decisionmakers are uninformed regarding the details of what happens when their decisions are implemented. The decisionmakers are the symbol-processing brains of the organization; the symbols they deal in may suggest very little of what the nerves, bones, and muscles actually do—even though, in the reality to which the metaphor relates, the nerves, bones, and muscles may be quite capable of describing it to each other.

Tacit skills may be teachable even though not articulable. Successful teaching presupposes the willingness of the pupil to engage in a series of trial performances of the skill and to attend to the teacher's critique of the errors made in these trials. Teachers may also provide model performances of the skill, which provide the pupil with an opportunity for imitative learning. Instruction of this sort may accomplish a radical reduction in the time and effort required for skill acquisition, relative to what would be required by the pupil proceeding on trial and error alone—but the situation nevertheless is vastly different from one in which knowledge is fully conveyed by communication alone.

A second subdimension identified in Figure 11-1 is the distinction between articulable knowledge that is articulated and articulable knowledge that is not. The latter situation may be illustrated by the case of a complex computer program that has gone through a number of major revisions since its documentation was last brought up to date. Simple answers to questions about the program's functioning could be articulated in principle but may not be articulable in fact if the information is no longer in someone's memory. Similar situations seem to arise frequently in manufacturing, where the actual process or product design being followed deviates systematically from the symbolically recorded design or plan. Personnel turnover or simple lapse of time may erase the organization's memory of the actual process or design if the production routine is not regularly exercised and thus remembered by doing. A related phenomenon is that a deviation from the nominal standard may remain unarticulated because it includes features that are to the advantage of an individual organization member but perhaps not to the organization as a whole.

In Figure 11-1, the fact that the not articulated position is placed to the left of the teachable position is intended to suggest the point that the failure to articulate what is articulable may be a more severe handicap for the transfer of knowledge than tacitness itself.

Observability in use, the second of the major continua in Figure 11-1, involves the extent of disclosure of underlying knowledge that is necessitated by use of the knowledge. The design of a product is a secret that is hard to keep if the product is made available for purchase (and inspection) by all comers in an open market. In general, the question at issue involves the opportunities that use makes available to someone who wishes to discover the underlying knowledge. The resources that such an individual has to apply to the task, relative to the costs of observation, should be taken into account in operationalizing this conceptual dimension. Also, the question of whether the observation is taking place with or without the cooperation of the organization or individual observed is a key contextual feature of the discovery task.

The complexity/simplicity dimension has to do with the amount of information required to characterize the item of knowledge in question. Here, as elsewhere in information theory, the notion of an amount of information must be interpreted in terms of the alternative possibilities from which a particular case must be distinguished. For example, the item in question might superficially have to do with the design of an automobile. But perhaps everything about the design is familiar throughout the relevant context except the ceramic material used in the spark plugs, which itself is distinguished from possible alternatives by its name. In that context, the apparently complex is actually simple.

Similar issues arise in connection with the final dimension. A single module in a microcomputer qualifies intuitively as an element of a system. A pocket calculator is at the opposite end of the spectrum; it is useful standing alone. In a context where all other elements of the microcomputer system are readily available, however, the individual module might be said to be useful by itself.

Strategic Significance

As suggested above, the left-hand ends of the continua in Figure 11-1 are unfavorable to knowledge transfer: Transfer of tacit knowledge, if possible at all, requires teaching; an element of a system may not be helpful if transferred without the rest of the system, and so forth. Ease of transfer is itself a decidedly ambiguous variable. From the strategic point of view, it is crucial here to distinguish *voluntary* from *involuntary* transfers of knowledge. Among the most important peculiarities of knowledge and competence as assets is that secure control of such assets is often very difficult to maintain. No one can walk out the gate of a steel plant or a refinery taking the economic value of the physical installation with him in his pocket, leaving a hollow shell behind. The same is not true of an R&D lab, since the pocket may contain an articulated statement of a simple item of knowledge whose value is substantially independent of the value of other knowledge that remains behind in the lab. And even though what is in the pocket may be only a copy of something that remains in the lab, it may suffice to make the original a hollow shell without economic value.

A recent *Fortune* article (Flax 1984) provides a handy list of twenty-one ways that companies snoop on their rivals, ranging from such familiar methods as hiring away rivals' employees and reverse engineering their products to more esoteric or exotic techniques such as getting customers to put out phony bid requests and buying competitors' garbage for analysis. Because it focuses on "snooping" activity, the list omits one major route by which knowledge may escape from control, the "fissioning" of the company as new, entrepreneurial enterprises are founded by its former employees.[8] For the same reason, it also omits the important category of voluntary disclosure through patent applications, advertising, and contract bidding.

The key strategic questions are (1) What sorts of knowledge and competence assets are worth developing and (2) how is value to be derived from those assets? As will be emphasized below, intrinsic differences among knowledge bases and other circumstances of different areas of technology and organization are important determinants of where newly developed assets tend to fall along the taxonomic dimensions identified above. To the extent this is true, the implications for strategic choice relate to which areas to be in. These implications in turn must be assessed in light of the previous section's emphasis on the initial state of the system as a fundamental determinant of value: If the company in question is in the toy business, it is not helpful to observe that the prospects for protecting knowledge assets are better in the chemical business. Less dramatic transformations of a company's knowledge and competence, however, may usefully be guided by asking where the new areas under consideration tend to fall along the taxonomic dimensions of Figure 11-1.

There do exist important opportunities for affecting the positions that particular knowledge developments take on these dimensions. The degree of articulation of anything that is articulable is partially controllable. The possibilities for controlling observability and resisting reverse engineering are illustrated by the practice of "potting" integrated circuit devices—encasing them in a resin that cannot be removed without destroying the device (Shapley 1978). In the case of process knowledge, hazards associated with observability in use may be reduced not only by restricting observation opportunities to employees but also by compartmentalizing knowledge within the company and restricting the opportunity for a full overview to a select few. The emphasis that Teece (1986) places on control of cospecialized assets in the protection of gains from innovation is interpretable in the present framework as involving recognition that virtually any innovation is at least potentially an element of a system in one or more ways. Acquiring control of the complementary elements of the system is a way to move away from independence and its attendant hazards of involuntary transfer.

Features that restrain involuntary transfer tend to inhibit voluntary transfer; likewise, actions undertaken to facilitate voluntary transfer may well facilitate involuntary transfer also. It is here that the question of how value is to be derived becomes crucial. On the assumption that value is maximized by exploiting the knowledge within the firm (and at approximately the current scale), the general rule is to keep to the left in Figure 11-1, to the extent possible. If, on the other hand, the appropriate course is to rapidly expand the use of the same knowledge within the company or to enter licensing agreements or partnerships concerning the technological or organizational competencies involved, then it is at least necessary to restrain the tendency to keep to the left and perhaps better to keep to the right. These observations do not suggest the full complexity of the problem because actually the value-maximizing choice of mode of exploitation of the knowledge is interdependent with the cost and effectiveness of directing its development to the left or to the right. If, for example, it appears unlikely that a process secret can be kept for long, regardless of the effort put into the attempt, then either rapid growth to exploit leadtime or licensing arrangements may be a superior exploitation mode. Such a choice may imply a drastic change in how the development is handled because many arrangements that would support the secrecy approach become counterproductive. Finally, the answer to the antecedent question of whether an entire area of activity is worth entering in the first place depends on the value achievable from an appropriate simultaneous choice of position on the taxonomic dimensions and mode of exploitation of the knowledge.

Heuristic Frames

The foregoing discussion is far from exhaustive either with respect to the dimensions on which knowledge states might be described or with respect to the control variables that can be employed to alter them. Under the former heading, for example, there is obviously a need for an approach to describing the *amount* of knowledge or competence held in a particular area; under the latter, there is the whole domain of the legal system and its various mechanisms that support or hamper efforts to protect knowledge assets. The discussion is at least suggestive of a general approach to the development of heuristic frames appropriate to the development and protection of knowledge and competence assets in a particular line of business. Consider once again the example of BCG experience curve doctrine. Mechanisms that have been suggested to account for the experience curve effect include skill development by individual workers and design improvements in both products and processes. Each of these three is no doubt real, but they represent very different sorts of knowledge assets in the taxonomic scheme of Figure 11-1 and are accordingly developed and tended by quite different means (control variables).

THE DIVERSITY OF INDUSTRIAL CONTEXTS

This section sets forth evidence that U.S. manufacturing industries present a diverse array of environments in terms of the characteristics of the productive knowledge on which they depend and the means that are effective in protecting knowledge assets. One obvious strategic implication of this diversity is that lessons derived from experience in one industry may be very misleading guides to knowledge-related strategic choices in another. Also, while the across-industry variation is demonstrably large, this does not imply that the within-industry variation is small. (Indeed, as just pointed out, the slope of a single experience curve may reflect a variety of mechanisms.) Consideration of the across-industry variation suggests that there may be a payoff to a more discriminating approach to the problems of a single business unit—a willingness to recognize, for example, that a particular situation arising in some branch of chemical manufacturing may be "like semiconductors" even though most of the situations encountered there are, naturally, "like chemicals."[9]

The evidence presented here derives from the Yale survey of R&D executives. This survey project, headed by Richard Levin in collaboration with Alvin Klevorick, Richard Nelson, and myself, obtained answers from R&D executives to a wide range of questions regarding the appropriability of gains from innovation and the sources of technological opportunity in the industries with which they are familiar. To circumvent problems of confidentiality regarding the practices of individual companies, the survey addressed respondents in their capacity as experts on innovation in particular lines of business, rather than as authorities on the practices of their own companies. We obtained 650 responses from executives involved in R&D management in 130 lines of business. There are eighteen lines of business, noncoincidentally including most of the major R&D performing industries, for which we received ten or more responses.[10]

The first questions of the survey asked respondents to record, on a seven-point Likert scale, their view of the effectiveness of various means of protecting the returns from innovation in their various lines of business. Table 11-1 records the exact phrasing of the question, along with mean effectiveness scores for patents to prevent duplication obtained from the eighteen industries for which we had ten or more responses.

The first notable feature of these results is that, with the single exception of petroleum refining, patents are consistently rated as more effective in protecting product innovations than process innovations. To interpret this pattern requires consideration of how the observability-in-use dimension of a knowledge asset interacts with the patent law. In general (and practices like "potting" notwithstanding), the design information embodied in a product is discoverable through reverse engineering by any purchaser who wants to apply the necessary resources. Contractual arrangements to forestall reverse engineering are effective in only a few cases involving narrow markets where all buyers are identified to the seller. Also, design information is articulable. By contrast, physical access to a production process can be restricted, and much process knowledge is tacit or unarticulated. Although there are cases in which knowledge of the process can be inferred from reverse engineering of the product, the general situation is that process knowledge need not be observable in use unless the producer permits it. Finally, there are many cases in which complex processes yield simple products. On all

TABLE 11-1   Effectiveness Ratings of Patents to Prevent Duplication

Question: In this line of business, how effective is each of the following means of capturing and protecting the competitive advantages of new or improved processes/products? (1) Patents to prevent competitors from duplicating the product, (2) Patents to secure royalty income, (3) Secrecy, (4) Lead time (being first with a new process/product), (5) Moving quickly down the learning curve, (6) Superior sales or service efforts. Scale: 1 = "not at all effective," 4 = "moderately effective," 7 = "very effective." (Mean scores are given for eighteen industries with ten or more respondents.)

Line of Business[a]	New Processes	New Products
Pulp, paper, and paperboard	2.58	3.33
Inorganic chemicals	4.59	5.24
Organic chemicals	4.05	6.05
Drugs	4.88	6.53
Cosmetics	2.94	4.06
Plastic materials	4.58	5.42
Plastic products	3.24	4.93
Petroleum refining	4.90	4.33
Steel mill products	3.50	5.10
Pumps and pumping equipment	3.18	4.36
Motors, generators, and controls	2.70	3.55
Computers	3.33	3.43
Communications equipment	3.13	3.65
Semiconductors	3.20	4.50
Motor vehicle parts	3.65	4.50
Aircraft and parts	3.14	3.79
Measuring devices	3.60	3.89
Medical instruments	3.20	4.73

a. See Table 11-2 for SIC codes.

these grounds, knowledge embodied in products is inherently more subject to involuntary transfer than process knowledge—the patent system aside.

As is apparent from Table 11-1, patenting is not always an effective response to this inherent vulnerability of product information. In relation to process knowledge, however, the patent system has specific and severe disabilities. Processes that involve an inarticulable "mental step" are not patentable. Insights into process arrangements that are of such broad scope as to amount to "ideas" or "scientific principles" are not patentable. Most important, a patent on a process that is not observable in use (without consent) is difficult to enforce because infringement is not directly observable and can at best be inferred, in the first instance, from circumstantial evidence. Finally, the patent application itself discloses information that might otherwise be protected by secrecy. In sum, patent protection is ineffective for processes relative to products because tacitness and non-observability are more characteristic of process than of product innovations. In addition, secrecy is a strong alternative to patenting for processes but a weak alternative for products.

A second significant observation derivable from Table 11-1 is that highly effective patent protection is by no means a necessary condition for technological progressiveness. At least, this is the conclusion that follows if we assume that common perception is correct in assessing such industries as computers, semiconductors, communications equipment, and aircraft as being highly innovative. Of the eight mean scores characterizing patent effectiveness for processes and products in these four industries, only one (semiconductor products) is above the humdrum midlevel—"moderately effective." A thorough analysis of this phenomenon is beyond the scope of the present discussion, but it is worth noting the obvious inference that if these industries manage to be innovative in spite of the lack of effective patent protection, other mechanisms presumably protect the gains from innovation. Some reflection on the nature of these industries and another glance at Figure 11-1 produce the suggestion that the prevalence of "complexity" and the status "part of a system" may play a key role in protecting innovative gains in these areas.

A third prominent feature of Table 11-1 is the high scores for patent effectiveness shown for a group of industries that are within the SIC chemicals group (SIC 28). Although the importance of patents in this area comes as no surprise—especially in the case of drugs—the survey results are nevertheless striking for the closeness of the association between patent effectiveness and the chemical industry. In Table 11-1, SIC 28 accounts for all four out of the top four mean scores in the product column, and four out of the top five in the process column—and the intruder (with the top score) is a close relative of the chemical business, petroleum refining.[11] Out of the full sample of 130 lines of business, there are only four for which patents are rated more effective than any of the nonpatent means of protecting gains from product innovation listed in question 1B. Two of those are drugs and pesticides, one is represented by a single respondent, the other is meat products (three respondents).

At least a part of this pattern is easily accounted for by reference to the taxonomic dimensions of Figure 11-1. Chemical products are plainly far to the right on the dimensions of articulability, observability in use, and independence (meaning in this case that there are markets for individual products as defined by the molecular structure). Indeed, with modern analytical techniques, chemical products (whether simple or complex) are essentially an open book to the qualified and well-equipped observer. In the absence of patents, this sort of knowledge would be highly subject to involuntary transfer. On the other hand, essentially the same characteristics make the property right conferred by a chemical product patent peculiarly sharply defined, distinctively invulnerable to "inventing around." (As is documented elsewhere in the survey results, "inventing around" is the leading reason given for ineffectiveness of patent protection.)

The rationale for the distinctive position of chemicals industries with respect to patent protection of new processes seems much less clear. Relatively tight process-product links may well be involved; for example, it may be unusually easy to infer process patent infringement from examination of the product.

A different perspective on the diversity of industrial contexts is provided by Table 11-2. This shows, for the same industries as Table 11-1, the method of protecting gains from process and product innovation that ranked highest in mean score. Note that one of the possible responses, patents to secure royalty income, never shows up in first place.[12] Patents to prevent duplication rank first only in drugs and in organic chemical products. Surprisingly, only in organic chemicals does secrecy hold first place as a means of protecting process innovation. Everywhere else, it is lead time or learning curve effects in the process column and lead time or sales and service efforts in the product column.

Finally, it should be noted explicitly that the industries in which we obtained ten or more responses from R&D executives are industries that are doing a substantial amount of R&D—and some mechanism must be protecting the results of that effort or it would not be going on. There is another industrial environment, not represented in Tables 11-1 and 11-2, where appropriability is low and not much R&D is done. This does not mean that knowledge and competence are strategically insignificant. It means that emphasis shifts from the production of innovation to the adoption of innovations produced elsewhere and to the competent use of competitive weapons other than innovation.

Table 11-2 Highest-Rated Methods of Protecting Gains from Innovation

Key: PD = parents to prevent competitors from duplicating the product, S = secrecy, LT = lead time, LC = moving quickly down the learning curve, SS = superior sales or service efforts. Numbers in parentheses are SIC codes for the line of business. (Industries and question are the same as in Table 11-1.)

Line of Business	Processes	Products
Pulp, paper, and paperboard (261, 262, 263)	LC	SS
Inorganic chemicals (2812, 2819)	LT	LT
Organic chemicals (286)	S	PD
Drugs (283)	PD	PD
Cosmetics (2844)	LT	LT
Plastic materials (2821)	LT	SS
Plastic products (307)	LC	SS
Petroleum refining (291)	LC	SS
Steel mill products (331)	LC	SS
Pumps and pumping equipment (3561)	LT	LT
Motors, generators, and controls (3621, 3622)	LT	SS
Computers (3573)	LT	LT
Communications equipment (3661, 3662)	LT	SS
Semiconductors (3674)	LC	LT
Motor vehicle parts (3714)	LC	LT
Aircraft and parts (3721, 3728)	LT	LT
Measuring devices (382)	LT-LC	SS
Medical instruments (3841, 3842)	LT	SS

SUMMARY

Considering the acknowledged importance of knowledge and competence in business strategy and indeed in the entire system of contemporary human society, it is striking that there seems to be a paucity of language useful for discussing the subject. Within each microcosm of expertise or skill, there is of course a specialized language in which *that* subject—or at least the articulable parts of it—can be discussed. At the opposite extreme, there is terminology of very broad scope. There are words like *information, innovation, skill, technology transfer, diffusion, learning,* and (of course) *knowledge* and *competence.* These name parts of the realm of discourse but do not do much to point the way toward advancing the discourse. The problems of managing technological and organizational change surely lie between these two extremes of low and high generality, and in that range there seems to be a serious dearth of appropriate terminology and conceptual schemes. Such, at least, has been the premise of this paper.

Like evolutionary theory, from which it partly derives, the approach to strategy sketched in earlier sections has a healthy appetite for facts. The first implementation challenge it poses is that of strategic state description—the development of a strategically useful characterization of those features of the organization that are not subject to choice in the short run but are influencable in the long run and are considered key to its development and success. From evolutionary theory comes the idea that a state description may include organizational behavioral patterns or routines that are not amenable to rapid change, as well as a more conventionally defined assets. It is by this route that a variety of considerations that fall under the rubrics *knowledge* and *competence* may enter the strategic state description. From the optimal control theory side comes, first, the insistence that a scheme intended to provide policy guidance must have some choices to relate to; there must be some control variables that affect the development of the state variables. Second, granting the adoption of present value or expected present value as a criterion, control theory provides an approach to the valuation of strategic assets, conventional, and unconventional. In particular, it offers the full imputation challenge of seeking out the present acorns from which the future golden oaks are expected to grow—information likely to be useful in the proper tending of the acorns.

Both control theory and evolutionary theory invoke the notion of state description in the context of formal modeling, and both pursue conclusions logically within the context of the model once it is set down. Without denying the possible usefulness of a formal modeling approach to particular strategic problems, I have proposed the informal, looser and more flexible concept of a heuristic frame—essentially, the control theory approach stripped down to a list of state descriptors and controls. The word *heuristic* serves as a reminder that a control theory model or any other elaboration of a heuristic frame is an elaboration of an educated guess about what matters and what can be controlled. The making of that guess may be the key step. A change of heuristic frame may make all the difference in terms of identifying those acorns from which future value will grow and in so doing dramatically affect the value actually realized. It is in the choice of heuristic frame, above all, that creative insight into strategic problems plays its role.

Another challenging problem is the subtask of the strategic state description task that involves the characterization of knowledge and competence assets. Such assets are extraordinarily diverse, not only (obviously) in their specific details but also in a number of identifiable dimensions of strategic significance. Some assets are subject to major hazards of involuntary transfer; others may prove highly resistant to affirmative efforts to transfer them pursuant to a sale or exchange. Among the control variables involved in the management of these assets are some that affect the hazards of involuntary transfer or the feasibility of voluntary transfer. It was suggested that the opposition between these two control goals is fundamental.

Finally, the diversity of knowledge contexts found in U.S. manufacturing industry (documented with evidence from the Yale survey of R&D executives) can be analyzed using the chapter's taxonomic scheme. It underscores the point that different approaches to the management of knowledge and competence assets, for understandable reasons, predominate in different industries.

The themes introduced in this chapter are not fully developed. There is much more to be done and said. If the gaps and loose ends are obvious, that at least suggests that a heuristic frame for the analysis of knowledge and competence assets has been put in place.

NOTES

1. The habits may well be sophisticated skills and the impulses leaps of passionate faith. Peters, in the paper cited, puts forward normative conclusions that emphasize the role of corporate leaders in the related tasks of (1) selecting, in an uncertain world, directions of skill development that will lead to long-term profitability and (2) guiding the development of these skills through the enunciation and legitimation of appropriate subgoals. He seems to be skeptical of the usefulness of any (intendedly) rational analytic framework in connection with step 1.

2. There is a well-known device for extending the range of goals represented in an optimization problem beyond that reflected by the formal criterion of the problem: Introduce constraints requiring that acceptable levels of other goal variables be achieved (see Simon 1964). This device is one available method for extending the propositions developed here. For example, "Maximize present value subject to acting in compliance with the law" is formally a close cousin of "Maximize present value," although it may be a very different thing substantively.

3. In one way or another, most contemporary theorists actively concerned with the theory of the firm and its internal organization seem to have adopted the nexus-of-contracts view. For a concise statement of this view, see the opening paragraph of Fama and Jensen (1985).

4. As a classroom example of this problem, I like to cite the following passage from a BCG publication, regarding the appropriate treatment of "dogs": "They can never be satisfactorily profitable and should be liquidated in as clever and graceful a manner as

possible. *Outright sale to a buyer with different perceptions can sometimes be accomplished"* (Conley 1970: 13, emphasis supplied). This is sound advice—but, of course, equally sound for stars, cash cows, and question marks as for dogs, if the buyer's perceptions differ sufficiently in the right direction. On the other hand, if no such buyer can be found for a dog, it is not at all clear that selling it makes sense.

5. In economic theory, the issue and principle of full imputation may be traced back at least to Wicksteed's concern with the exhaustion-of-the-product problem in production theory (Wicksteed 1894). For a sophisticated discussion of profitability and imputation, see Triffin (1949: ch. 5).

6. Failure can be explained by deficiencies in these various respects—although luck seems to be more widely acknowledged as an explanation for failure than for success.

7. A noteworthy example of the latter genre is Salinger (1984), which gives impressive evidence that an R&D stock (accumulated expenditure) variable is an important determinant of profitability when the latter is measured by Tobin's q. This approach to assessing profitability is in much better conformity with the valuation discussion in this chapter than approaches based exclusively on accounting measures.

8. The term *fissioning* is used by Charles A. Ziegler (1985: 104), who provides an interesting account of the process, concluding that "it can be unwise for corporate leaders to overestimate the efficacy of legal precautions and countermeasures and to underestimate the debilitating effect on the parent firm that successful fissioning can produce."

9. There are analogous implications for public policy. For example, in the light of the evidence presented below, it is clear that patent policy is a tool of dramatically different significance in different industries. It is, accordingly, an inappropriate focus for policy attention arising from general (as opposed to industry-specific) concerns about the innovativeness of U.S. industry (see Levin 1985).

10. The lines of business were those defined by the Federal Trade Commission, which correspond primarily to four-digit SIC manufacturing industries, occasionally to groups of four-digit industries or to three-digit industries. Lines of business that report zero R&D expenditures were excluded from the sample, as were highly heterogeneous ones. The starting point for our list of R&D performing firms was the *Business Week* annual R&D survey list, which includes all publicly traded firms that report R&D expenses in excess of 1 percent of sales or $35 million. This gives the survey excellent coverage as measured by R&D expenditure but largely omits the perspective of small, entrepreneurial firms. For further details on the design of the survey and an overview of its results, see Levin, *et al.* (1984).

11. The anomalies relative to this relationship are cosmetics (actually "perfumes, cosmetics and toilet preparations") (an industry which does not seem to share the characteristics of the chemicals club in spite of being SIC 2844) and steel mill products (SIC 331), which score high on patent effectiveness for new products in spite of being remote from the chemicals club.

12. By contrast, the analysis of situations in which patents are used to secure royalty income does occupy a very prominent place in the theoretical economics of innovation.

REFERENCES

Bellman, R. 1957. *Dynamic Programming*. Princeton, N.J.: Princeton University Press.

Blakeslee, S. 1985. "Clues Hint at Brain's Two Memory Maps." *New York Times* (February 19): C1.

Conley, P. 1970. *Experience Curves as a Planning Tool*. Boston: Boston Consulting Group.

Cyert, R.M., and J.G. March. 1963. *A Behavioral Theory of the Firm*. Englewood Cliffs, N.J.: Prentice-Hall.

Dorfman, R., P.A. Samuelson, and R.M. Solow. 1958. *Linear Programming and Economic Analysis*. New York: McGraw-Hill.

Fama, E.F., and M.C. Jensen. 1985. "Organizational Form and Investment Decisions." *Journal of Financial Economics* 14: 101–19.

Flax, S. 1984. "How to Snoop on Your Competitors." *Fortune* (May 14): 29–33.

Greiner, L.E. 1983. "Senior Executives as Strategic Actors." *New Management* 1: 11–15.

Levin, R. 1985. "Patents in Perspective." *Antitrust Law Journal* 53: 519–22.

Levin, R., A.K. Klevorick, R.R. Nelson, and S.G. Winter. 1984. "Survey Research on R&D Appropriability and Technological Opportunity." Working paper, Yale University.

Nelson, R.R., and S.G. Winter, 1982. *An Evolutionary Theory of Economic Change*. Cambridge, Mass.: Belknap Press of the Harvard University Press.

Peters, T.J. 1984. "Strategy Follows Structure: Developing Distinctive Skills." In *Strategy and Organization: A West Coast Perspective*, edited by G. Carroll and D. Vogel. Mansfield, Mass.: Pitman.

Polanyi, M. 1962. *Personal Knowledge: Toward a Post-Critical Philosophy*. New York: Harper Torchbooks.

Pontryagin, L.S., V.G. Boltyanskii, R.V. Gamkrelidze, and E.F. Mischenko. 1962. *The Mathematical Theory of Optimal Processes*. New York: Interscience.

Porter, M.E. 1980. *Competitive Strategy: Techniques for Analyzing Industries and Competitors*, New York: Free Press.

Salinger, M.A. 1984. "Tobin's *q* Unionization, and the Concentration-Profits Relationship." *The Rand Journal of Economics* 15: 159–70.

12

The Persistence and Transfer of Learning in Industrial Settings

Linda Argote, Sara L. Beckman, Dennis Epple

The presence of a learning curve has been documented in many industries. Yet we know little about why learning occurs. For example, is learning attributable to accumulating experience of production workers or management, to increasing sophistication of capital equipment, or to improved coordination of the production process? Similarly, there is little evidence regarding the extent to which learning is transferred across organizations. Further, the presumption that learning is associated with cumulative output implies that learning persists through time, but there is little evidence about the extent to which learning persists. Our goals in this paper are to examine empirically the persistence and transfer of learning in organizations.

These issues are clearly important. The dynamics of learning are important issues for organizations in pricing, hiring employees, planning production schedules and anticipating the behavior of rivals. The learning curve has been used as a base for predicting the cost of replacement labor (Kilbridge 1962), for gauging the effects of training (Levy 1965), for determining cost savings from overseas production (Jucker 1977), for making marketing decisions, and for setting manufacturing strategy (Hayes and Wheelwright 1984). The rate and transfer of learning are also central concerns for antitrust policy (Spence 1981).

In the next section, we review previous work on the learning curve and develop the research questions for the current study. Following this, we discuss the methods and data used in the analysis and present results on the persistence and transfer of learning. We then apply the results to Lockheed's production of the L-1011 (cf. *Wall Street Journal*, 1980a, p. 12). The paper concludes with an interpretation of the results and a discussion of their implications for theory and practice.

Reprinted by permission, Linda Argote et al., "The Persistence and Transfer of Learning in Industrial Settings," *Management Science*, Volume 36, Number 2, February 1990. Copyright © 1990 The Institute of Management Sciences (currently INFORMS), 2 Charles Street, Suite 300, Providence, RI 02904 USA.

OVERVIEW OF PREVIOUS RESEARCH

Early investigations of learning focused on the behavior of individual subjects. These investigations revealed that the time required to perform a task declined at a decreasing rate as experience with the task increased (Thorndike 1898; Thurstone 1919; Graham and Gagné 1940). The term "learning curve" was coined to denote this characteristic learning pattern.

More recently, researchers interested in the behavior of individuals have focused on the process through which individuals learn and modify their problem-solving strategies (Anzai and Simon 1979). Newell and Rosenbloom (1981) and Mazur and Hastie (1978) provide recent reviews of research on learning by individual subjects. Examining the performance of individuals in organizations, Kelsey et al. (1984) found that as the experience of surgeons increased, their success rates at angioplasty procedures increased. The performance of small groups also fits the characteristic learning-curve pattern (Leavitt 1951; Guetzkow and Simon 1954; Baloff 1967).

A pattern similar to that observed for individuals and small groups has also been found at organizational (e.g., Wright 1936; Hirsch 1956; Alchian 1963) and industry (e.g., Sheshinski 1967) levels. At these levels of analysis, the phenomenon, or close variants of it, is alternatively referred to as a learning curve, an experience curve, or learning by doing. At the organizational level of analysis, the first published documentation of the learning curve is provided by Wright (1936), who observed that unit labor inputs in airframe production declined with cumulative output. Preston and Keachie (1964) found that unit total costs as well as unit labor costs declined with cumulative output. They also demonstrated a dependence of unit labor costs on both the rate of output and cumulative output.

Rapping (1965) provided particularly convincing evidence of learning by doing at the organizational level. Rapping employed data from several organizations producing the same product—emergency shipyards that produced the Liberty Ship during World War II. Rapping demonstrated that the observed increase in the rate of output with cumulative production was not due simply to increased inputs of labor and capital, or to increasing exploitation of economies of scale, or to the passage of time.

Other empirical work on the learning curve in organizations has focused on investigating whether learning by doing occurs in other industries and on investigating the functional form of the learning curve (Yelle 1979). Indeed in a recent paper, Lieberman (1984) concluded that while the learning curve has achieved widespread practical acceptance, little is known about the precise nature of the learning process. Similarly, Yelle (1979) indicated that identifying factors favoring an accelerated rate of learning is a promising area for future research. Joskow and Rose (1985) suggested that examining the persistence of learning in organizations is also an important area for additional research.

THE RESEARCH QUESTIONS

In this research, we examine whether learning persists within organizations and whether it transfers across organizations. Concerning persistence, theoretical research and simulation results have pointed out the implications of forgetting for planning and scheduling (Sule 1983; Smunt and Morton 1985; Smunt 1987). In addition, there is much evidence in the psychological literature that if the practicing of a task by an individual is interrupted, forgetting occurs (Ebbinghaus 1885). While interference from other tasks causes forgetting, forgetting occurs when performance is delayed even if there is no interference (Anderson 1985; Wickelgren 1976). When performance is resumed, it is typically inferior to when it was interrupted but superior to when it began initially (e.g., see Kolers 1976).

A small number of empirical studies have examined the effects of an interruption in production on learning in organizations. For example, Hirsch (1952) and Baloff (1970) found that when performance was resumed after an interruption at a firm, it was lower than the level achieved prior to the interruption. Batchelder, Boren, Campbell, Dei Rossi and Large (1969) presented an example of a "scallop" learning curve in which manufacturing costs rise abruptly and then decline. According to Batchelder et al., the "scallop" is generally caused by a major interruption in the production process.

Even though there is some evidence that "forgetting" may occur in organizations, the assumption is often made in the organizational learning curve literature that learning is cumulative—that it persists through time and does not evidence depreciation. In fact, most empirical analyses of learning in organizations are based on this assumption and hence use cumulative output as the measure of learning (e.g., see the many studies cited in Yelle's review). Further empirical investigation of persistence in industrial settings is clearly needed.

The current study examines the persistence of learning in multiple organizations. We develop a procedure for estimating the amount of depreciation that occurs while controlling for inputs of labor and capital. Controlling for input levels is particularly important in field research on organizations because it is important to demonstrate that any decrease observed in productivity after an interruption or change in the rate of output is not due to changes in these factors.

We also examine the transfer of learning—whether production experience acquired in one organization transfers to another.[1] Concerning transfer, Zimmerman (1982) found evidence of transfer of learning in the construction of nuclear power plants. Zimmerman noted, however, that firm-specific learning was more significant than nonfirm specific learning. Joskow and Rose (1985) did not find statistically significant evidence of transfer of industry experience in the construction of coal-burning generating units.

The organizations in our data set appear to have promoted transfer of knowledge. The organizations produced the same product and its design was standardized (Lane 1951). A central agency was responsible for purchasing, approving plant layout and technology, and supervising construction. The central agency also had engineers, auditors, and inspectors stationed at each organization. Thus, mechanisms for the transfer of knowledge existed. In the current study, we examine empirically whether transfer occurred.

METHOD

Sources of Data

The data set is based on data from the construction of Liberty Ships during World War II (Fisher 1949).[2] The Liberty Ship was built in 16 different shipyards. On average, two months were required to build a Liberty Ship. A large number were produced—2708. A standard design was adopted and produced with minor variation in all of the yards. Parts were standardized, procured by a central authority, and distributed to the yards (Lane 1951).

All of the yards producing the Liberty Ship began production during 1941 or 1942. These were new yards, known as Emergency Shipyards, constructed under the authority of the U.S. Maritime Commission. The Liberty Ship was the first ship to be produced in any of the yards, and it was the only ship produced by the yards during a significant part of the war. The vast majority of workers employed in the Emergency Shipyards had no prior experience in shipbuilding (Fisher 1949).

Hence, the data are from a virtually unique situation. A large number of a single homogeneous product were produced from homogeneous raw materials in a large number of organizations with workers who shared a common level of prior industry experience. These features of the Liberty Ship program come as near as one is likely to encounter in the field to controlling for a host of important factors (e.g., prior experience of workers, product characteristics, input characteristics) that are difficult to control for statistically in most production environments.

Fortunately, the yards in the sample began production at different times, produced at very different scales of operation, and experienced different rates of labor turnover. Therefore, these data allow us to study the persistence of learning within shipyards and the transfer of learning across shipyards.

Key Variables

The symbols we use throughout the paper and the variables they represent are listed below and described in greater detail in the text that follows.

Symbol	Variable
t	Calendar time in months; $t = 1$ in January 1941
q_{it}	Tonnage (in thousands) produced in yard i in month t
H_{it}	Labor hours (in hundreds) in yard i in month t

W_{it} — Shipways used in yard i in month t

$Q_{it} = \sum_{s=0}^{t} q_{is}$ — Cumulative output in yard i through month t

$A_t = \sum_{t=1}^{13} Q_{it}$ — Aggregate cumulative output through month t

K_{it} — Knowledge acquired in yard i through month t

$AK_t = \sum_{t=1}^{13} K_{it}$ — Aggregate knowledge acquired through month t

S_t — Month production started in yard i

Hire_{it} — Number of new hires per hundred employees in yard i in month t

Sep_{it} — Number of separations per hundred employees in yard i in month t

Tonnage produced per month refers to the weight of all vessels or portions of vessels produced during a month. Womer (1984) demonstrated that erroneous inferences may be drawn from empirical analyses of learning if the measure of output is based on units finished in a given month, and the period of production exceeds a month. This problem does not arise in our investigation since output is based on tonnage constructed in a given month.

Shipways are the structures upon which the ships were built. Following Rapping (1965), shipways in use is our measure of capital inputs. In our analysis, data from 13 of the 16 yards that produced Liberty Ships are used. Data on one or more variables were missing for the other yards.

Analysis Plan

We estimated models in which output depends on the inputs of labor (labor hours), capital (shipways), and on other variables.[3] Specifically, we estimated production functions of the following form:

$$Ln\ q_{it} = a_0 + \sum_{i=2}^{13} a_i D_i + \alpha\ Ln\ H_{it} + \beta\ Ln\ W_{it} + \gamma\ Ln\ K_{it-1} + \delta' Z_{it} + u_{it} \tag{1}$$

where

$$K_{it} = \lambda K_{it-1} + q_{it} \text{ and} \tag{2}$$

$$u_{it} = \rho_1 u_{it-1} + \rho_2 u_{it-2} + \rho_3 u_{it-3} + \varepsilon_{it}. \tag{3}$$

In equation (1), the D_i are dummy variables for the shipyards. These dummy variables are included to capture unmeasured yard-specific factors such as land that are relatively constant through time. Variable K_{it} is the stock of knowledge accumulated by yard i at date t. As equation (2) indicates, this stock increases with output. Equation (2) allows for the possibility that the stock of knowledge depreciates over time by inclusion of the parameter λ which must lie in the interval [0, 1]. If $\lambda = 1$, the accumulated stock of knowledge is simply equal to lagged cumulative output, the conventional measure of learning. By estimating λ, we obtain an estimate of the persistence of learning. As equation (1) indicates, knowledge acquired through the end of the preceding month, K_{it-1}, appears in the production function for month t. Thus, past but not current output appears on the right-hand side of equation (1).

The vector Z_{it} in equation (1) varies from regression to regression and represents other variables that may influence productivity. The error u_{it} is assumed to be serially correlated as shown in equation (3).[4] The choice of a third-order autoregressive error is a result of our analysis of the data and is explained shortly.

The monthly data have two limitations. First, the number of shipways in use by a shipyard is reported on an annual, not a monthly basis. Hence, in our analysis, we set the number of shipways in use in each month of the year for a given yard equal to the annual average for that yard. Second, monthly production is reported as output per shipway per month, not output per month. Hence, to calculate output per month, we multiplied output per shipway per month by the average number of shipways in use per year. The annual data do not have these limitations. We performed comparable analyses with the annual data and found similar results. Hence the limitations of the monthly data do not appear to be serious. Key findings from our analysis of the annual data are also presented.

Womer (1979) emphasized the importance of integrating the neoclassical production function and learning by doing. Because our data are from several organizations that differed significantly in scale of operation, we are able to undertake this integration successfully. By controlling for inputs of labor and capital, we are able to separate increases in productivity due to learning from increases in productivity due to increasing exploitation of economies of scale. In addition, calendar time is controlled for to separate the effect of technical progress associated with the passage of time from productivity improvements associated with increasing cumulative output.

RESULTS

We first discuss results concerning the persistence and transfer of learning. Other potential explanations for our findings are then investigated including adjustment costs, choice of functional form, method of estimation, and economies of scale.

The Persistence of Learning

Results on persistence are presented in Table 12-1.[5] The models were estimated by maximum likelihood.[6] The maximum likelihood estimate of λ for the

TABLE 12-1   Results Concerning the Persistence of Learning*

	(1)	(2)	(3)	(4)	(5)
Constant	−3.91 (12.72)	−3.74 (9.73)	−3.85 (11.75)	−3.83 (11.87)	−3.52 (10.95)
Labor hours ($\text{Ln } H_{it}$)	0.16 (5.14)	0.18 (5.18)	0.16 (4.60)	0.15 (4.38)	0.14 (4.09)
Shipways ($\text{Ln } W_{it}$)	1.15 (21.83)	1.08 (21.02)	1.15 (21.77)	1.13 (21.84)	1.12 (19.38)
Knowledge ($\text{Ln } K_{it-1}$)	0.65 (31.42)		0.71 (9.54)	0.71 (17.82)	0.67 (29.96)
λ	0.75[a]		0.75[a]	0.85	0.70[a]
Cumulative output ($\text{Ln } Q_{it-1}$)		0.44 (15.74)	−0.04 (0.72)		
Calendar time (t)				−0.01 (3.33)	
New hires ($\text{Ln } \text{Hire}_{it}$)					0.003 (0.22)
Separations ($\text{Ln } \text{Sep}_{it}$)					−0.019 (1.09)
R^2	0.9911	0.9900	0.9912	0.9912	0.9905
Ln L	379.047	358.254	379.321	380.463	375.680
N	337	337	337	337	327

*Unstandardized coefficients are reported, with associated t-statistics in parentheses. Ln L is the natural logarithm of the likelihood function.
[a]Significantly different from one ($p < 0.000001$).

model shown in Column (1) of Table 12-1 is 0.75.[7] The estimation procedure does not yield a standard error for λ.[8] However, using the distribution of the likelihood ratio, we have determined that a 93% confidence interval for λ is roughly (0.65, 0.85). The hypothesis $\lambda = 1.0$ is very strongly rejected. Hence, the conventional measure of learning, cumulative output, significantly overstates the persistence of learning.

Indeed, these results indicate a rapid rate of depreciation. A value of $\lambda = 0.75$ implies that, from a stock of knowledge available at the beginning of a year, only 3.2% (0.75^{12}) would remain one year later. Thus, if the stock of knowledge is not replenished by continuing production, it depreciates rapidly. Even with a value of λ as high as 0.90, only 28% of a given stock of knowledge would remain one year later.

The contrast of Columns (1) and (2) of Table 12-1 provides further evidence that learning depreciates and that our knowledge variable is a better measure of learning than the conventional measure, lagged cumulative output. Column (1) is identical to Column (2) except that Column (1) includes the knowledge variable whereas Column (2) includes the conventional measure of learning. The log of the likelihood function in Column (1) is significantly greater than the log of the likelihood function in Column (2), $x^2 = 41.59$, $df = 1$, $p < 0.000001$.

Results presented in Column (3) of Table 12-1 show the effect of including the conventional measure of learning, lagged cumulative output, and the knowledge variable in the same model. When lagged cumulative output is included, the value of λ that maximizes the likelihood function is 0.75, as in Column (1). Moreover, cumulative lagged output has a small, statistically insignificant coefficient. This is further evidence that the knowledge variable captures the effects of learning better than cumulative output does.

In Column (4) calendar time is introduced to capture the possibility that technical change associated with the passage of time rather than learning is responsible for productivity improvements in shipbuilding. The negative coefficient for the time variable indicates that this is not the case. Further results concerning the time variable are discussed later in the section on more general production functions.

The depreciation of knowledge could be related to turnover. Therefore, labor turnover is included in the model shown in Column (5) of Table 12-1. There, the rate of new hires and the rate of separations were included as explanatory variables.[9] As can be seen from Column (5), these variables together do not contribute significantly to explaining changes in productivity. Additional analyses (available on request) revealed that neither variable makes a significant contribution when included separately. The estimate of the depreciation parameter in Column (5), $\lambda = 0.70$, indicates that knowledge depreciates rapidly when the effects of labor turnover are controlled for.

The results presented in Table 12-1 indicate that learning is acquired through experience in production. They also indicate that learning does not persist—knowledge acquired through production depreciates rapidly.[10] With the exception of the model that included calendar time, estimates of λ, the depreciation parameter, are all significantly less than one.

Transfer of Learning

Results on the transfer of learning are reported in Table 12-2. If knowledge acquired through production transfers across yards, the coefficient of AK_{t-1}, the knowledge variable summed across all yards, should be positive and significant. As can be seen from Column (1) of Table 12-2, this variable has a negative coefficient. This negative coefficient does not support the hypothesis of a transfer of

TABLE 12-2   Results Concerning the Transfer of Learning*

	(1)	(2)	(3)	(4)
Constant	−3.79 (12.73)	−3.65 (10.03)	−3.37 (9.52)	−3.40 (10.04)
Labor hours ($Ln\ H_{it}$)	0.18 (5.42)	0.13 (4.10)	0.13 (4.00)	0.14 (3.95)
Shipways ($Ln\ W_{it}$)	1.16 (21.64)	1.10 (22.03)	1.08 (22.11)	1.11 (19.34)
Knowledge ($Ln\ K_{it-1}$)	0.70 (29.47)	0.58 (18.80)	0.56 (16.72)	0.76 (15.31)
λ	0.70[a]	0.85[b]	0.88[b]	0.76[c]
Aggregate knowledge ($Ln\ AK_{t-1}$)	−0.06 (2.45)			−0.06 (1.66)
Start date (S_i)		0.027 (5.23)		
Calendar time (t)				−0.007 (2.34)
Aggregate cumulative output prior to start date ($Ln\ A_{S-1}$)			0.0003 (4.37)	
New hires ($Ln\ Hire_{it}$)				0.001 (0.11)
Separations ($Ln\ Sep_{it}$)				−0.015 (0.89)
R^2	0.9913	0.9897	0.9896	0.9906
$Ln\ L$	381.168	353.86	352.4115	377.6213
N	337	337	327	327

*Unstandardized coefficients are reported, with associated t-statistics shown in parentheses. $Ln\ L$ is the natural logarithm of the likelihood function.
[a]Significantly different from one ($p < 0.000001$).
[b]Significantly different from one ($p < 0.001$).
[c]Significantly different from one ($p < 0.05$).

learning. Similarly, when lagged cumulative output summed across all yards is included as an explanatory variable, it has a negative coefficient (results available on request).

Column (2) of Table 12-2 presents the results of our test of the hypothesis that yards with later start dates are more productive than yards with earlier start dates. The model in Column (2) was estimated without dummy variables for shipyards. Since the start dates can be written as a linear combination of the yard dummies, the coefficients would not be identified if the start dates and the yard dummies were both included.[11] The significant positive coefficient on variable S, the start date, in Column (2) of Table 12-2 suggests that yards with later start dates were more productive than yards with early start dates.

We also included cumulative output in all yards prior to start date as an explanatory variable to capture knowledge potentially available to each yard at the date it began production (see Column (3)). The variable also has a significant positive coefficient, indicating that when yards began production they benefited from production up to that date at other yards.[12]

Finally, we estimated a model that included all variables of interest. The start dates and aggregate cumulative output prior to the start dates could not be included in this model since these variables are perfectly correlated with the shipyard dummy variables. These results, which are presented in Column (4) of Table 12-2, are very similar to those reported earlier. The knowledge variable is positive and highly significant, and the depreciation parameter is significantly less than one. Thus, these results provide further evidence that knowledge acquired through production depreciates rapidly.

Robustness of the Results

In this section, we explore other potential explanations of our findings. Costs of changing the rate of output are often emphasized in discussions of production activities (e.g., Asher 1956). For example, Lockheed executives frequently mentioned the difficulties encountered when they increased the rate of production of the L-1011 (*Wall Street Journal*, 1980b, p. 19). We investigated the importance of adjustment costs in our data by including variables measuring the rate of change in input levels from one period to the next. While there is evidence that adjustment costs may be present in the Liberty Ship program, our results on the persistence and transfer of learning (available on request) are unchanged by the inclusion of the adjustment-cost variables.

We also investigated whether different results would be obtained with a more general specification of the production function. The analyses presented in Tables 12-1 and 12-2 employed the Cobb-Douglas specification. We performed additional analyses using the more general translog specification (Berndt and Christensen 1973). The translog model introduces $(\text{Ln } H)^2$, $(\text{Ln } W)^2$, and $\text{Ln } H \text{ Ln } W$ in addition to the terms appearing in the Cobb-Douglas production function. We estimated the translog for all versions of the model in Tables 12-1 and 12-2. In all cases except Column (2) of Table 12-1, the additional terms introduced for the translog are significant ($p < 0.05$). Estimates for λ in these alternative equations range from 0.62 to 0.80 and are all significantly less than one. Moreover, the coefficient estimate of the calendar time variable (which was negative and significant in Column (4) of Table 12-1) is smaller in magnitude and not significant in the translog model. Thus, the results with the more general translog model reinforce and amplify the results on transfer, persistence, and turnover reported earlier.

Use of cumulative output, the conventional measure of learning, in logarithmic form as in equation (1) implies that unit cost converges to zero as cumulative output increases. It may be that cumulative output is the correct measure of learning but that unit cost converges to a positive number rather than to zero. To investigate this possibility, we estimated Cobb-Douglas and translog production functions with both Ln K and $(\text{Ln } K)^2$ as predictors. This quadratic function, evaluated at values of K less than the value at which the function reaches a minimum, can approximate a function with a positive asymptote—even with no depreciation of learning. The maximum likelihood estimate of λ was significantly less than one when learning was included as a quadratic function. This provides further evidence that knowledge acquired through learning by doing depreciates rapidly (results available upon request).

All of the results reported here were obtained by use of ordinary least squares. Since there may be simultaneity in the choice of inputs and outputs, we estimated several of the equations using the nonlinear two-stage least-squares procedure of Amemiya (1974). The results were virtually identical to those obtained using ordinary least squares.[13]

The results consistently exhibit evidence of economies of scale in shipbuilding. For example, the results in Column (1) of Table 12-1 indicate that an increase in hours and shipways of one percent would result in a 1.31 percent increase in output, other things constant.[14] The knowledge variable, K, is highly significant when measures of labor hours and shipways are included in the models. Thus, the results indicate that when input effects and economies-of-scale effects are controlled for, there is strong evidence of learning.

Figure 12-1 illustrates the effects of economies of scale and depreciation on unit costs. In this simulation, input levels were held constant at the sample mean for the first 13 months of yard operation. The levels of inputs were halved in month 14 and held constant thereafter. The reduction in inputs caused an immediate increase in unit costs, indicated by the vertical line at the date of the reduction. This increase in unit costs is due to scale economies: the reduction in inputs results in a more than proportionate reduction in output. The increase in costs thereafter is due to the depreciation of knowledge. The reduction in inputs led to a reduction in output. This reduction in output then reduced the knowledge variable, K, because the gains in knowledge from current production were not sufficient to offset the losses in knowledge from depreciation of the previous period's stock. If inputs were held constant indefinitely at their new level, the stock of knowledge would eventually decline to a level sustained by production.

Finally, to test the generalizability of our results, especially to modern production environments, we obtained data for the production of an advanced jet produced in the 1970s and 1980s. Since these data were from a single firm, we

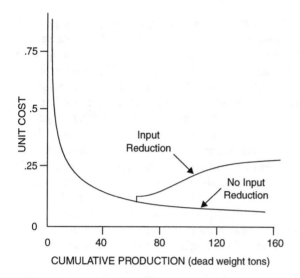

FIGURE 12-1
The Relationship Between Unit Costs and Cumulative Production When Inputs Are Reduced to Half Their Initial Levels

were able to examine persistence but not transfer. We found evidence of depreciation of knowledge in the production of the advanced jet. Thus, there is evidence that the results on persistence generalize to other production environments.

APPLICATION OF PERSISTENCE RESULTS

In this section, we apply our results on persistence to Lockheed's production of the L-1011 and suggest a possible explanation for the limited learning benefits Lockheed experienced. Our results on persistence indicate that cost forecasts based on cumulative output are likely to contain large errors for production programs in which there are variations in the rate of output over time. The production of the L-1011 TriStar was characterized by wide variations in the rate of output. Lockheed produced 17 planes in 1972, 39 in 1973, and 41 in 1974 (Lockheed Annual Report, 1972, p. 1; 1974, p. 8). Production dropped to 25 in 1975 (*Wall Street Journal,* 1976, p. 2), to 16 in 1976 (*Wall Street Journal,* 1977, p. 11), and to 6 in 1977 (*Aviation Week and Space Technology,* 1979, p. 32). Eight planes were produced in 1978 (*Wall Street Journal,* 1980b, p. 19). The rate of production was then increased to 25 per year until February 1981 when production was reduced to 18 per year (*Wall Street Journal,* 1981a, p. 10). Additional reductions to 12 or fewer per year were scheduled (*Wall Street Journal,* 1981C, pp. 1, 22) and plans to phase out production of the plane were announced on December 7, 1981 (*Wall Street Journal,* 1981b, p. 3).

For a wide range of values of the depreciation parameter, λ, in equation (2), Lockheed's production rates imply that the knowledge variable for the L-1011 peaked in late 1974 or early 1975 and then declined. A high value of the knowledge variable implies, of course, a low level of production costs. Based on these observations and on the hypothesis that Lockheed experienced depreciation of knowledge, we examined published reports to determine whether Lockheed's costs were relatively low in 1974 and 1975, and whether those costs rose subsequently as rates of production were reduced.

Lockheed estimated in 1973 that it would reach the point where production costs fell below price in mid-1974 (*Wall Street Journal*, 1974, p. 1). In November 1975, Lockheed reported that production costs were, in fact, less than the price at which each plane was being sold (*Wall Street Journal*, 1975, p. 1). Thus, it appears that production costs were below price during the period in which the knowledge variable K would have been highest if a depreciation parameter value on the order of that estimated in this paper is used. Cuts in production occurred in late 1975, and costs rose to exceed price—a situation that apparently persisted for the remainder of the production program (*Wall Street Journal*, 1980a, p. 12). The price at which the L-1011 sold increased more rapidly than inflation during this period, but production costs increased even more rapidly.[15]

A detailed analysis of L-1011 data would be required to test the hypothesis that depreciation of knowledge occurred. For example, it would be necessary to determine that the increase in costs that occurred when production was reduced was not due to scale economies, to the inclusion of overhead on fixed capital in the calculation of variable production costs, to changing wage rates,[16] or to adjustment costs. The pattern of costs reported by Lockheed, however, is consistent with the depreciation hypothesis. Given the huge sums of money lost by Lockheed on the TriStar program, averaging more than $125 million per year over the decade ending in 1980 (*Business Week*, 1980, p. 88), improved strategies for forecasting costs are clearly of great importance.

Reinhardt (1973) criticized Lockheed's analysis of the L-1011 program for omitting the opportunity cost of nonrecurring expenses for developing technology and production facilities for the L-1011. In his forecast of recurring production costs, Reinhardt used cumulative production as the measure of learning and arrived at a conclusion similar to Lockheed's: production costs would be below price at about the 50th plane. Our results on depreciation suggest that production costs would rise if the rate of production fell. Thus, it appears that allowing for depreciation of knowledge would have led to even more pessimistic forecasts than Reinhardt's analysis indicated.

CONCLUSION

Our results on persistence indicate that knowledge acquired in production depreciates rapidly. The conventional measure of learning, cumulative output, significantly overstates the persistence of learning. Controlling for labor turnover does not alter this conclusion.

These results on the lack of persistence of organizational learning are consistent with results in psychology on the lack of persistence of individual learning. Further, the results on the insignificance of turnover are consistent with the persistence results. Knowledge depreciates very rapidly—much more rapidly, than the rate of labor turnover.

Concerning transfer, our results indicate that shipyards beginning production later in the war were more productive than yards with early start dates. The initial gain in productivity may have been due to learning by doing in the design and construction of shipyards and the equipment used in them as well as to learning by doing in the construction of ships. Once shipyards began production they did not benefit from learning at other yards.

Why knowledge depreciates is an interesting question for future research. Theoretically, knowledge could depreciate because individuals forget how to perform their tasks or because individuals leave and are replaced by others with less experience. While there is no evidence that turnover contributed to depreciation in the Liberty Ship environment, it might matter in other organizational contexts. The jobs of production workers in the Liberty Ship program were highly standardized and designed to be low in skill requirements (Lane 1951). Turnover might matter more in contexts where employees are highly skilled and jobs are less standardized.

Depreciation could also be due to technological obsolescence. This might occur, for example, if a part is redesigned and new techniques must be learned to manufacture it. Technological obsolescence could also be due to process changes that make old skills obsolete.

Depreciation might also result from lost or inadequate organizational records. An interesting example of lost records occurred at the Steinway piano company.[17] Lenehan (1982) describes the difficulty Steinway had putting a discontinued piano, for which the company did not have any records, back into production.

The Steinway example illustrates how knowledge can depreciate when production is discontinued. Steinway's efforts to put the discontinued piano back into production also illustrate where and how knowledge can be embedded in organizations. An engineer at Steinway's New York plant, who had one of the models at home, took it apart and made drawings from the existing piano. He also located records at Steinway's Hamburg factory. In addition, the engineer tracked down an old foreman who loaned him his "black book," which contained very valuable information about how to make the piano. This example is consistent with theoretical treatments of organizational learning which suggest that knowledge can, to some extent, be embedded in individual employees, in the structure and culture of the organization and its records and routines, and in the organization's products and technology (e.g., see Hirsch 1952; Hayes and Wheelwright 1984; Levitt and March 1988).

While our results do not enable us to identify directly where knowledge was embedded in the Liberty Ship organizations, they suggest that certain factors were not prime sources. For example, the insignificance of the turnover variable suggests that the departure of direct production workers was not a prime determinant of depreciation. The initial gain in productivity experienced by shipyards beginning production later in the war may suggest that part of the knowledge acquired in the Liberty Ship program was embedded in technology. The results indicating rapid depreciation within shipyards, however, suggest that learning was not totally embedded in technology, since if it were, we should not see such rapid declines in productivity. Further support for this conclusion is provided by the finding that yard-specific production history was highly significant in explaining shipbuilding productivity, but neither time nor aggregate cumulative output was positively associated with productivity improvements. An interesting hypothesis, which is consistent with the results, is that learning was embedded in the various organizations—in their standard operating procedures, methods of communication and coordination, and shared understandings about how work is to be done (cf. March and Simon 1958; Levitt and March 1988).

If our result on depreciation turns out to be a fundamental feature of learning by doing, it has important strategic implications. A strategy of adopting high output levels during initial periods of production followed by relatively lower rates of output may be an effective way to increase productivity if learning is related to cumulative output (cf. Conley 1970), but is not necessarily preferable to a policy of relatively uniform production through time if learning is tied only to recent output. Further, in industries where learning does not persist, a firm with relatively low cumulative output such as a recent entrant to an industry need not be at a competitive disadvantage if its recent output levels are comparable to those of its rivals.

The results on depreciation also have important implications for forecasting production costs. Failure to allow for depreciation may result in forecasts with systematic errors. This is particularly likely to occur when a conventional learning curve based on cumulative output is estimated from a past production program and then used to forecast costs on a future program. If depreciation occurs and if the rate of output on the past program differs from that expected for the planned program, then the cost forecasts will contain systematic errors.

In closing, our results suggest that there is a substantial component of organizational learning that depreciates rapidly. Our results also provide evidence of a type of transfer: organizations beginning production later are more productive than those with early start dates. Once organizations begin production, however, they do not appear to benefit from learning at other organizations. It will be important to undertake further empirical research to determine the conditions under which our results concerning the persistence and transfer of learning hold. It will also be important to identify factors affecting the rate of learning and "forgetting" in organizations.[18]

NOTES

1. The psychological research on transfer typically examines how performing one task affects the performance of another task by the same individual. This research is not particularly relevant for examining transfer across organizations in the current study since there was virtually no movement of individual production workers across them.

2. Rapping (1965) also used these data in his investigation of whether learning occurred in the Liberty Ship program. The current study uses the data set to examine the persistence and transfer of learning.

3. Data on output are available from the beginning of production in each yard, but observations on other variables typically are unavailable until the yard has been operating for a month or more. Hence, the first month of production never appears in our sample. Consequently, K_{it-1} is always greater than zero and Ln K_{it-1} is always defined.

4. The error term ε_{it} in equation (3) is assumed to be serially uncorrelated and uncorrelated (in large samples) with all variables other than u_{it} on the right-hand side of equation (1). Furthermore, the ε_{it} are assumed to be mutually uncorrelated. The serial correlation coefficients are assumed to be the same across all shipyards.

5. The coefficients of the yard-specific dummy variables are not of particular interest so are not reported. A joint test of the null hypothesis that there are no yard-specific effects is rejected at a very high significance level ($p<0.001$), so important yard-specific effects appear to be present. Yard-specific dummy variables are included in all analyses, except where otherwise indicated.

6. Estimation is done using the following search procedure. Values of λ in the interval [0, 1] are chosen. With λ fixed, the remaining parameters are readily estimated by standard procedures for estimating regression models with autocorrelated errors. Hence, for each chosen value of λ, the remaining parameters are estimated. We began with a search over values of λ at increments of 0.05 in the interval [0, 1] to identify the subinterval in which the function reaches a maximum and then located the maximum by searching that subinterval at increments of λ of 0.01. The maximum likelihood estimates for the overall model are then the value of λ and the values of the associated coefficients which yield the largest value of the likelihood function. This procedure is equivalent to nonlinear search procedures that vary all parameters simultaneously, but is computationally easier to implement. This scanning procedure for maximum likelihood estimation is discussed in Goldfeld and Quandt (1972) and developed in greater detail by Dhrymes (1966).

7. The serial correlation coefficients are not of particular interest so are not reported. Third-order serial correlation coefficients all reached at least the 0.05 level of significance. This is not surprising since production of a ship required an average of two months, and longer periods were required early in production. Estimates of the other parameters are not sensitive to the order of serial correlation. For example, with either first or second-order autocorrelation, the maximum likelihood estimate of λ for the model in Column (1) of Table 12-1 is 0.80. Since autocorrelation coefficients up to third-order are significant, we adopted the third-order specification for the remaining analyses.

8. The standard errors of the remaining coefficients are computed treating λ as a known parameter. This may result in some understatement of the standard errors of the coefficients and a corresponding overstatement of the t-statistics. Therefore, all conclusions regarding significance of alternative measures of learning are based on likelihood ratio tests.

9. This run has fewer observations than previous runs because of missing data for rates of hires and separations. Hence, the likelihood function values for this equation cannot be compared to those for other equations in Table 12-1.

10. A referee expressed the concern that our persistence finding might possibly be an artifact of estimating monthly output by multiplying monthly production per shipway by an annual measure of shipways in use. This is a valid concern that, ideally, we would like to address by use of a direct measure of monthly production. Since we were unable to obtain such a measure of monthly production, we investigated the persistence issue using annual data (for which all variables are measured for the same time unit). We contrasted the explanatory power of lagged output (i.e., output in the previous year) with that of lagged cumulative output. Specifically, we estimated a model that included labor hours, shipways, lagged cumulative output, lagged output, and time. The coefficient of lagged output was positive and significant, $t=2.09$, $df=40$, $p<0.05$, while the coefficient of lagged cumulative output was negative and insignificant. These results indicate that recent experience is a significant predictor of learning while cumulative experience is not. Thus, the annual results support those obtained for the monthly data.

11. The equation in Column (2) of Table 12-2 is nested in Column (1) of Table 12-1. Because the equation in Column (1) of Table 12-1 has dummy variables (not shown in the table) that capture differences in productivity across yards due to differences in start dates as well as other yard-specific effects, the lower R^2 in Column (2) of Table 12-2, compared to that of Column (1) of Table 12-1, is to be expected.

12. This is the one issue on which our analyses of annual and monthly data differ. In the analysis of annual data, there is no evidence that yards with later start dates were more productive initially than yards with early start dates. Data disaggregated to monthly observations permit more precise measurement of the effects of start date than the annual data do. Hence, in this one instance of a difference between the annual and monthly analyses we are inclined to think that the results of the monthly analysis are more informative.

13. As instruments, we used current and lagged values of real wages, shipyard dummy variables, time and time squared, lagged endogenous variables (output, shipways, labor hours) and current and lagged exogenous variables. An appendix that explains the logic underlying our choice of instruments and presents the NL2SLS estimation results is available on request.

14. The results indicate that an increase in shipways would result in a more than proportionate increase in output, other things constant. One would expect that the incremental gains from adding shipways would diminish if a large number of additional shipways were added. Our results, including those with the translog production function, indicate that the yards did not add a sufficient number of shipways for this diminution to be encountered.

15. The price planes were sold for in 1975 was $20 million. Adjusted for inflation using the producer price index, this is equivalent to a price in 1968 dollars of $12.58 million. In 1982, the L-1011 was sold for more than $50 million per plane. The corresponding price in 1968 dollars is $18 million. Thus, in 1975, production cost per plane was less than $12.58 million in real terms while in 1982, production cost was greater than $18 million in real terms.

16. This problem does not arise in our analysis of the Liberty Ship program because we use physical units of inputs and output rather than dollar values.

17. We are grateful to one of the referees and the Associate Editor for suggesting this very interesting example.

18. This material is based upon work supported by the National Science Foundation under Grants RII-840991 and SES-8808711 and by the Center for Teaching and Research in Integrated Manufacturing Systems at Stanford University. Parts of the project were completed while the first author was a Visiting Assistant Professor and the second author was a Doctoral Candidate in the Department of Industrial Engineering and Engineering Management at Stanford University and the third author was a National Fellow at the Hoover Institution, Stanford University. The work has been presented at Carnegie Mellon University, Duke University, the University of Illinois, the University of Michigan, the University of Virginia, Stanford University, the 1987 ORSA/TIMS Meeting in St. Louis, and the 1987 Conference on Current Issues in Productivity at Rutgers University. The authors wish to thank participants in these forums, the reviewers, and Rukmini Devadas, Paul Goodman, Howard Gruenspecht, Paul Joskow, Robert Kaplan, Daniel Levinthal, Marvin Lieberman, John Muth, and Gerald Salancik for their very helpful comments.

REFERENCES

Alchian, A., "Reliability of Progress Curves in Air-frame Production," *Econometrica*, 31 (1963), 679–693.

Amemiya, T., "The Nonlinear Two-stage Least-squares Estimator," *J. Econometrics*, 2 (1974), 105–110.

Anzai, Y. and H. A. Simon, "The Theory of Learning by Doing," *Psychological Rev.*, 86 (1979), 124–140.

Asher, H., *Cost-Quantity Relationships in The Air-frame Industry*, Rand Corporation, Santa Monica, CA, 1956.

Aviation Week & Space Technology, "TriStar Production Costs Offset Lockheed Profits," (October 15, 1979), 32.

Baloff, N., "Estimating the Parameters of The Startup Model—An Empirical Approach," *J. Industrial Engineering*, 18 (1967), 248–253.

———. "Startup Management," *IEEE Trans.*, EM-17 (1970), 132–141.

Batchelder, C. A., H. E. Boren, H. G. Campbell, J. A. Dei Rossi and J. P. Large, *An Introduction to Equipment Cost Estimating*, Rand Corporation, Santa Monica, CA, 1969.

Berndt, E. R. and L. R. Christensen, "The Translog Function and The Substitution of Equipment, Structures, and Labor in U.S. Manufacturing 1929–68," *J. Econometrics*, 1 (1973), 81–113.

Business Week, "The TriStar's Trail of Red Ink," (July 28, 1980), 88.

Conley, P., "Experience Curves as a Planning Tool," *IEEE Spectrum*, 7 (1970), 63–68.

Dhrymes, P. J., "On the Treatment of Certain Recurrent Nonlinearities in Regression Analysis," *Southern Economic J.*, 23 (1966), 187–196.

Ebbinghaus, H., *Memory: A Contribution to Experimental Psychology* (Transl. by Henry A. Ruger and Clara E. Bussenius and with an introduction by Ernest Hilgard, 1964), Dover, New York, 1885.

Fisher, G. J., *A Statistical Summary of Shipbuilding Under the U.S. Maritime Commission During World War II*, Historical Reports of War Administration, United States Maritime Commission, 1949.

Goldfeld, S. M. and R. E. Quandt, *Nonlinear Methods in Econometrics,* North-Holland, Amsterdam, 1972.

Graham, C. H. and R. M. Gagné, "The Acquisition, Extinction, and Spontaneous Recovery of A Conditioned Operant Response," *J. Experimental Psychology,* 26 (1940), 251–280.

Guetzkow, H. and H. A. Simon, "The Impact of Certain Communication Nets upon Organization and Performance in Task-oriented Groups," *Management Sci.,* 1 (1954), 233–250.

Hayes, R. H. and S. C. Wheelwright, *Restoring our Competitive Edge: Competing through Manufacturing,* Wiley, New York, 1984.

Hirsch, W. Z., "Manufacturing Progress Functions," *Rev. Economics and Statist.,* 34 (1952), 143–155.

———, "Firm Progress Ratios," *Econometrica,* 24 (1956), 136–143.

Joskow, P. L. and N. L. Rose, "The Effects of Technological Change, Experience, and Environmental Regulation on the Construction Cost of Coal-burning Generating Units," *Rand J. Economics,* 16 (1985), 1–27.

Jucker, J. V., "The Transfer of Domestic-Market Production to a Foreign Site," *AIIE Trans.,* 9 (1977), 321–329.

Kelsey, S. F., S. M. Mullin, K. M. Detre, H. Mitchell, M. J. Cowley, A. R. Gruentzig and K. M. Kent, "Effect of Investigator Experience on Percutaneous Transluminal Coronary Angioplasty," *Amer. J. Cardiology,* 53 (1984), 56C–64C.

Kilbridge, M., "A Model for Industrial Learning Costs," *Management Sci.,* 8 (1962), 516–527.

Kolers, P. A., "Reading a Year Later," *J. Experimental Psychology: Human Learning and Memory,* 2 (1976), 554–565.

Lane, F. C., *Ships for Victory: A History of Shipbuilding under the U.S. Maritime Commission in World War II,* The Johns Hopkins Press, Baltimore, 1951.

Leavitt, H. J., "Some Effects of Certain Communication Patterns on Group Performance," *J. Abnormal and Social Psychology,* 46 (1951), 38–50.

Lenehan, M., "The Quality of the Instrument," *The Atlantic Monthly,* 250 (1982), 32–58.

Levitt, B. and J. G. March, "Organizational Learning," *Ann. Rev. Sociology,* 14 (1988), 319–340.

Levy, F. K., "Adaptation in the Production Process," *Management Sci.,* 11 (1965), B136–B151.

Lieberman, M. B., "The Learning Curve and Pricing in the Chemical Processing Industries," *Rand J. Economics,* 15 (1984), 213–228.

Lockheed Aircraft Corporation, *Lockheed Annual Report,* Corporate Publications, Burbank, CA 1972.

———, *Lockheed Annual Report,* Corporate Publications, Burbank, CA 1974.

March, J. G. and H. A. Simon, *Organizations,* Wiley, New York, 1958.

Mazur, J. E. and R. Hastie, "Learning as Accumulation: A Reexamination of The Learning Curve," *Psychological Bulletin,* 85 (1978), 1256–1274.

Newell, A. and P. S. Rosenbloom, "Mechanisms of Skill Acquisition and the Law of Practice," In J. R. Anderson (Ed.), *Cognitive Skills and their Acquisition,* Lawrence Erlbaum, Hillsdale, NJ, 1981, 1–55.

Preston, L. E. and E. C. Keachie, "Cost Functions and Progress Functions: An Integration," *Am. Economic Rev.,* 54 (1964), 100–107.

Rapping, L., "Learning and World War II Production Functions," *Rev. Economics and Statist.,* 47 (1965), 81–86.

Reinhardt, U. E., "Break-Even Analysis for Lockheed's Tri Star: An Application of Financial Theory," *J. Finance,* (1973), 821–838.

Sheshinski, E., "Tests of the Learning by Doing Hypothesis," *Rev. Economics and Statist.,* 49 (1967), 568–578.

Smunt, T. L., "The Impact of Worker Forgetting on Production Scheduling," *Internat. J. Production Res.,* 25 (1987), 689–701.

——— and T. E. Morton, "The Effect of Learning on Optimal Lot Sizes: Further Developments on the Single Product Case," *IIE Trans.,* 17 (1985), 33–37.

Spence, A. M., "The Learning Curve and Competition," *Bell J. Economics,* 12 (1981), 49–70.

Sule, D. R., "Effect of Learning and Forgetting on Economic Lot Size Scheduling Problem," *Internat. J. Production Res.,* 21 (1983), 771–786.

Thorndike, E. L., "Animal Intelligence: An Experimental Study of The Associative Processes in Animals," *The Psychological Rev.: Ser. Monograph Supplements,* 2 (1898), 1–109.

Thurstone, L. L., "The Learning Curve Equation," *Psychological Monographs,* 26 (1919), 1–51.

Wall Street Journal, "Lockheed is Planning a Write-down of $600 Million on Its TriStar in a Complex Financial Restructuring," (June 3, 1974), 1.

———, "Lockheed Net Soared 108% in 3rd Period but Outlook for TriStar Sales is Dismal," (November 7, 1975), 1.

———, "Lockheed Plans L-1011 Charges of $515 million," (March 31, 1976), 2.

———, "Lockheed Is Trying to Interest Airlines in Shorter-range Version of L-1011 Jet," (March 16, 1977), 11.

———, "Lockheed Loses Hope TriStar Program Will Show Profit but Sees Improvement," (May 14, 1980a), 12.

———, "Lockheed Losses on TriStar Grew in 2nd Quarter," (June 20, 1980b), 19.

———, "Lockheed to Cut L-1011 Production by Fall, Fueling Speculation on Plane's Survival," (July 1, 1981a), 10.

———, "Lockheed Plans to End Output of L-1011 Jet," (December 8, 1981b), 3.

———, "Delayed Takeoff: Stalled Jetliner Makers May Not Rise Steeply Even If the Airlines Do," (December 9, 1981c), 1, 22.

Wickelgren, W. A., "Memory Storage Dynamics," In W. K. Estes (Ed.), *Handbook of Learning and Cognitive Processes,* 4, Lawrence Erlbaum Associates, Hillsdale, NJ, 1976, 321–361.

Womer, N. K., "Learning Curves, Production Rate, and Program Costs," *Management Sci.,* 25 (1979), 312–319.

———, "Estimating Learning Curves from Aggregate Monthly Data," *Management Sci.,* 30 (1984), 982–992.

Wright, T. P., "Factors Affecting the Costs of Airplanes," *J. Aeronautical Sci.,* 3 (1936), 122–128.

Yelle, L. E., "The Learning Curve: Historical Review and Comprehensive Survey," *Decision Sci.*, 10 (1979), 302–328.

Zimmerman, M. B., "Learning Effects and the Commercialization of New Energy Technologies: The Case of Nuclear Power," *Bell J. Economics*, 13 (1982), 297–310.

13

Two Strategies for Economic Development: Using Ideas and Producing Ideas

Paul M. Romer

The central claim of this paper is that the difference between the economics of ideas and the economics of objects is important for our understanding of growth and development. A subsidiary claim is that academic and policy discussions in these areas might be more fruitful if we spent less time working out solutions to systems of equations and more time defining precisely what the words we use mean. The notion that ideas are different from objects is both familiar and obvious. In the economic analysis of patents, for example, there is a long tradition of recognizing the unique characteristics of ideas as economic goods. The content of the claim lies in the assertion that these differences are more subtle than some presentations suggest and that they matter for aggregate-level policy analysis.

All too often, economists concerned with the economy as a whole have been willing to treat the economics of ideas as a footnote to the rest of economic analysis—important for understanding some of the details but not something that changes how we think about big policy questions. A neoclassical model with perfect competition and exogenous technological change continues to frame many, if not most, policy discussions of growth and development. Ideas are routinely ignored.

In what follows, two kinds of support are offered for the claim that ideas should be our central concern: abstract arguments about the economic attributes of ideas and descriptions of the role that ideas played in two cases of successful economic development. The abstract arguments presented in the first part of the

From *Proceedings of the World Bank Annual Conference on Development Economics 1992.* Copyright © 1993 The International Bank for Reconstruction of Development/The World Bank. Reprinted by permission.

Paul M. Romer is a professor at the University of California, Berkeley. The author would like to thank conference participants and the discussants for much useful feedback. Detailed comments by George Akerlof, Curtis Eaton, Richard Lipsey, and David Romer were also very helpful. This work was supported by National Science Foundation grant SES 9023469.

paper proceed from the observation that ideas are extremely important economic goods, far more important than the objects emphasized in most economic models. In a world with physical limits, it is discoveries of big ideas (for example, how to make high-temperature superconductors), together with the discovery of millions of little ideas (better ways to sew a shirt), that make persistent economic growth possible. Ideas are the instructions that let us combine limited physical resources in arrangements that are ever more valuable.

As economic goods, ideas differ from objects in ways that are more subtle than traditional aggregate models allow. The familiar description of an idea as a public good like a lighthouse beacon overlooks the fact that many ideas are controlled by private individuals who respond to market incentives. An equally misleading approach is to equate ideas with human capital and to treat them as conventional private goods. This misses the notion, correctly suggested by the public good analogy, that an idea can be used by many people at the same time. Adding external effects or spillovers to human capital and physical capital comes no closer to capturing the essential attributes of ideas. Externalities suggest incomplete control or appropriability, but they do not capture the absence of opportunity costs that is the key characteristic of an idea. The combination of some degree of private control and an absence of opportunity costs means that ideas are neither public goods nor private goods—nor a mixture of the two.

To address a frequently expressed objection to this description of an idea, the abstract discussion acknowledges that ideas are used in fixed proportions with objects that do have an opportunity cost. For example, the bit string representing a computer program can be used by an unlimited number of people with no loss of functionality for the first user. In practice, however, it takes a floppy disk to make a copy of the bit string for another user, and the floppy disk does have an opportunity cost. The distinction between capital and labor is useful even though both are needed to produce output; so is the distinction between the bit string and the floppy disk.

The abstract analysis of ideas has special relevance for poor countries. Industrial countries possess a stock of ideas that could yield large increases in standards of living if they were put to use throughout the world. Moreover, since the use of an idea by one person does not limit its use by someone else, the large potential gains available to developing countries need not come at the expense of industrial countries.

In the few instances in which ideas have been controlled by international aid organizations, we can see just how large the gains from worldwide dissemination can be. The idea behind the smallpox vaccine has now eliminated this disease from every country on earth. The simple idea behind oral rehydration therapy has saved the lives of millions of children who would otherwise have died from diarrhea.

These examples suggest the magnitude of the gains that ideas can offer, but they are not typical. Most ideas with economic value are not controlled by a charitable organization willing to bear the costs of dissemination. Instead, they are controlled by people who will not incur the costs needed to share what they know unless they have a monetary incentive to do so. As a result, the gains from the dissemination of ideas will not be realized if distortions, weak institutions, and bad political structures prevent the holders of ideas from sharing in the gains that accrue when the ideas are brought to a new geographic area.

For this reason, the logic behind the economics of ideas supports the new development orthodoxy that a policy of openness with few distortions offers the potential for large gains in poor countries. The experience in Mauritius, the first of the two economies considered below, supports this view. A poor island whose prospects for development once seemed very bleak, Mauritius successfully exploited a development strategy that consisted almost entirely of trying to make use of ideas that already existed in industrial countries by encouraging foreigners to produce there. This is the first of the two strategies noted in the title of this paper: using ideas. Judging from the increased receptivity of many poor countries to direct foreign investment, it appears that this strategy is gaining favor.

Yet as important as this strategy can be during the early stages of development, the analysis also suggests that there may be limits to how far it can take an economy. Both the experience in the second economy discussed, Taiwan (China), and the logic behind the analysis of ideas suggest that some interventions may encourage growth at intermediate stages of development. Taiwan pursued the second strategy described in the title—producing ideas—and intervention by the government seems to have contributed to the strategy's success.

Most economists would acknowledge that some kinds of intervention to support the production of ideas are appropriate. Few would challenge the assertion that governments should subsidize education and some forms of research. If one follows the logic of the economics of ideas, one sees that there is no basis in economic theory (as opposed to political theory) for restricting government intervention to support for education and research.

Many economists are also convinced that restrictions on trade and direct foreign investment are bad policy instruments for encouraging development. Yet the evidence from Taiwan (China) suggests that those policies were useful there. These observations can be reconciled by adding a political and institutional analysis to the economic analysis. An economic analysis based on the economics of ideas suggests that trade and investment restrictions can be growth-enhancing only if they are complemented by other policies such as support for education and rigorous standards of performance for protected firms. To be effective, these policies must be implemented by a government that is immune to the political pressures associated with rent-seeking and that possesses a competent and relatively honest bureaucracy. Because these conditions are not met in most of the world, restrictions on trade and investment will almost always be counterproductive. The challenge is to find better forms of government intervention, ones that have better economic effects and pose fewer political and institutional risks.

The temptation for economists, however, has always been to duck the complicated political and institutional issues that this kind of analysis raises and instead to work backward from a desired policy conclusion to a simple economic model that supports it. According to this approach, if we want to discourage counterproductive restrictions on trade and foreign investment in most countries of the world, then the right model is one with perfect markets so that intervention can be shown to be everywhere and always a mistake.

The motivation behind this paper comes from a belief that the poor people of the world will be better served if we resist this temptation and meet head-on the intellectual challenge presented by the economics of ideas. In industrial countries a number of government interventions have evolved to encourage the production and dissemination of ideas. Examples include patents, copyrights, laws to protect trade secrets, subsidies for education at all levels, peer-reviewed research grants, and agricultural extension services. These interventions have been relatively free of political manipulation and, despite some weaknesses, are generally regarded as having had a positive effect.

The same arrogance that made people at the turn of the century think that almost everything had already been invented sometimes leads us to think that there is nothing left to discover about the institutions that can encourage economic development. It is conceivable that the institutions now present in industrial countries exhaust the list of beneficial interventions that would fit the circumstances of low- and middle-income countries. It is far more likely that there are undiscovered institutional arrangements that would work even better. We will never know if we always look at the evidence through a theoretical lens that does not let us consider this possibility.

MODELS AND METAPHORS

Most theoretical discussions of economic growth revolve around a few mathematical equations built from abstractions such as an aggregate production function. Because of its simplicity, theorists sometimes call such a system of equations a toy model to distinguish it from a multiequation simulation or forecasting model. The label is apt because a good theoretical model should be as easy to manipulate in one's head as the mental image of a child's toy. That is, a successful model invokes a metaphor, and the metaphor has a subtle but pervasive effect on the reader's understanding of the principles behind the equations and his or her belief in the accuracy of its description of the world. To show how one model can obscure our vision of the role of ideas and how a different model can highlight their role, it helps to start by being unusually explicit and concrete about the metaphors behind the math.

A Toy Model

One of the great successes of neoclassical economics has been the elaboration and extension of the metaphor of the factory that is invoked by a production function. To be explicit about this image, recall the child's toy called the Play-Doh Fun Factory. To operate the Fun Factory, a child puts Play-Doh (a form of modeling compound) into the back of the toy and pushes on a plunger that applies pressure. The Play-Doh is extruded through an opening in the front of the toy. Depending on the particular die used to form the opening, out come solid Play-Doh rods, Play-Doh l-beams, or lengths of hollow Play-Doh pipe.

We use the Fun Factory model or something just like it to describe how capital (the Fun Factory) and labor (the child's strength) change the characteristics of goods, converting them from less valuable forms (lumps of modeling compound) into more valuable forms (lengths of pipe). In most applications we imagine that the characteristics being changed are physical characteristics such as shape, chemical composition, or connections with other objects. We push the model slightly when we recognize that the date and location at which a good is available are also relevant characteristics, ones that can be changed by storage and transport. We push the model much further by extending the list of characteristics that can be changed to include a description of who holds property rights. Wallis and North (1986) estimate that by 1970 the transformation of property rights accounted for nearly one-half of gross national product in the United States, so this last extension is particularly important.

The Fun Factory metaphor is powerful because our intuition about production can be pushed to encompass transformation activities and levels of economic analysis far removed from the factory floor. When a worker with a welding rig attaches parts on a car, when a driver with a semitrailer truck moves the car, when a dealer with a showroom sells the car, when a banker with a computer prepares the loan, and when an agent with a tow truck repossesses the car, labor and capital are used to change the characteristics of the underlying goods. In this kind of analysis, the productive unit can range from a household to a firm or industry, even to the nation or the world as a whole.

The production function and the Fun Factory metaphor have been widely used in the neoclassical analysis of aggregate growth. Yet in this analysis the neoclassical model has been successful primarily at establishing a diagnosis by exclusion. Economic growth cannot be understood solely in terms of the accumulation of physical capital and labor—the fundamental concepts in the underlying metaphor. This insight, of course, was Solow's famous result (1957), and it stands to this day despite an enormous effort at refining the econometric techniques for measuring a growth-accounting residual and at extending the notion of effective labor to allow for accumulation of human capital. The formal growth-accounting evidence, historical accounts, and everyday experience all suggest that something extra, something like innovation, invention, technological change, or the discovery of new ideas, is needed to understand and explain growth. Yet, having made this point, the Fun Factory metaphor offers no guidance about what an idea is, where ideas come from, and how the presence of ideas might matter for development strategy.

Other Toy Models

Another child's toy is a chemistry set. For this discussion, the set can be represented as a collection of N jars, each containing a different chemical element. From the child's point of view, the excitement of this toy comes from trying to find some combination of the underlying chemicals that, when mixed together and heated, does something more impressive than change colors (explode, for example). In a set with N jars, there are 2^N-1 different mixtures of K elements, where K varies between 1 and N. (There are many more mixtures if we take account of the proportions in which ingredients can be mixed and the different pressures and temperatures that can be used during mixing.)

As N grows, what computer scientists refer to as the curse of dimensionality sets in. The number of possible mixtures grows exponentially with N, the dimension of this system. For a modestly large chemistry set, the number of possible mixtures is far too large for the toy manufacturer to have directly verified that no mixture is explosive. If N is equal to 100, there are about 10^{30} different mixtures that an adventurous child could conceivably put in a test tube and hold over a flame. If every living person on earth (about 5 billion) had tried a different mixture each second since the universe began (no more than 20 billion years ago), we would still have tested less than 1 percent of all the possible combinations.

Within the metaphor of the chemistry set, it is obvious what one means by an idea. Any mixture can be recorded as a bit string, an ordered sequence of 0s and 1s of length 100. The bit at position j is set to 1 if element j is included in the mixture. In the crude representation used here, an idea is the increment in information that comes from sorting some of the bit strings into two broad categories: useful ones and useless ones. To represent this information, we can add two more bits on the end of each bit string describing a mixture. These are set at 00 if we know nothing about its properties, 10 if it is a useful mixture, and 01 if it is useless.

When a useful mixture is discovered and its trailing bits are changed from 00 to 10, the discovery makes possible the creation of economic value. It lets us combine raw materials of low intrinsic value into mixtures that are far more valuable. Once we have the idea, the process of mixing will require its own Fun Factory (specialized capital and labor). For example, the bit string representing nylon requires a chemical processing plant and skilled workers. Important as these tangible inputs are, it is still the idea itself that permits the resulting increase in value. In this fundamental sense, ideas make growth and development possible.

The potential for continued economic growth comes from the vast search space that we can explore. The curse of dimensionality is, for economic purposes, a remarkable blessing. To appreciate the potential for discovery, one need only consider the possibility that an extremely small fraction of the large number of possible mixtures may be valuable.

There is a branch of physical chemistry that literally cooks up mixtures from the periodic table of elements. New mixtures to be evaluated are selected on the basis of theory, experience, and guesswork. Supporters call this "exploratory synthesis"; detractors call it "heat and beat" or "shake and bake" chemistry. A group of French chemists cooked up one of the 10^{30} possible mixtures, one consisting of lanthanum, barium, copper, and oxygen. More than a decade later, scientists at IBM decided to test the superconductivity properties of the resulting ceramic, even though the prevailing wisdom suggested that it violated several of the basic rules required of a candidate for a good superconductor. The IBM team won the Nobel Prize in physics for their discovery that this mixture became a superconductor at temperatures far exceeding those for all the known superconductors.

This "high-tech" example of a valuable mixture suggests only a small part of the enormous scope for making discoveries of economic importance. If a garment factory requires 52 distinct independent steps to assemble a shirt, there are $52! = 10^{68}$ different ways to order these steps in sequence. The number 52 is a useful reference point because it arises with another familiar toy, a deck of cards. The number of possible orderings for the 52 assembly operations is the same as the number of possible ways to arrange a shuffled deck of cards.

Even though it arises from a very simple toy, a number such as 10^{68} is very big, even in comparison with numbers like 10^{30}. (The total number of protons and electrons in the visible universe is estimated to be on the order of 10^{79}.) For any realistic garment assembly operation, almost all the possible sequences for the steps would be wildly impractical, but if even a very small fraction of sequences is useful, there will be many such sequences. It is therefore extremely unlikely that any actual sequence that humans have used for sewing a shirt is the best possible one.

Corporations that understand this point recognize that there will always be at least as much scope for improvement through large numbers of small changes in the way things are done in a manufacturing process as through laboratory research. Accordingly, they have promoted worker experimentation and systems for encouraging wide adoption of discoveries made on the line.

Conventional wisdom tends to suggest that all the important ideas come from research labs and that nothing remains to be discovered about mundane activities such as assembly line operation or garment assembly—but conventional wisdom completely missed the potential for "continuous improvement," as implemented in Japanese automobile assembly, just as it missed the potential for high-temperature superconductors made from ceramics. To understand growth, we need to understand not only how big ideas, such as high-temperature superconductors, are discovered and put to use but also how millions of little ideas, such as better ways to assemble shirts, are discovered and put to use. To understand development, we need to understand how both kinds of ideas, but especially the millions of small ones, can be used and produced in a developing country.

Human Capital

It is possible to add human capital to both the Fun Factory and the chemistry set models, and it is instructive to do so. In the Fun Factory model there are only two basic kinds of inputs, human and nonhuman. Physical capital is an aggregate of many different durable nonhuman inputs. The concept of human capital lets us recognize and aggregate different kinds of human inputs. One person may be more productive than another, just as one machine may be more valuable than another. Some of the differences in productivity among workers are the result of investments and are durable, so the analogy with capital is close.

As powerful as this analogy is in labor economics, it sheds little light on the fundamental processes that generate growth. In some proximate sense it must be true that increases in human capital and physical capital explain the increases in value that we have experienced. But what does it really mean to say that the average worker today has several times the effective labor power of a worker in the last century? In a biological sense the population of workers today is virtually identical to the population that existed then.

To see how the same physical objects can be arranged in more valuable ways, consider first an example involving physical capital. The computer that I used to write this paper is about fifty times faster than the one I used just ten years ago, yet it is constructed from just about the same assortment of aluminum, copper, steel, plastic, silicon, and other raw materials. It is manufactured in about the same way and is sold for about the same price.

Now consider human capital. In my brain there are different physical connections between my neurons. These connections store the commands I need to use the new computer and new word-processing software. Just as my new computer is a more productive piece of physical capital, I have more valuable human capital than I did ten years ago.

From the point of view of the chemistry set model, the increase in the value of human and physical capital that is possible using fixed tangible inputs is just like the increase in value that arises when elements such as lanthanum, barium, oxygen, and copper are combined to make a high-temperature superconductor. The knowledge that one mixture or arrangement is more valuable than another is just like the knowledge that changing the layout in a microprocessor increases its processing power, that a different design for a hard disk will increase its storage capacity, or that storing the bit string representing the word-processing software on my hard disk will make the computer more useful. It is also just like the knowledge that reading a software manual rearranges connections in my brain and makes my human capital more valuable. (For later reference, note that on-the-job experience with the software is also extremely important for establishing and reinforcing these connections.)

In some accounting sense the combined increase in the value of human and physical capital explains the increased productivity in word-processing experienced in my office. But to explain productivity growth through these increases in human and physical capital begs the question of where the increased value of the capital originates. The increased value is created by new ideas. Whether it takes the form of a hardware design, software code, or an instruction manual, an idea is used to mix or arrange roughly the same physical ingredients in ways that are more valuable. And in each case, these ideas can be represented as pure pieces of information, as bit strings.

Ideas are therefore the critical input in the production of more valuable human and nonhuman capital. But human capital is also the most important input in the production of new ideas. Physical capital (a computer, for example) is sometimes used in an ancillary way, but a trained person is still the central input in the process of trial and error, experimentation, guessing, hypothesis formation, and articulation that ultimately generates a valuable new idea that can be communicated to and used by others.

Because human capital and ideas are so closely related as inputs and outputs, it is tempting to aggregate them into a single type of good. After all, structures and equipment are different goods, and they both fit rather well in the category of physical capital. It is important, nevertheless, to distinguish ideas and human capital because they have different fundamental attributes as economic goods, with different implications for economic theory.

Attributes of Economic Goods

Figure 13-1 illustrates a two-way classification of different types of economic goods that has been useful in the economics of public finance. The vertical axis measures the degree of control or excludability (or appropriability) that is feasible for a good. The left-hand column lists rival goods—goods that are object-like in the sense that they have an opportunity cost. (The label "rival" reflects the fact that you and I are rivals for the use of one of these goods.) The right-hand column lists nonrival goods, which are like bit strings in the sense that everyone can use them at the same time.

As traditionally defined, a private good in public finance is one that lies in the upper-left-hand corner of the figure; it is both rival and fully excludable. According to this definition, human capital is as close to a perfect private good as one can get. There is no way for anyone to take advantage of my ability to remember commands for my word processor without getting my permission; therefore my ability is fully excludable or is subject to complete control by me. And because

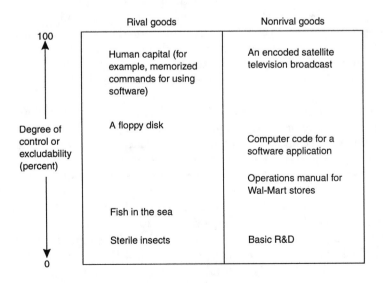

FIGURE 13-1   Economic Attributes of Selected Goods

there is also no way for many people to make use of my ability at the same time, it is a rival good.

Many economists will find these assertions surprising. We often assert that there are spillovers from human capital, such as incomplete control or excludability. We also have an intuition that since I can teach others to do what I can do, what I know is nonrival. After I teach them, we will all be using the same computer commands at the same time.

These imprecise statements are the result of a failure to distinguish among human capital, the ideas that help produce human capital, and the ideas that human capital can produce. My human capital is literally a set of connections between neurons. Converting this rival good into a nonrival good—for example by putting what I know into comprehensible prose on paper—is a time-consuming activity. Once what I know is expressed in words, it can indeed be used by many people (neglecting for now the trivial cost of making a photocopy). As each person reads my words, the nonrival bit string represented by the text is converted back into the rival human capital. Human capital is therefore used to produce ideas, and ideas are used to produce human capital, but human capital and ideas are conceptually distinct goods. They occupy different places in Figure 13-1 and have different implications for economic analysis.

The bit strings, or the how-to manual for using software, would be nonrival, not the connections in my brain. The bit string would also be difficult to control, as every software firm knows. For most of the successful computer programs, someone has written a book that is a substitute for the original manual and can be used by someone who has bootleg copies of the code for the program.

When I bought my software, I purchased a manual, several floppy disks, and the legal right to use the bit string representing the computer code. I used the manual to produce some human capital that is easy for me to control. The floppy disks themselves are somewhat harder to control because they could be stolen. For this reason they are listed farther down the column of rival goods. The software code is even harder to control because it can be taken without the knowledge of the owner. This feature tends to make all nonrival goods less excludable and more difficult to control.

Because nonrivalry and limited control are correlated in practice, many informal discussions of ideas do not distinguish carefully between the two concepts, but for economic analysis the difference is important. Private firms survive in the business of writing and selling very costly computer code: therefore they must be able to assert some control over it. Software code is, however, the quintessential nonrival good. Most ideas of economic significance lie in the upper right portion of Figure 13-1. They are nonrival and at least partially excludable.

Such goods are very different from the goods in the lower left side of the figure, the ones that are rival but impossible to control. Fish in the sea are the most familiar example for economists. Only one person can eat a fish. Sterile insects used to prevent the reproduction of agricultural pests are another example. A sterile male insect can mate with unsuspecting fertile insects in one valley or the other, but not in both at the same time. Because it is so difficult to establish property rights over these kinds of goods, market outcomes are inefficient. We overfish, and we underprovide sterile insects. Our understanding of the policy implications of this part of the figure is very clear. Property rights should be provided where possible—for example, tradable rights to catch fish. Where this is not possible, as in the case of the insects, the government must supply the good and use its tax power to cover the costs.

Although the sterile insects seem to be examples of public goods in the everyday use of the term (things that are provided by the government), the formal definition of a public good used by economists is one that lies in the lower right of Figure 13-1; it is a good that is both nonexcludable and nonrival. Basic scientific research is perhaps the best example of a pure public good in this sense. Our understanding of how vaccines prevent disease and how drinking water mixed with electrolytes can prevent death from diarrhea both come from public support for basic research.

In the left-hand column (the rival goods), the policy implication is to move up the column—to create property rights whenever possible and to make them as strong as possible. For nonrival goods, this conclusion does not follow. Property rights to a nonrival good always imply a market price for the good that is higher than its opportunity cost because the opportunity cost is zero. As the usual analysis of patents suggests, strong property rights and the resulting monopoly profits are desirable because they create an incentive to discover new ideas, but they are undesirable because the difference between price and marginal cost creates distortions.

Depending on the type of good involved, we craft different solutions to this conflict between the two conditions required for efficiency. In some cases it is relatively clear which directions for new discoveries are worth pursuing, and the social cost of setting a price higher than marginal cost is very high. In these cases—for example in public health—the government pays for the research and gives the results away. In other cases the government has no mechanism for deciding what to produce, and the social costs of prices higher than marginal cost seem trivial—for example, in the production of popular music (which these days is literally a bit string on a compact disc). In areas such as biotechnology and software it is unclear exactly how we should proceed. We do not know whether a gene fragment or a programming concept such as overlapping windows should be protected by law or, if so, whether the law of copyrights, patents, or trade secrets should be used.

For thinking about growth and development, the important implications of Figure 13-1 are as follows. First, the distinction between objects and ideas (between rival and nonrival goods) is far more important than the concept of excludability or control or the related concepts of spillovers and externalities. An approach to economic policymaking that neglects nonrival goods will miss most of the interesting issues.

Second, nonrival goods have the unique feature that their value depends on the size of the market in which they can be used. This is obvious for an idea such as the vaccine that is treated as a pure public good but is equally true for nonrival goods such as software or even ideas about how to run a discount store. If Bill Gates could have sold software only in Washington state, or if Sam Walton could have opened discount stores only in Arkansas, they would have been millionaires, at best, instead of the billionaires they became. This is the other side of the gains from trade that ideas can generate if they are widely used.

Third, any discussion of an economy in which nonrival goods such as software are privately provided must allow for departures from price-taking. The textbook description of perfect price-taking competition is logically inconsistent with the private provision of nonrival goods. Even in a case in which a bit string (for example, computer code) must be sold together with an object (for example, a floppy disk), monopoly pricing must still apply. The package consisting of the code and the disk will have a positive marginal cost equal to the cost of the disk, but the package must still sell for a price higher than marginal cost, or no one would be able to earn a return on effort devoted to writing software. Casual empiricism suggests that software sells for a price that is 10 to 100 times marginal cost.

Fourth, and finally, there is no hope that a decentralized equilibrium in which new ideas are discovered will be first-best Pareto optimal. The usual justification for the welfare theorems in terms of price-taking does not apply. No comparable justification on the basis of the Coase theorem will work unless it replicates the essence of a government—a decisionmaker with powers of coercion over everyone else in the economy.

This last point is clear only in a general equilibrium setting, which perhaps explains why it has not been adequately emphasized. In partial equilibrium analysis, price-setting by a monopolist is consistent with Pareto optimality if control or the ability to contract is strong enough. For example, we know that a perfectly discriminating monopolist or a monopolist who charges a two-part tariff can produce the efficient level of output in a partial equilibrium model.

This partial equilibrium analysis simply does not extend to the economy as a whole. It violates a fundamental adding-up condition. Output for any particular activity can be written as $y = f(k, h; a)$, where h and k are lists of all the different human and nonhuman rival goods that are used in production and a is the idea or knowledge that makes this activity possible. For fixed a, we can think of the production of y in terms of the Fun Factory metaphor. By a standard replication argument, f is homogeneous of degree 1 in the rival goods that must be replicated to make a copy of the existing activity. But Euler's theorem tells us that h and k will exhaust the total value of output in this activity if competition is used to allocate these goods and they are paid their value marginal products. Nothing will be left to pay for a.

What is true for one activity is equally true for the economy as a whole. If aggregate output is written as $Y = F(H, K; A)$, F will be homogeneous of degree 1 in the human and nonhuman rival inputs. It is therefore impossible to use prices to allocate H and K between different activities and at the same time provide the incentives for discovering ideas, A. There is not enough income in the economy as a whole to go around. (See Romer 1990a for an elaboration of this point.)

TWO ISLANDS

The challenge now is to use the analytical framework outlined above to discuss the different economic activities taking place in Mauritius and in Taiwan (China). In both economies government policy is attuned to the role of ideas. In Mauritius policy changes in the 1970s and 1980s made it attractive for entrepreneurs from Hong Kong to put their ideas to use there. As a result, the citizens of Mauritius achieved large increases in income and employment. A more clear-cut case of the gains from trade could hardly be imagined. In Taiwan (China) ideas from the rest of the world are not merely put to work with domestic labor. To a much greater extent than in Mauritius, the government intervened in market exchange in its attempts to encourage the domestic production and exploitation of ideas that can earn a return on world markets.

Using Ideas: Mauritius

Table 13-1 reports some basic economic and social indicators for Mauritius over the interval from 1960 to 1985. For comparison, data are also presented for two economies with similar ethnic and economic backgrounds, India and Sri

TABLE 13-1   Economic Performance, 1960–88

Indicator	Mauritius	India	Sri Lanka	Taiwan China
Rate of growth of income per capita, 1960–88	2.8	0.9	1.3	6.4
Rate of growth of population, 1960–88	1.7	2.2	1.9	2.2
Income per capital, 1960 1985 U.S. dollars	2,000	600	1,400	950
Share of investment in GDP, 1960–88	12	17	21	23
Literacy rate, 1960	60	28	75	54
Primary school enrollment rate, 1960	98	61	95	96
Average years of schooling, labor force, 1986	4.5	1.9	6.2	8.4

%, except as otherwise specified.
Sources: For income, investment, and population, Heston and Summers (1991); for literacy and schooling, Levine and Renelt (1992).

Lanka, and for Taiwan (China), which is discussed below. In Mauritius the share of investment in gross domestic product (GDP) is no better than that in the other three economies and in the Heston-Summers data used here, it is substantially lower.[1] Investment in human capital, while better than in India, is not outstanding. Income per capita at the beginning of the sample period was higher than in the other three economies because of the high income earned by the wealthy owners of sugar plantations, but the distribution of income was very uneven.

When Mauritius was preparing for independence from Great Britain in the 1960s, prospects for development did not seem promising. The economy was dependent on sugar exports for 99 percent of its exports. James Meade, commissioned by the British government to comment on economic policy, entitled his 1961 report "Mauritius: A Case Study in Malthusian Economics" and devoted it to a discussion of how to cope with a real wage that would inevitably fall as population on the island grew. Young people with higher levels of education were encouraged to emigrate, but it was feared that not enough would leave. A local import-substituting manufacturing sector existed only because of protective tariffs.[2]

Since independence in 1968, the political situation has been fluid, almost to the point of instability. Up to the present, corruption, fraud, and drug trafficking have been a continuing source of government scandals. Political parties are organized along ethnic and religious (primarily Hindu and Muslim) divisions. There has been no majority government since independence. The emergence of a left-leaning party and the strikes that it organized in 1971 provoked an assassination attempt instigated by members of a rival party. This led to public riots and a state of emergency that lasted until 1976. Unions were suspended, and union and party leaders were arrested.

The average growth rate for per capita income of nearly 3 percent a year during 1960–88 was achieved despite the terms of trade shocks experienced by all primary goods exporters in the 1970s. Sugar prices soared in the early part of the decade, then fell dramatically in the second half just as oil prices went up. This led to predictable macroeconomic difficulties (budget deficits, inflation, and a balance of payments crisis), followed by a period of austerity and adjustment that was associated with zero growth during the five years from 1978 to 1982. Most of the growth that took place came in two brief spurts, one in the first part of the 1970s and the other in the latter part of the 1980s.

Despite all this, Mauritius stands out as a significant and surprising success story when compared, for example, with India and Sri Lanka. The only obvious candidate for explaining the success of Mauritius is the island's policy of supporting an export-processing zone (EPZ), which made investment attractive to foreigners. The EPZ was an administrative arrangement; it involved no geographic restrictions and no special investment in infrastructure. The main policies in this arrangement were unrestricted, tariff-free imports of machinery and materials, no restrictions on ownership or repatriation of profits, a ten-year income tax holiday for foreign investors, a policy of centralized government wage-setting, and an implicit assurance that labor unrest would be suppressed and wage increases would be moderate.

From the inception of the arrangement in 1971, employment in the EPZ grew to 17,000 workers by 1978, a significant number on an island with a total population of about 1 million. Over this same interval GDP per capita grew at 9 percent a year, fueled partly by the EPZ and partly by favorable sugar prices and harvests. During the macroeconomic difficulties between 1978 and 1982 EPZ employment growth slowed and almost ceased. Once the government had completed its adjustment process, growth resumed with a vengeance. Income and corporate tax rates were halved in 1983 (from about 70 to about 35 percent). Both domestic and foreign investment in the EPZ increased sharply. In 1982 the unemployment rate stood at 22 percent and total employment in the EPZ at about 20,000 workers. By 1988 the economy had essentially reached full employment through the addition of 70,000 jobs in the EPZ. In 1970 agriculture employed 60,000 people and the EPZ did not exist. In 1990 agriculture employed 46,000 workers and the EPZ employed 90,000, about one-third of all workers on the island. Jobs added in the EPZ accounted for two-thirds of the total increase in employment between 1970 and 1990.

Manufacturing in the EPZ is concentrated almost exclusively in garment production and was developed almost entirely because of the participation of entrepreneurs from Hong Kong who were drawn to Mauritius because of contacts with the small ethnic Chinese population on the island. These entrepreneurs were motivated by the prospect of lower wages, a location free from the threat of expropriation by the mainland Chinese government, and a country of origin that would not be subject to quota limits set by the United States and the European Economic Community (EEC). Investors from Hong Kong now hold nearly three-quarters of the foreign investment in the EPZ.

According to one observer (quoted in Bowman 1991), "textile entrepreneurs flocked to the island bearing sewing machines" because of the EPZ arrangements. In the Fun Factory model, this inflow of capital must explain the increase in employment and output that subsequently took place. A little reflection suggests that the entrepreneurs brought much more than physical capital, for Mauritius had long enjoyed special trade status with the EEC, and sewing machines could always have been purchased on the open market. Nor were foreigners essential as a source of the savings needed to finance investment in physical capital; domestic savings ultimately accounted for a substantial fraction of total investment in the EPZ.

The entrepreneurs did bring a crucial array of ideas about the textile and garment business, including ideas on the specific kind of equipment to use, how to manage a small factory, how to manage relations with textile importers in the industrial countries, how to successfully exploit loopholes in quota limits, and hundreds of other ideas about running a modern garment assembly operation, such as knowledge of the sequence to use in sewing a shirt.

In a model with no ideas or in which ideas are already available throughout the world, it is difficult to explain the experience of Mauritius. If investment in physical capital is the cause of growth, one must understand why domestic invest-ment did not take place prior to the arrival of the foreigners but did subsequently, and why it took place only in garment production. If a scarcity of human capital explains why people on Mauritius were poor, this surely could not have changed much in the interval between 1972 and 1979 or between 1982 and 1989. More-over, if human capital were all that mattered, why did Mauritius do so much bet-ter than Sri Lanka, which had a much better record in education?

In a world in which ideas are under private control, events in Mauritius are easy to understand. Suppose that agricultural output is a constant returns-to-scale function of land, T, labor, L, and capital, K: $F(T, K, L)$ (F for farm). We can sum-marize garment output in the form $G(K, L; A)$, where A takes on the values 0 or 1 (G for garment). Output of garments is zero if $A = 0$ because no one knows how to run a garment operation. If an entrepreneur does know, $A = 1$ and garments are a constant returns-to-scale function of sewing machines, K, and labor, L.

When $A = 0$, wages are equal to the marginal product of labor in agricul-ture. For large L, wages can be very low. Sewing machines are freely available for sale at the price p_K, but none are imported because no one knows how to put them to use. Farm equipment is imported, funded either by domestic savings or by for-eign investment. Investment in Mauritius earns the same rate of return as in the rest of the world. Wages were low not because of any restrictions on flows of fi-nancial capital or inadequacy of domestic capital investment but because the idea, A, needed for garment production was not in use there.

Now suppose that a single textile entrepreneur learns of the low wages on Mauritius, brings knowledge of A, and sets up shop. Sewing machines will now be imported. Income and employment will increase. An examination of many such cases could lead one to conclude that investment, particularly investment in ma-chinery, causes rapid economic growth. (See DeLong and Summers 1991 for cross-country evidence of the correlation between investment in machinery and growth.) What detailed knowledge of the history of Mauritius shows is that in-vestment was the proximate, but not the fundamental, cause of the growth that took place. It was the knowledge, A, brought by the foreigners that caused both the investment and growth.

To represent the private returns for putting an idea to use, let $\pi(L, p_G, p_K)$ denote the restricted profit function for a single entrepreneur who employs L units of labor on Mauritius and faces a price for sewing machines p_K. Since $G(K, L; A)$ is homogeneous of degree one in K and L, the profit function π defined by

$$\pi(L, p_G, p_K) = \max_K p_G(K, L; 1) - p_K K$$

will be linear in L. The entrepreneur is a monopsonist in the labor market in Mau-ritius, as depicted in Figure 13-2. The excess supply curve for labor faced by the entrepreneur (which is the same as the marginal productivity curve in agriculture) is upward-sloping. The marginal product of labor for the entrepreneur is con-stant. The single entrepreneur will employ labor up to the point where wages are equal to w in the figure.

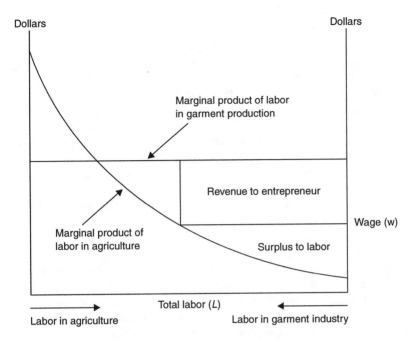

FIGURE 13-2   Labor Market with a Monopsonist Entrepreneur

   Workers in Mauritius are exploited in the sense that w is strictly less than the marginal product of labor. Yet they also receive a pure surplus or windfall gain from the entry of the entrepreneur (the area labeled "surplus to labor" in the figure). The entrepreneur collects the monopsony rectangle denoted "revenue to entrepreneur." Workers in agriculture also gain at the expense of landholders.
   The usual analysis of government policy when faced with this kind of monopsonist recommends a minimum wage. By setting the minimum wage at close to the marginal product of labor in garment assembly, the government can drive the monopsony profits to zero, encourage the efficient level of employment, and capture the largest possible surplus for workers.
   The problem with this analysis is that it neglects the possibility that the textile entrepreneurs will not come if they are not offered a large enough profit. Coming to Mauritius is a costly activity, and these entrepreneurs have alternative uses for their time and energy. Welfare on the island is increasing when the minimum wage is raised from the monopsony level, but only up to the point at which the ex post monopoly revenue captured by the textile entrepreneur is just enough to offset the initial cost of coming there. Beyond this point, an increase in the minimum wage makes welfare on the island drop precipitously, back to the Malthusian equilibrium anticipated by Meade.
   Extracting surplus from foreigners can therefore be a risky proposition, especially if policy decisions are made in the absence of knowledge about the potential entrants and their costs and alternative opportunities. The dangers of setting

too high a value for the minimum wage apply equally to other costs imposed on foreigners—costs such as burdensome customs procedures, high required domestic equity participation, high explicit taxes, high implicit taxes collected as bribes, ex post extraction of rents by organized labor, or poor provision of services by government agencies. An authoritative central government that can centralize the decisionmaking process and lower the total rent extracted from potential investors can generate substantial benefits for the nation as a whole if it changes the EPZ from one that has not attracted any substantial foreign participation (and there are many of these in the world) to one that is attractive. (For a more detailed description of this problem of decentralized extraction of rents, see the analysis of corruption by Shleifer and Vishny 1992.)

The analysis suggests not only that attempts by the government to extract rents may be strongly counterproductive but also that the government must be strong enough to prevent this kind of extraction by other actors in the economy. The government might even be able to improve welfare by subsidizing the entry of the entrepreneur. If the fixed costs for the entrepreneur of coming to the island are greater than the monopsony profit but smaller than the sum of this profit plus the surplus to workers, the government could offer part of the surplus to induce the entrepreneur to come. In the more realistic case in which a large number of firms, rather than a single monopolist, contemplate entry, the government might even facilitate collusion among the foreign firms to preserve their profits after entry.

Viewed in this way, the timing of the investment in Mauritius is easier to understand. The state of emergency, the banning of unions, and the imposition of centralized government wage-setting were crucial steps leading to the first wave of investment by foreigners. Resolution of government budget difficulties, a devaluation that reduced real wages for workers, and cuts in effective tax rates were the decisive actions in bringing about the second wave of investment. It is also relevant that while employment and income did increase substantially in Mauritius, the government made good on its pledge of wage moderation. Real wages have been allowed to increase very little in garment assembly. Now that full employment has been reached, there are signs that the government is moving away from the previous policy of wage moderation. How it will handle the next phase of development is not yet clear.

What is worrisome about a strategy of encouraging foreigners to employ low-skilled, low-cost labor is that the equilibrium wage for unskilled labor may be very low—even lower than the wages now earned on Mauritius. In the industrial countries during most of this century, A and H have been high and growing in relation to the small quantity of L present in these countries. Because of restrictions imposed by poor countries, labor in the rest of the world was segregated from labor in industrial economies. The restrictions were no doubt encouraged by domestic firms that wanted protection from foreign competition in output markets and in the labor market but may also have been fostered by a fear of exploitation. As a result, wages for L kept pace with growth in A and H in industrial countries.

Now many poor countries understand the advantages that come from removing these restrictions, and a very large quantity of labor from developing nations is on the verge of entering the worldwide market. For example, there are more than 125 EPZs in developing countries, with most of the increase in numbers coming in the last half of the 1980s. Mainland China and even India are now opening to the rest of the world. In addition, improvements in transport and communication have reduced the costs faced by an entrepreneur who wants to move production elsewhere in the world. The first countries to integrate their labor markets with markets in industrial countries experienced relatively large wage gains, but as more labor from other developing countries enters the market, wages will have to fall.

There is already evidence of this process in the pressure on wages for unskilled labor in industrial countries, especially the United States. Skill differentials are increasing as real wages for unskilled labor remain stagnant or fall. In industries where production in low-wage countries can most easily be undertaken (textiles, for example), there is already in place an extensive system of quotas designed to protect wages in industrial countries. Countries such as Mauritius can therefore expect to be squeezed from two sides. There will be more competition from other countries with low labor costs and increased trade barriers in industrial countries.

In the very long run, the fall in wages will be partially offset by increases in worldwide stocks of K and H. Suppose that the ratio of these stocks to the world stock of labor L reaches the ratio that now prevails in industrial countries. A striking implication of the analysis of ideas as economic goods is that worldwide integration of markets will permanently increase wages for H in relation to wages for L. As emphasized in the discussion of ideas, the value of an idea increases with the size of the market. Because the production of ideas is human-capital-intensive, increased worldwide economic integration will drive up the returns to human capital in relation to returns to labor. There are large gains from trade that arise from worldwide integration. Unfortunately for poor people and poor countries, the gains will be captured disproportionately by the most highly skilled workers. (See Romer 1990b or Grossman and Helpman 1992 for formal models that illustrate this point.)

For a small economy, investing in schooling may not by itself be enough for it to become involved in the production of ideas, where the high returns to human capital lie. The production of ideas requires human capital, but it also requires access to existing ideas. A country like Sri Lanka that invests heavily in education but remains isolated from all the economically important ideas that are in use in industrial countries has no hope of ever becoming a player in the global production of ideas. Recall that before Mauritius opened the EPZ, its policy was to encourage migration of educated youths, for whom there were no prospects on the island.

A more worrisome possibility is that the relatively open strategy toward the rest of the world pursued by Mauritius, or even a strategy of totally free trade, may not be sufficient to bring local human capital into use in the production of ideas. It is easier to use ideas in a small country than it is to begin producing ideas. It takes a relatively narrow range of ideas to open up a particular activity such as a garment factory. Because of constant returns to scale, the market incentives will then be to increase production of the associated good without incurring the cost of starting another activity. In Mauritius only one idea has been put to work because almost all of the EPZ output is in garments. Prospects for developing new products—that is, for producing ideas—are therefore quite weak.

Taiwan (China)

Authorities in Taiwan (China) used a wide variety of approaches to encourage the use of ideas there, with the explicit intention of shifting to the domestic control and production of ideas. Generally speaking, the government moved from a period of import substitution during the 1950s and 1960s toward an export-oriented strategy in the 1970s and 1980s. More recently it has placed increased emphasis on human capital and research subsidies similar to those used in industrial economies, but in applications with specific commercial goals. The pattern of intervention in several different industries illustrates the eclectic and flexible approach used by the government to achieve its aims.[3]

In the early 1950s the government gave special attention to the textile industry, which got its start with mainlanders who came to Taiwan (China) with their knowledge and looms. Early policy supports included tariffs and quantitative limits on imports of yarn and finished products, restrictions on entry for new firms, and controlled access to raw materials. In the early years the government supplied raw cotton to spinning mills and bought all the finished yarn, which it then supplied to firms with looms. Later the government used cheap credit to encourage firms to operate at larger scales and to integrate vertically, relying on the local office of a U.S. engineering firm to evaluate individual requests for credit. Exports grew rapidly from 1952 to 1958, the year when the island became a net exporter of textiles. After the exchange rate regime was changed in 1958 to encourage exports, textile exports to the United States grew so rapidly that quota limits were imposed in 1961.

To diversify the textile industry away from cotton, the government encouraged a move into synthetic fibers, acting primarily as an intermediary between domestic firms and foreign firms with advanced technologies. By 1954 the domestic chemical industry could produce most of the intermediate inputs needed to make rayon. With the help of advisers from the United States, the government brought together a U.S. firm and several local textile firms and supervised the negotiations leading to the creation of a joint venture that began production in 1957. The U.S. firm provided the planning, the equipment, and worker training. In 1962 this joint venture, in collaboration with a state financing agency, created another joint venture to make nylon, this time relying on technology from a Japanese firm. As private firms began to enter the synthetic fibers industry in the late 1960s and 1970s, they relied increasingly on licensing instead of joint venture agreements. The government continued to assist in finding foreign partners with technology to share and in negotiating the terms of the technology agreements, over which it retained authority for final approval. By 1981 Taiwan (China) was the fourth biggest producer of synthetic fibers in the world.

The electronics industry started like the textile industry, building from a domestic base in radio assembly that was protected by restrictions on imports. As in synthetic fibers, radio assembly was aided in the early years by a technology agreement with a foreign firm. Then, in the 1960s, the government set up an EPZ designed to encourage electronics assembly by foreign firms. By 1965 twenty-four U.S. firms had made arrangements for production in Taiwan (China). The industry developed around a few large foreign assemblers and many small domestic suppliers of components. A government-supported electronics working group assisted in marketing, training of personnel, and product expositions. In 1973 the government opened the Industrial Technology Research Institute (ITRI), which supported advanced training programs for engineers. The Electronics Research and Service Organization (ERSO), which operates under itri, supplied the first basic input-output system (BIOS) used in Taiwanese clones of IBM personal computers. More recently ERSO supported a move into semiconductor design and fabrication, opening a model shop for wafer fabrication and negotiating a technology transfer agreement with a U.S. firm. The government has begun to aggressively court Taiwanese nationals who had been trained and were employed in electronics and other high-technology fields in the United States. By 1968 electronics was second only to textiles in total exports, and in 1984 it became number one.

Over time the government in Taiwan (China) has increasingly emphasized exports and has moved away from the traditional import-substituting model of development. It is largely for this reason that Taiwan is regarded as an open, or at least an outward-oriented economy. It has nevertheless continued to employ many restrictions designed to protect and develop domestic industry. Proposals for foreign investment outside of an EPZ must be approved by the government and are often subject to conditions that limit sales in the domestic market, mandate local-content requirements, or set export targets.

Three cases are indicative of the general pattern. When the Singer Sewing Machine Company asked permission to open a manufacturing plant in the 1960s, the government required that within one year the company purchase more than 80 percent of its parts domestically. Singer did facilitate technology transfer and helped upgrade the domestic components industry but was not able to meet its goal by the end of the first year. The agreement with the government was then renegotiated. When the National Distiller and Chemical Corporation from the United States proposed the construction of a polyethylene plant, it was given a five-year tax holiday, permitted to sell in a domestic market that was protected from imports for three years, and allowed unlimited repatriation of profits. In return, the government insisted that after five years the firm would convert to a joint venture, with half of the equity held by residents of Taiwan (China). When Proctor and Gamble opened a plant in the 1970s, it was required to export 50 percent of its output.

Export requirements were initially imposed to generate foreign exchange but were increasingly used to guarantee that a foreign company would bring to Taiwan (China) a technology sophisticated enough to compete in world markets. It is anticipated that through the company's purchases from suppliers, through the experience of workers, and sometimes through mandated sales of equity, aspects of this technology will diffuse to Taiwanese citizens. In general, negotiations with foreign firms are characterized by a wide latitude for discretion and by agreements that are customized to fit the circumstances (and bargaining strength) of each foreign investor. Aggressive targets are set but are subject to renegotiation on the basis of new information.

Explicit tariff barriers have fallen, but nontariff barriers continue to be used as indirect subsidies for domestic firms. Imports of foreign equipment and intermediate inputs are subject to a complicated system of discretionary administrative control designed to support domestic suppliers of a good. One Taiwanese study cited by Wade estimates that in 1984 about half of all imports by value were subject to some form of nontariff barrier. In addition, government officials monitor detailed reports of imported inputs used by foreign firms, watching for cases in which they can arrange for a domestic supplier to provide the imported goods.

A key characteristic of government intervention in Taiwan (China) is the freedom and authority with which government officials can act. Three examples tell the story. The chief economic planner for the government once ordered the public destruction of 20,000 low-quality domestic light bulbs and threatened to liberalize imports if quality did not improve. The government approved the arrangement with Singer Sewing Machines despite the opposition of domestic sewing machine manufacturers, who ultimately benefited from the improved quality of the parts industry. In 1982 the government granted a two-year import ban on videocassette recorders (VCRS) to protect two domestic manufacturers from Japanese competitors. After one year the government gave a public warning that it would bring in a foreign firm in a joint venture if the prices and technology of the domestic firms did not achieve world standards by the end of the two-year ban. The protected firms did not live up to this standard, and eighteen months after the initial ban the government approved a joint VCR production venture between Sony and a new Taiwanese firm.

Some economists see the success of Taiwan (China) as a vindication of laissez-faire. Others attribute it to an explicit industrial policy that steered the economy into a sequence of important activities. A third interpretation is that the particular industrial activities undertaken in Taiwan were determined primarily by market forces and followed the general pattern observed in other countries at similar stages of development (Pack 1992). According to this view, what mattered was not the government's steering but its use of the accelerator. Taiwan moved very rapidly through the stages of industrial development, in large part because of its success in gaining access to and control of foreign technology. This is reflected in a high rate of measured productivity growth, which stands in contrast to the low productivity growth recorded in rapidly developing economies where growth is driven by extremely high rates of capital accumulation. (See Young 1992 for a discussion of Singapore and Pack 1988 for a general description of this phenomenon.)

The description in the previous section of the gains from using ideas suggested reasons why government intervention might be useful. Ideas that are privately controlled create more economic value when they are introduced into an economy than the holder of the idea can extract. A description of the opportunities for producing ideas reinforces this point.

The discussion of production on Mauritius focused on a single manufacturing activity and did not consider the production of ideas at all. Suppose that there are many different manufacturing activities which can be indexed by j, and suppose that each activity requires its own idea A_j:

$$Y = F(T, K, L) + \sum_j G_j (K_j, H_j, L_j, A_j)$$

Suppose as well that search, the production of new ideas, depends on human capital, H_A, used exclusively in search, and on the entire list $(A_1, A_2, \ldots)$ of ideas that are in use within a specified geographic area. Suppose also that success in search also depends on the amount of human capital that is used in production in each of the manufacturing activities. $(H_1, H_2, \ldots)$ through a process of "discovering" by doing:

$$\dot{A} = S[H_A, (A_1, A_2, \ldots), (H_1, H_2, \ldots)].$$

Finally, recall the example of learning how to use computer software by using it. To capture this, we can write human capital acquisition as a function of the use of specialized human capital on the job in a conventional learning-by-doing specification:

$$\dot{H}_j = \mu H_j.$$

Note that this description of the accumulation of new ideas and new human capital relies on two different kinds of joint product assumptions. Someone with human capital of type j who is employed in activity j produces manufactured good j, produces more human capital of type j, and (occasionally) makes new discoveries of the "better ways to sew a shirt" variety.[4]

In this complete model it is clear that when a new idea comes into an economy, it helps domestic citizens in three ways. First, as noted above, the new idea creates a surplus for unskilled labor by making possible a new productive activity in which it can be employed. Second, it creates opportunities and production of specialized human capital through on-the-job training. In effect, it creates a new opportunity for investing in human capital, and the returns from this investment may be very high. Finally, it increases the productivity of research and discovery. If enough such ideas are present, this may tip the economy from a no-discovery equilibrium to one in which many new products and processes are discovered.

It is possible that the firm that brings an idea to an economy can capture part of these additional gains. For example, it may be able to get educated employees to work at a lower wage in exchange for the opportunity to acquire human capital on the job. Even if this is true, the firm is likely to capture less than 100 percent of the gains—perhaps substantially less. And economists widely agree that a firm captures very little of the gains that its ideas create for others engaged in research.

For all these reasons, the social return to having an idea like the technology for polyethylene in use in an economy may be substantially greater than the private gain that foreign holders can capture. Thus, subsidies from the government to attract these ideas may be essential to get them to come. (Recall the three-year protection from competing imports offered to the polyethylene plant.) The total gain for domestic citizens, net of the cost of the subsidy, may still be very large.

POLICY AND POLITICS

In the United States the Congress gives research grants directly to some colleges and universities. Success in attracting these grants depends on the effectiveness of the lobbying firm employed by the school and on the seniority and committee assignments of local senators and representatives. Because neither the quality of previous research nor the quality of the proposed research plays any important role in allocating these grants, observers have concluded that they encourage rent-seeking but not good science.

In many countries direct and indirect subsidies are granted to firms through measures such as tariff and nontariff restrictions on competing imports. Success in attracting these subsidies depends on the political power of the beneficiaries. Because neither success in introducing new ideas into an economy nor success in reaching worldwide standards for price and quality play any role in the allocation of these subsidies, most observers have concluded that these interventions encourage rent-seeking but not economic development.

One might conclude from the U.S. experience that the government should never give grants to support research. One might even follow the fashion in economics and construct a model to show that the market provides the optimal level of research. Neither conclusion is warranted. We know that there is a valid economic justification for supporting basic scientific research at universities. We also know that some institutional arrangements for allocating grants (mandates from Congress) do not achieve the intended goal but that other arrangements (peer review) do a reasonably good job.

Despite frequent protestations to the contrary, the economic case for intervention to encourage the use of ideas in developing economies is at least as strong as the economic case for supporting basic research in industrial economies. The problematic assertion is that it is possible to create institutions analogous to peer review that can undertake beneficial economic intervention. The required institutions may not exist, and it may not be possible to create them in a given country.

Laissez-faire may be a second-best solution, but we must recognize that deciding whether this is the case depends at least as much on political and sociological analysis as on economic analysis.

Together with the economic analysis outlined above, my amateur political and sociological analysis leads me to the following general conclusions. First, there is much evidence suggesting that the specific arrangements used in Taiwan (China) cannot achieve their goals in a modern democracy or in most open political systems. (For a good summary of the evidence from political science showing that a Taiwanese system of discretionary bureaucratic decisionmaking is not feasible in the United States, see Wilson 1989.) To succeed, these arrangements must be part of a larger political system that can support wide latitude for discretion on the part of a strong, authoritarian government that is willing and able to override parochial interests. In addition, these arrangements require a configuration of bureaucratic competence and ruthless dedication to national economic success that is relatively rare and may be impossible to sustain.

Contemporary evidence suggests that interventionist institutions may not continue to function well even in economies such as Japan, Taiwan (China), Singapore, and the Republic of Korea, where they seem until now to have been a success. In these countries the experience with extensive intervention extends only through the working career of one—perhaps uniquely dedicated—generation of bureaucrats working in an unusual political environment. In Korea the powers of the state, traditionally used to support the large corporations, were turned against the Hyundai group when its head became a candidate for the presidency. In Japan concern with corruption is growing at the same time as the system for allocating political power shows signs of being more openly contested. Neither development bodes well for the long-run viability of a system based on honest, independent bureaucrats with extensive discretionary power.

Until other politically viable institutions for fostering development can be discovered, the one safe piece of advice to offer developing countries is that integration with world markets offers large potential gains. The gains from using someone else's ideas come from a source that is different from the classical gains from trade. The division of the gains may not correspond to intuitive notions of fairness, but they can be very large and very important nonetheless. This is absolutely clear for a small country such as Mauritius, but it is equally clear for the very large and rapidly growing economy on mainland China. The gains it receives from interaction with Hong Kong and Taiwan (China) far outweigh the small and risky gains that might be achieved through a more tightly controlled industrial policy.

The other safe counsel is to increase savings and schooling, but both of these activities require a reduction in current consumption that may be very costly for the poorest countries. Formal education also works with a long lag. In contrast, openness to investments by foreigners bearing ideas costs nothing, except perhaps a bit of national pride. On-the-job training can in many cases be even more effective than classroom education in developing human capital. Once gains in income from direct foreign investment are forthcoming, high savings and large investments in schooling are easier to finance and can be used to lay the groundwork for further gains in income.

Beyond this, cautious attempts to encourage the development of local expertise may be valuable. For example, government-financed setting of standards and support for advanced training for people in the private sector may be appropriate. These activities are politically safer than direct subsidies for private firms, which inevitably carry a much greater risk of capture and political manipulation and are difficult to make contingent on the desired actions by firms.

In the event that a government does undertake some form of subsidy for firms, the market in the rest of the world must always be used as the benchmark by which success is judged. Protection from foreign competitors is therefore the worst possible way to offer a subsidy for undertaking some activity. Attempts to imitate Taiwan (China) can all too easily end by yielding the closed markets and stagnation of India and Brazil.

Finally, having issued all of the cautions about the risks of intervention and the limits imposed by political and institutional constraints, one must not lose sight of the endogenous nature of political and institutional constraints. Just as in a child's chemistry set, there is far more scope for discovering new institutional arrangements than we can possibly understand. In the United States, if we had naively applied the theory of rent-seeking to the analysis of research grants, we would have concluded that government support for research can never be effective. We would not have invented peer review after World War II.

As the world becomes more and more closely integrated, the feature that will increasingly differentiate one geographic area (city or country) from another will be the quality of public institutions. The most successful areas will be the ones with the most competent and effective mechanisms for supporting collective interests, especially in the production of new ideas.[5]

The challenge for economic analysis is therefore somewhat delicate. We must take seriously the economic opportunities presented by the potential for producing new ideas and for diffusing existing ideas to the widest possible extent. In so doing, we must recognize that ideas are economic goods which are unlike conventional private goods and that markets are inherently less successful at producing and transmitting ideas than they are with private goods. We must be willing to learn from cases where collective action has been socially productive. The experience of Taiwan (China) can teach us something about what is feasible from an economic or technological point of view, even if that island's politics and institutions could not and should not be replicated elsewhere. We must be open to the possibility of the discovery of new kinds of institutions for supporting the production and use of commercially relevant ideas.

Yet at the same time we must send the correct signals to developing countries about what is possible given existing political constraints. Here, the experience in Mauritius is likely to be a better guide, especially in the early stages of development. There is much that can be gained merely by using ideas produced elsewhere. There is great risk in adopting interventions, especially protectionism.

NOTES

1. According to the national income accounts data of the World Bank (see Levine and Renelt 1992), Mauritius, India, and Sri Lanka all invest about 20 percent of GDP. The Heston-Summers numbers adjust nominal investment spending to correct for variation in relative cost of capital goods in different countries. In principle, the real investment numbers from Heston and Summers are more relevant, but the downward adjustment for investment in Mauritius seems implausibly large.
2. The account that follows is drawn is from World Bank data and from published studies by Gulhati and Nallari (1990) and Bowman (1991).
3. This account is drawn from Wade (1990).
4. See Romer (1990b) for a discussion of a basic model with a manufacturing sector and a separate research sector in which search builds on existing ideas. Grossman and Helpman (1992. ch. 8) cover the case assumed here in which only ideas that are available locally can be used in research. They derive the result that government intervention in support of research may be necessary to move a geographic region out of a corner equilibrium with no research. Glaeser and others (1991) describe the theoretical motivation for allowing a diverse set of ideas to enter as inputs in the search process for new ideas and offer evidence from different cities in the United States that supports the importance of this effect. Empirical support for the idea that human capital is acquired on the job in developing countries can be found in the survey of experience in EPZs by Rhee, Katterbach, and White (1990). For example, they find that many managers of domestic firms operating in the EPZ in the Dominican Republic were once employees of foreign-owned firms in the EPZ.
5. For a discussion of the role of infrastructure and development and suggestive elaboration of the parallel between development in poor countries and in U.S. cities, see Rauch (1986, 1992).

REFERENCES

Bowman, Larry W. 1991. *Mauritius: Democracy and Development in the Indian Ocean.* Boulder, Colo.: Westview.

DeLong, J. Bradford, and Lawrence H. Summers. 1991. "Equipment Investment and Economic Growth." *Quarterly Journal of Economics* 106 (May): 445–502.

Glaeser, Edward L., Hedi D. Kallal, Jose A. Scheinkman, and Andrei Shleifer. 1991. "Growth in Cities." NBER Working Paper 3787. Natural Bureau of Economic Research, Cambridge, Mass.

Grossman, Gene M., and Elhanan Helpman. 1992. *Innovation and Growth in the Global Economy.* Cambridge, Mass.: MIT Press.

Gulhati, Ravi, and Raj Nallari. 1990. *Successful Stabilization and Recovery in Mauritius.* EDI Development Policy Case Series, Analytical Case Study 5. Washington, D.C.: World Bank.

Heston, Alan, and Robert Summers. 1991. "The Penn World Table (Mark5): An Expanded Set of International Comparisons, 1950–1988." *Quarterly Journal of Economics* 106 (May):327–68.

Levine, Ross, and David Renelt. 1991. "A Sensitivity Analysis of Cross-Country Growth Regressions." *American Economic Review* 82 (September):942–63.

Meade, James. 1961. "Mauritius: A Case Study in Malthusian Economics." *Economic Journal* 71 (September):521–35.

Pack, Howard. 1988. "Industrialization and Trade." In Hollis Chenery and T. N. Srinivasan, eds., *The Handbook of Development Economics*. New York: North-Holland.

———. 1992. "New Perspectives on Industrial Growth in Taiwan." In Gustav Ranis, ed., *Taiwan: From Developing to Mature Economy*. Boulder, Colo.: Westview.

Rauch, James. 1986. "The Transfer of Production from Rich to Poor Countries." *Journal of Development Economics* 23:41–53.

———. 1992. "Does History Matter Only When It Matters Little? The Case of City-Industry Location." Working Paper, Department of Economics, University of California, San Diego.

Rhee, Young Whee, Katharina Katterbach, and Janette White. 1990. "Free Trade Zones in Export Strategies." Industry Series Paper 36. World Bank, Industry and Energy Department, Washington, D.C.

Romer, Paul M. 1990a. "Are Nonconvexities Important for Understanding Growth?" *American Economic Review* 80 (May):97–103.

———. 1990b. "Endogenous Technological Change." *Journal of Political Economy* 98 (October):S71–S102.

Index